I0013929

Kazi I

Energy Balanced Topology for Sensor Networks

Muhevmin Sakib

Kazi Muheymin Sakib

Energy Balanced Topology for Sensor Networks

Maximising Network Lifetime

VDM Verlag Dr. Müller

Impressum/Imprint (nur für Deutschland/ only for Germany)
Bibliografische Information der Deutschen Nationalbibliothek: Die Deutsche Nationalbibliothek
verzeichnet diese Publikation in der Deutschen Nationalbibliografie; detaillierte bibliografische
Daten sind im Internet über http://dnb.d-nb.de abrufbar.
Alle in diesem Buch genannten Marken und Produktnamen unterliegen warenzeichen-, marken-
oder patentrechtlichem Schutz bzw. sind Warenzeichen oder eingetragene Warenzeichen der
jeweiligen Inhaber. Die Wiedergabe von Marken, Produktnamen, Gebrauchsnamen,
Handelsnamen, Warenbezeichnungen u.s.w. in diesem Werk berechtigt auch ohne besondere
Kennzeichnung nicht zu der Annahme, dass solche Namen im Sinne der Warenzeichen- und
Markenschutzgesetzgebung als frei zu betrachten wären und daher von jedermann benutzt
werden dürften.

Coverbild: www.purestockx.com

Verlag: VDM Verlag Dr. Müller Aktiengesellschaft & Co. KG
Dudweiler Landstr. 99, 66123 Saarbrücken, Deutschland
Telefon +49 681 9100-698, Telefax +49 681 9100-988, Email: info@vdm-verlag.de
Zugl.: Melbourne, RMIT University, Diss., 2008

Herstellung in Deutschland:
Schaltungsdienst Lange o.H.G., Berlin
Books on Demand GmbH, Norderstedt
Reha GmbH, Saarbrücken
Amazon Distribution GmbH, Leipzig
ISBN: 978-3-639-12817-8

Imprint (only for USA, GB)
Bibliographic information published by the Deutsche Nationalbibliothek: The Deutsche
Nationalbibliothek lists this publication in the Deutsche Nationalbibliografie; detailed
bibliographic data are available in the Internet at http://dnb.d-nb.de.
Any brand names and product names mentioned in this book are subject to trademark, brand or
patent protection and are trademarks or registered trademarks of their respective holders. The use
of brand names, product names, common names, trade names, product descriptions etc. even
without a particular marking in this works is in no way to be construed to mean that such names
may be regarded as unrestricted in respect of trademark and brand protection legislation and
could thus be used by anyone.

Cover image: www.purestockx.com

Publisher:
VDM Verlag Dr. Müller Aktiengesellschaft & Co. KG
Dudweiler Landstr. 99, 66123 Saarbrücken, Germany
Phone +49 681 9100-698, Fax +49 681 9100-988, Email: info@vdm-publishing.com
Melbourne, RMIT University, Diss., 2008

Copyright © 2009 by the author and VDM Verlag Dr. Müller Aktiengesellschaft & Co. KG and
licensors
All rights reserved. Saarbrücken 2009

Printed in the U.S.A.
Printed in the U.K. by (see last page)
ISBN: 978-3-639-12817-8

Energy Balanced Topology for Sensor Networks

Maximising Network Lifetime

Kazi Sakib

February 17, 2009

Acknowledgement

Zahir Tari, Peter Bertok
and My Family.

Special thanks to the Australian Research Council and the Distributed Systems and Networking group at RMIT University.

Contents

List of Figures

ix

List of Tables

Chapter 1

Introduction

1.1   Issues in Sensor Networks

The miniaturisation and increased communication capabilities of sensors has enabled their ubiquitous and invisible deployment anywhere at anytime. For example, sensors can be deployed in Mars to sense the atmosphere analysing and predicting the weather of Mars [Hong et al., 2002]. A network of 4000 sensors deployed by Intel in a semiconductor manufacturing plant performs predictive maintenance of machinery [Krishnamurthy et al., 2005]. Invention of bio-sensors even allow those tiny devices to co-exist with haemoglobin to monitor every physical change inside their human host [Schwiebert et al., 2001]. These deployments of sensors require a collaborative network to accomplish a common task such as acquiring the complete data set of a monitored phenomenon.

The exciting prospects of what sensor networks can bring come with numerous challenges. An architectural overview of typical resource-limited sensors and sensor networks is given in Chapter 2. These networks are likely to be composed of potentially hundreds or thousands of tiny sensor nodes that are required to function autonomously, usually without access to renewable energy resources [Ganesan et al., 2004].

The set of challenges in sensor networks are diverse, the fundamental ones relating to node organisation, also referred as topology or network formation, are the main focus of this book. The key challenges in sensor node organisations are as follows.

- **Limited Energy Reserves and Energy Efficiency**

    A sensor node can only be equipped with limited energy reserves such as 1.5 Amphours at 3 Volt [Crossbow, 2007b]. For this reason, good management of energy usage is extremely important in a sensor network. Sensors are usually unattended in the field. In most cases, renewing energy is not feasible or even impossible. Techniques that utilise energy reserves efficiently can keep sensor nodes operational for a relatively long period of time without any human intervention.

Energy efficiency affects the operational lifetime of a sensor network. For example, in a multi-hop sensor network, sensor nodes operate in multiple modes by performing sensing and data forwarding, and the exhaustion of some nodes can seriously degrade network performances. To prolong the operational lifetime of a sensor network, energy efficiency must be considered in almost every aspect of network design. An energy-efficient network protocol or algorithm can provide significant power savings in individual sensor nodes and thus extend the operational lifetime of an entire network.

- **Sensor Node Density and Scalability**

  Future networks are predicted to accommodate large numbers of sensors that operate cooperatively to perform a sensing task. Network scalability is one of the main hurdles to achieve this objective [ElBatt, 2004]. Scalability indicates the network's ability to handle growing amounts of work in a graceful manner and be readily enlarged. Gupta and Kumar [2000] show that the one-to-one transport capacity of wireless ad-hoc networks scales as $O(\sqrt{N})$ where N is the node density, but this scaling law does not hold when node density grows to infinity. ElBatt ElBatt [2004] argues that this conclusion may not be true for sensor networks where spatially close sensors may have correlations among their sensing tasks.

- **Unattended Nodes and Self-Organisation**

  Sensor networks usually operate unattended, and nodes often fail. In such a case, nodes should dynamically organise themselves to cope with the changing environment. A self-organising system is defined as "a system where a collection of units coordinate with each other to form a system that adapts to achieve a goal more efficiently" [Collier and Taylor, 2004]. Sensor nodes should be self-organising as the ad-hoc deployment of these unattended nodes requires the system to form a covered and connected network. For each sensor node, there is a defined cost (for example, energy consumption) of sensing, processing and communicating, and for each sensor network there is a defined task to accomplish (for example, tracking a moving object) with a defined set of constraints, such as minimum tracking error and energy consumption. The node organisation technique also should take those constraints into account while forming the network.

- **Limited Resources and Control Overhead**

  A typical small sensor node has low end processors, small memory and limited energy reserves. These require algorithms that can perform with minimum control overhead. However, there are trade-offs between control packet overhead, energy efficiency and algorithmic performances. For example, self-organisation is extremely important for a rapidly changing network environment, but node re-organisation increases the control overhead with the increase of node density. On the other hand, energy overhead (consumed energy to re-organise) is directly proportional to the number of control packets generated [Cordeiro and Agrawal, 2006], so high control overhead also implies energy inefficiency.

- **Limited Network Lifetime and Lifetime Maximisation**

  Due to limited resources, the lifetime of a sensor network is also limited. Ideally, a network should become ineffective only when all the nodes become exhausted. In reality, the lifetime of a sensor network is the minimum time up to which the network is functionally effective. A network is functionally effective, if it can monitor the entire sensor field and collect sensed data with a predefined Quality of Service (QoS). For example, in some military applications, data should be delivered accurately within a certain period of time, otherwise the data is useless. For this reason, network lifetime or network effectiveness depends on the required degree of coverage and connectivity by applications.

  Network lifetime maximisation problem has been mostly studied from the indirect perspective of energy conservation [Dong, 2005]. However, energy conservation is not the same problem as network lifetime maximisation. Energy efficient, low cost network protocols or algorithms can extend node lifetime, but network lifetime depends on more than an individual node's energy conservation because a network can still sense and collect data despite a node failure. The impact of individual node energy conservation on network lifetime cannot be ignored, but a network can extend its lifetime more by best utilising limited node resources.

In order to form sensor networks that can cope with the numerous future applications, the challenges described above must be addressed. While some of these challenges can be dealt with through technological improvements, not all of them can be solved this way. For example, while processor speed and memory technologies have achieved significant improvements, battery life improves on average only 5 to 10% each year [Starner, 2003]. Therefore, instead of relying on the improvement of battery lifetime to solve the limited energy problem for sensor nodes, the focus should be on designing network protocols that are more energy efficient and lifetime maximising. Similarly, sensor nodes have limited resources so it is important to design protocols that have low control overhead and make efficient use of available resources.

1.2   Research Questions

Node organisation has been a subject of extensive study in typical distributed systems [Stallings, 2007; Coulouris et al., 2005; Sinha, 1997]. These works were based on the assumption that nodes such as PCs and servers have limitless resources and are strongly connected in a static network topology. This assumption however does not hold where sensor nodes have strict resource constraints and are vulnerable. A sensor network may need to change its topology with the change of environment, such as weather, or with the change of targeted phenomenon, such as a moving object.

In this book, a novel network formation technique is proposed for sensor networks which accommodates energy constraints, changing environments and limited processing and memory capabilities. The objective is to form the network in such a way that the network will be functional for an extended period of time, with given sensor node limitations. In particular, the following main research questions are pursued.

1. What is a sensor node organisation technique that can extend network operational lifetime while accommodating large number of deployed nodes? Existing node organisation techniques have been studied in the context of sensor networks [Heinzelman et al., 2002; Cerpa and Estrin, 2004; Sohrabi et al., 2004]. It has been found that these techniques have limits in extending lifetime because of their less efficient network energy management.

2. To be able to cover the entire sensor field, redundant node deployment is common. What is the effect of redundant node deployment on network operational lifetime? Can we organise nodes by temporarily deactivating redundant nodes? While some redundant node elimination techniques have been proposed [Tian and Georganas, 2005;

Zou and Chakrabarty, 2005; Xing et al., 2005], they cannot identify the maximum possible redundant node set due to their imprecise redundancy calculation. In some cases they do not even consider control overhead, and so waste precious energy.

3. Sensor nodes are vulnerable in nature because they can often fail due to various reasons including exhaustion of energy or external hindrances. To extend the network operational lifetime further, can we reuse deactivated redundant nodes to replace failed nodes? Techniques for identifying failed nodes have been studied widely in the context of traditional distributed networks [Zhuang et al., 2005; Ranganathan et al., 2001; Tai et al., 2004]. These techniques cannot be used in sensor networks because they do not consider communication overhead and cannot deal with the dynamic restructuring of sensor nodes.

4. Which is the best replacement of a failed node that can maintain network effectiveness the longest? Choosing a good replacement node is critical because there is a trade-off between finding the best replacement nodes and overhead. What is the ideal policy that can identify the best failed node replacement from already deactivated neighbours and can extend the network operational lifetime?

1.3   Research Contributions

In answering the above research questions, our research contribution to the node organisation in a sensor network is summarised as follows.

Formation of Energy Balanced Clusters

The first contribution is the development of an energy balanced network formation technique that can organise nodes with a low control overhead and can maximise node and network operational lifetimes. In this technique, called Energy Balanced Clustering (EBC), nodes deterministically organise themselves into clusters based on their capabilities such as residual energy levels, so that the network can dynamically restructure when the environment changes. This enables the best utilisation of limited energy reserves and protects nodes from being exhausted unexpectedly. Thus, a network remains effective for an extended period of time by reducing wastage of energy reserves. The algorithm analysis shows that the computational complexity and energy overhead are linear for EBC.

Detailed analytical models of EBC and various existing node organisation techniques have been developed for better understanding of their performance from a theoretical perspective. These models provide a simple way to compare the lower bound of network lifetime of existing techniques. The analytical result shows that this lower bound when using EBC is at least around 15% higher than that of the existing techniques.

Extensive simulation has been performed to study the performance of EBC for three different lifetime definitions - when first node becomes exhausted, when first network partition occurred and when half of the deployed nodes become exhausted. Results show that compared to existing node organisation techniques, EBC extends the network lifetime by at least 10% more for various lifetime definitions. EBC maximises the lifetime because of its energy balancing measures, as the results show that the standard deviation of residual energy levels is at least 20% less than that of the existing techniques.

Elimination of Redundant Nodes

The second contribution is a redundant node identification and deactivation scheme that reduces the impact of excess energy consumption by redundant nodes on network operational lifetime. The scheme, called Self-Calculated Redundancy Check (SCRC), improves the accuracy of node redundancy calculation by utilising the local information of sensor field and deployed nodes. Using local information, a sensor field is divided up by a sensing grid and a sensor node's sensing region becomes a subset of the sensing points. Each of the nodes then calculates redundancy by checking the coverage degree of its sensing region. This maximises the set of deactivated redundant nodes, and thus maximises network operational lifetime. Algorithm analysis shows that the time, message and space complexity of SCRC is linearly proportional to the number of neighbours of a node. The simulation study shows that compared to existing redundant node identification techniques, SCRC can identify 5 to 10% more redundant nodes for various node distribution methods.

A detailed analytical study of expected number of redundant nodes under uniformly random and Poisson node distributions have also been conducted. The results obtained demonstrate the potentially redundant node's behaviour under those node distribution models. The simulation results show that SCRC is consistent with the analytical results.

6

Detection of Failed Sensor Nodes Asynchronously

The third contribution is the proposal of an asynchronous failed node detection mechanism which supports sensor nodes monitoring neighbouring nodes with low control overheads. The mechanism, called Asynchronous Failed Sensor node Detection (AFSD), differs from traditional distributed failure detection techniques by addressing the vulnerability of a failure detector in sensor networks due to limited resources. It highlights the importance of dynamic selection of failure detectors with the change of environments. Instead of periodic probing, AFSD uses data packets exchanged between nodes to predict a failed node and the prediction is verified using a consensus mechanism. The use of data packets reduces control overhead to an acceptable level for a resource limited sensor node.

A theoretical study proves that AFSD is *complete* by detecting all failed nodes and is *accurate* by avoiding false positives. Complexity analysis shows that the control, energy, and time overhead of AFSD are linearly proportional to the number of neighbours and gateways. The experimental result shows that AFSD is consistent with the analytical result obtained from the complexity analysis, and that it is at least three times more energy efficient than any of the existing methods. The result also shows that the average time to detect an AFSD failed node is at least as good as other existing methods when the packet generation rate is high.

Replacing Failed Nodes with Redundant Nodes

The final contribution is the introduction of a new concept, called policy for failed node replacement, and the proposal of three specific failed node replacement policies to improve network operational lifetime. Failed node replacement is considered as the repairing of network holes created by failed nodes. Existing hole repairing techniques are analysed, and it is shown that none of them utilises the existing node deployment, instead, they use either mobile robots or additional node redeployments. The proposed failed node replacement policies take the advantages of redundant node deployment and replaces failed nodes with those.

In the first proposed policy, called Directed Furthest Node First (DFNF), an active node that encountered a failed neighbour and a network hole, re-activates an inactive neighbour to repair the hole. The inactive neighbour is selected based on its location, distance and the hole direction. The second policy, called Weighted Directed Furthest Node First (WDFNF), is an extension of the first policy where an active node, having detected a failed node first, assigns a weight to each of its inactive neighbours based on its direction and distance with respect to the hole. By considering both distance and direction, WDFNF can select a pseudo ideal replacement for a failed node. Finally, Best Fit Node (BFN) policy is proposed to identify the appropriate replacement node with a higher control and energy overhead. In BFN, all the active nodes encountering a coverage hole participate in the replacement procedure. As a result, BFN can select an ideal replacement node by considering all inactive neighbours of a failed node.

Analytical study of failed node replacement policies showed that in the best case scenario, the energy and control overhead of DFNF and WDFNF are constant, and it is in the quadratic order of node density for BFN. In the worst case, the overhead increases linearly in the order of node density for DFNF and WDFNF, and control overhead increases in the cubic order for BFN.

Extensive simulations of DFNF, WDFNF and BFN have been conducted to evaluate their performance. The policies tested include network lifetime, Quality of Coverage (QoC) and redundant node usage. Test results show that DFNF and WDFNF can maintain the same performance as BFN when the network is extremely dense.

1.4 Book Structure

The rest of this book is structured as follows.

- Chapter 2 provides background information related to sensor network topology. Sensors, sensor networks and sensor network applications are discussed, together with a description of the network model used in the remainder of this book.

- Chapter 3 addresses the problem of how to efficiently organise nodes for sensor networks. Existing node organisation techniques are studied analytically and evaluated through simulation. Furthermore, a low cost and network lifetime maximising clustering mechanism is proposed where network energy consumption is balanced to reduce the wasted energy after a network fails.

- The effects of redundant node deployment on network lifetime are studied in Chapter 4. Related work on redundant node identification and deactivation is presented. This is followed by the proposal of a low overhead and accurate node redundancy calculation scheme, SCRC, that reduces the impact of redundant energy consumption on network lifetime. The proposed method is evaluated and compared to existing redundancy identification approaches through simulation.

- Chapter 5 addresses the issue of node failure for sensor networks. The use of data packets exchanged between nodes to assist failure detectors in making failed node detection decisions is investigated. Existing synchronous and asynchronous failure detection schemes are described. The AFSD method is also proposed in this chapter together with evaluations and discussions.

- Policies to replace failed nodes are introduced in Chapter 6 to exploit redundant node deployments. The aim of those policies is to improve network effectiveness in case of active node failures. Three failed node replacement policies are proposed, and their performance is evaluated against each other analytically and experimentally.

- Finally, the conclusion is drawn in Chapter 7 where the research aim and achievements are summarised and possible directions for future research are discussed.

Chapter 2

Background

This chapter provides the background for the work presented in this thesis. In the following, sensors and sensor networks are described with network design criteria. This is followed by a survey on sensor network applications and future trends. Finally, the network model this thesis is based upon is described.

2.1 Sensors

A Sensor is a device that stimulates to an input (for example, temperature, pressure, light) and produces a functionally related output usually in a user understandable form (for example, electrical or optical signal). Sensors are classified according to the type of phenomenon they detect, such as thermal, electromagnetic, mechanical, optical, chemical or acoustic sensors.

Recent advances in wireless communications and electronics have enabled low-cost, low-power, multi-functional sensors that are small in size and able to communicate across short distances [Akyildiz et al., 2002]. It is assumed that sensor devices, sometimes called sensor nodes, are equipped with small form-factor processors, limited storage capacity, wireless communication capabilities (transceiver/radio) and sensors [Tubaishat and Madria, 2003]. Some of the well known sensor nodes are IMote [Crossbow, 2007a], Crossbow Mica [Crossbow, 2007b] and Telos [Polastre et al., 2005]. An IMote sensor node with its comparative size is shown in Figure 2.1. Figure 2.2 shows an architectural overview of a sensor node and important components of a sensor node are described below.

Figure 2.1: An IMote Sensor Node from Intel Research [Intel Corporation, 2007].

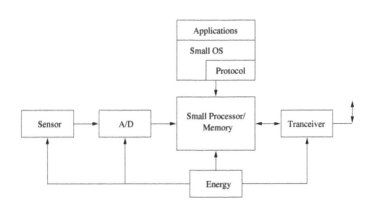

Figure 2.2: Architectural Overview of a Sensor Node.

Table 2.1: Comparison of Existing Sensor Nodes

Platform	Year	Micro-controller	Memory (ROM,RAM)	References
Mica	2002	ATMEL AtMega128	128 KB, 4 KB	[Crossbow, 2007b]
Telos	2004	TI MSP430	60 KB, 10 KB	[Polastre et al., 2005]
IMote2	2006	Intel PXA271	256 KB, 32 KB	[Crossbow, 2007a]

Processor and Memory

The miniaturisation of sensor nodes requires special processors which are small in size and have limited processing capability. Examples of such processors with full operating system (for example, TinyOS [University of California, Berkeley, 2007]) support include ATMEL At-Mega128L, AT90LS8535, Intel PXA271 and Texas Instruments MSP430 [Lynch and OReilly, 2005]. These processors use advanced low power RISC (Reduced Instruction Set Computer) architecture[1]. An important feature of these micro-controllers is power saving capability. For example, MSP430 has six different power modes, ranging from fully active to fully powered down. The power saving mode helps to design network protocols to extend node and network lifetimes by keeping unnecessary nodes in an inactive state.

Size and cost constraints on sensor nodes result in corresponding constraints on memory as well. Sensor nodes have a very simple memory architecture. All primary memory is accessible to all services running on a sensor node via a single address space. Most of these architectures do not have features such as memory management units (MMUs) or privileged mode execution to isolate program data and code. For this reason, applications and algorithms for sensor nodes need to be memory-conscious. Micro-controllers and memory sizes of some existing sensor nodes are given in Table 2.1.

Operating Systems

A sensor node needs a small, highly portable, multitasking operating system developed for use on a resource-constrained networked system. Some of the existing sensor node operating

---

[1]RISC architecture uses an instruction set reduced both in size and complexity of addressing modes, in order to enable efficient implementation of compilers with greater instruction level parallelism [Patterson and Hennessy, 1998].

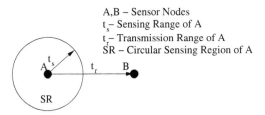

Figure 2.3: Sensing Range, Transmission Range and Sensing Region of a Sensor Node.

systems are TinyOS [University of California, Berkeley, 2007], SOS [University of California, Los Angeles, 2007] and Contiki [Dunkels et al., 2004]. Among them TinyOS is more popular in the sensor network research community [Hellerstein et al., 2003].

TinyOS supports complex, concurrent programs with very low memory requirements for example, many applications fit within 16KB of memory, and the core OS is 400 bytes [Levis et al., 2005]. This flexible operating system built from a set of reusable components that are assembled into an application-specific system. Levis et al. [2005] show that TinyOS supports an event-driven concurrency model, asynchronous events, and deferred computation, called tasks. In addition, TinyOS provides a list of services for applications and also provides facilities for creating new services for sensor networks. Such facilities help researchers to design and build various sensor network related protocols or algorithms.

Sensing Range

The ability to sense any arbitrary region within the sensor field is a fundamental requirement of a sensor node. Sensor devices have a limited sensing coverage area that depends on the sensitivity of the sensing instrumentation such as light range [Miluzzo et al., 2006].

Most of the existing work considers only two dimensional sensing and assumes that the sensing range of a sensor node is uniform in all directions, so the sensing or coverage region is a circle (disk) of radius equivalent to the sensing range [Zhou et al., 2004; Xing et al., 2005]. The disk model assumes that if an event happens at a distance less than or equal to the sensing range from the sensor location, that event will be detected. On the other hand, an event occurring at a distance greater than the sensing range cannot be detected at all. This assumption also makes network coverage maintenance protocols less complex to design and analyse [Zou and Chakrabarty, 2004; Kumar et al., 2004].

In this thesis, it is assumed that a sensor node has a fixed sensing range and the sensing coverage of a sensor node is uniform in all directions. This simplification allow to assume that the sensing region of a sensor node is a circle where the radius of the circle is the sensing range of the sensor node as shown in Figure 2.3.

Transmission Range

Sensor nodes are deployed in a field and forward their sensed data using a transceiver. Transmission range of a sensor node depends on the energy required to transmit a data packet within a certain distance. Dai and Wu [2005] show that the minimum transmission power required to sustain a link between nodes i and j depends on the distance of i and j. If r is the distance between nodes i and j, the required transmission power can be modelled as follows.

$$P_{ij} = r^{\alpha} \qquad (2.1)$$

Where α is between 2 and 4. For this reason, an optimum transmission range is identified to minimise the transmission power [Dai and Wu, 2005]. Like sensing range, it is assumed in this thesis that the transmission is of uniform strength in all directions, and the transmission range of a sensor node is always greater than or equal to its sensing range.

Energy Reserves and Consumption

Due to the size constraints, sensor nodes have limited energy reserves. Existing sensor nodes such as Mica2 uses AA batteries of about 1.5 Amp-hours (Ah) at 3V [Crossbow, 2007b]. Trends in miniaturisation suggest that the drops of sensor and battery sizes are not proportional. Battery sizes are not dropping at the same rate as sensor sizes, so node energy reserve is an important issue. For example, Lynch and OReilly [2005] show that a standard 3V CR2450 lithium coin cell has an energy density of $240\text{mAh}/cm^3$, and a sensing application requiring 4mAh per day with a twelve month deployment would require $6.1cm^3$ of battery. In one test deployment of Mica2 motes, Mainwaring et al. [2002] show that an environmental monitoring application had a daily energy requirement of 8.14mAh.

Sensor nodes consume different amounts of energy at different stages. For example, on average a Mica2 sensor draws 8mA in active mode and $>15\mu\text{A}$ in sleep mode [Crossbow, 2007b]. The power consumption of receiving and transmitting data packets are also different such

14

Table 2.2: *Comparison of Various Node Energy Consumptions [Polastre et al., 2005]*

Platform	Active Mode	Sleep Mode	Transmit	Receive
Mica2	75mW	33μW	42mW	29mW
Telos	3mW	15μW	38mW	35mW
Mote2	50mW	20μW	4317nJ/bit	2028nJ/bit

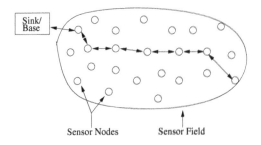

Sink/Base

Sensor Nodes   Sensor Field

Figure 2.4: *Sensor Nodes Distributed in a Sensor Field.*

as a UC Mote consumes 2028nJ/bit while receiving and 4317nJ/bit while transmitting [Hill et al., 2000]. Power consumptions of various sensor nodes are given in Table 2.2.

2.2 Sensor Networks

A sensor network is usually a wireless network consisting of spatially distributed sensor nodes to cooperatively monitor physical or environmental conditions such as temperature, sound, vibration, pressure, motion or pollutants at different locations [Culler et al., 2004]. A sensor network composed of a large number of sensor nodes that are densely deployed in the sensor field is shown in Figure 2.4. Sensors usually communicate with each other using a multi-hop data communication approach. The routing of data ends at special nodes called sinks or base stations that are special type of machines with enhanced capabilities over simple sensor nodes since they do complex data aggregation.

2.2.1 Network Design Criteria

Sensor networks have a wide variety of applications in systems with vastly differing requirements and characteristics. Important network design criteria that relates to our research are discussed below.

Random Vs. Predetermined Node Deployment

The deployment of sensor nodes in the sensor field may be performed in several ways. Nodes may be deployed at random (for example, by dropping them from high above) or at predetermined positions. Deployment may be a one-time activity or may also be a continuous process, with more nodes being deployed when the network is already active [Romer and Mattern, 2004]. In this thesis, it is assumed that nodes will be deployed in such environments (for example, in a disaster area or even in a battle field) where node deployment location may not be known a priori, so the node deployment is random and one-time. However, protocols that are proposed are also applicable to a network with predetermined and continuous node deployment.

Optimum Vs. Redundant Node Deployment

Sensor networks can be classified as fixed/traditional or ad-hoc networks. In a fixed sensor network, node deployment locations are known and using the location information, an optimum number of nodes can be deployed. In an ad-hoc sensor network, sensor location is not known a priori so random sensor deployment methods are used [Megerian and Potkonjak, 2002]. This is required when individual node placement is infeasible, such as battlefield or disaster areas. To compensate the lack of exact positioning, nodes are redundantly deployed in such networks. In this research, it is assumed that the node placement is not known a priori, so random and redundant node deployment is used.

Static Vs. Mobile Network

Sensor networks can be static or mobile according to the movability of deployed nodes. Sensor nodes may be attached to or carried by mobile entities, and sensor nodes may possess automotive capabilities. Romer and Mattern [2004] also show that node mobility can result from environmental influences such as wind or water. However, in this thesis, nodes are assumed to be static and network protocols for mobile sensor networks are left for future work.

Homogeneous Vs. Heterogeneous Network

Sensor networks can be homogeneous (that is, all the sensor nodes are architecturally identical) or heterogeneous (that is, nodes can be architecturally different) [Duarte-Melo and Mingyan, 2002]. For simplicity, a homogeneous sensor network is considered to consist of nodes that are mostly identical from hardware and software points of view. However, each node has a separate and unique ID to distinguish from others. In chapter 4, to identify the effect of sensing range on node redundancy, sensing range is varied with respect to transmission range.

Partial Vs. Complete Network Coverage

Network coverage measures the degree of coverage over the area of interest by sensor nodes [Dhillon and Chakrabarty, 2003]. Sometimes only parts of the area of interest are covered by the sensor nodes (for example, in a wild-life monitoring network). In other cases, the area of interest is completely covered by sensors (for example, in a security surveillance system). Redundant coverage may also be needed, that is multiple sensors cover the same physical location depending on the application. Unless otherwise explicitly stated in this thesis a network is called effective if it can provide complete network coverage.

Intermittent Vs. Complete Network Connectivity

If any two sensor nodes in the network can communicate with each other (possibly via multi-hop communications), the network is connected [Ghosh and Das, 2006]. In a sensor network, nodes can be scheduled to be inactive most of the time and participate in data routing occasionally - this is intermittent connectivity. Nodes in a network may also be connected all the time, which is complete network connectivity. Some of the applications may need more than complete connectivity and require redundant connectivity between nodes. In this thesis, a network is considered effective if it can provide (redundant or non-redundant) complete network connectivity.

2.2.2 Applications

Wireless sensor networks enable a paradigm shift in the science of monitoring, and constitute the foundation of a broad range of applications related to security, surveillance, military, medical, and environmental monitoring. They can significantly improve the accuracy and density of scientific measurements of physical phenomena because large numbers of sensors can directly be deployed where experiments are taking place [Estrin et al., 1999]. Some existing real life applications of sensor networks are given below.

Military Applications

Sensor network research was initially driven by military applications, such as battle-field surveillance and enemy tracking. One of the earliest applications of such networks was for anti-submarine warfare, like the Sound Surveillance System (SOSUS) used during the cold war. SOSUS is now used by the National Oceanographic and Atmospheric Administration (NOAA) of USA for monitoring events in the ocean such as seismic and animal activity, and named as Integrated Undersea Surveillance System (IUSS) [Nishimura and Dennis, 1994].

During the cold war, networks of air defence radars were also developed and deployed to defend the continental United States and Canada. This air defence system has evolved over the years to include aerostats as sensors and Airborne Warning and Control System (AWACS) planes, and is also used for drug interdiction [Chong and Kumar, 2003].

Habitat Monitoring

Cerpa et al. [2001] describe habitat monitoring as a driver application for wireless sensor networks, and they propose a tiered architecture for such applications for monitoring moving phenomenon. One of the example of habitat monitoring is Great Duck Island (GDI) system. In August 2002, researchers from UCB/Intel Research Laboratory deployed a Mote-based tiered sensor network on Great Duck Island, Maine, to monitor the behaviour of storm petrel [Mainwaring et al., 2002]. Other than that, Remote Ecological Micro-Sensor Network (REMSN) [Biagioni and Bridges, 2002] is a research project at the University of Hawaii that built a wireless network of environmental sensors to investigate why endangered species of plants will grow in one area but not in neighbouring areas.

Wireless sensor networks help farmers in assessing the requirements for crop and stock management by regularly monitoring animal behaviour and environmental conditions [Corke et al., 2006; Butler et al., 2006]. Scientists are using mobile sensors on cows to study their behaviour where sensors are linked by radio to another network monitoring the local field environment [Butler et al., 2004].

Environment Monitoring

Environment monitoring networks span large geographic areas to monitor and forecast physical processes such as environmental pollution, flooding etc. CORIE (COlumbia RIEver) [Steere et al., 2000] is an example of such applications, where a number of stationary sensor nodes are deployed across the Columbia river estuary and a mobile sensor station collects information from them. Another example of environment monitoring is the Automated Local Evaluation in Real-Time (ALERT). The network was developed by the national weather service of USA in the 1970's, and provide important real-time rainfall and water level information to evaluate the possibility of potential flooding [ALERT, 2007]. Currently ALERT is deployed across most of the western United States, and it is heavily used for flood alarming in California and Arizona.

For the Queensland Centre for Native Floriculture, CSIRO (Commonwealth Scientific and Industrial Research Organisation) developed a wireless sensor network that provides horticulturalists with a better understanding of the environment inside a greenhouse [CSIRO, 2007], and knowledge about what can grow in specific climates.

Medical Applications

Applications in health monitoring include tele-monitoring of human physiological data, tracking and monitoring of doctors and patients inside a hospital etc. An interesting project of medical sensor networks is the Smart Sensors and Integrated Micro-systems (SSIM) [Schwiebert et al., 2001] where retina prosthesis chips that consisting of 100 micro-sensors are built and implanted within a human eye. Those sensors collaborate with each other allowing patients with no vision or limited vision to see at an acceptable level. The idea of embedding wireless biomedical sensors inside human body is promising and applications for such a technique include general health monitoring and cancer detectors.

In-home Applications

The Smart Kindergarten [Srivastava et al., 2001], a sensor-based wireless network for early childhood education envisioned that interaction-based instruction method will soon replace the traditional stimulus-responses based methods.

The smart home concept is another example of a real-life in-home sensor network. In Smart Home Vacuum (SHV), a goal driven task planning (GDTP) engine is developed [Chen et al., 2006]. The engine is implemented in wireless vacuum systems to maximise cleaning efficiency.

2.2.3 Future Applications

Recent advances in Micro-Electro Mechanical Systems (MEMS) and wireless communication technology produced inexpensive miniaturised sensor nodes. This promises future applications of large scale, widely distributed sensor networks. The ad-hoc and unattended nature of sensor networks makes it even more attractive for military and other risk-associated applications. Some of the potential future applications include - Space exploration [Hong et al., 2001], Unmanned aerial vehicles [Sinopoli et al., 2003], Robotic landmine detection [Santana et al., 2005], Border surveillance [Chong and Kumar, 2003], Traffic control [Chong and Kumar, 2003], Bushfire monitoring and response [Mendis et al., 2006], Wearable network [Lorincz et al., 2007], Home automation [Oh et al., 2005] etc.

2.3 The Network Assumptions

In this section, the network assumptions used in this thesis are described. All subsequent discussions are based upon the following.

A sensor network comprises a specific region of interest and a set of sensor nodes to monitor that region. To collect data from sensors, another set of special nodes, called sinks or base stations, are deployed. Based on sensing and transmission ranges, nodes form an ad-hoc network. Each of these important entities are described below.

- **Sensor field**: Sensor nodes are deployed in a region of interest, called sensor field. A sensor field is represented by a 2D grid, whose dimension is $X \times Y$ as shown in Figure 2.5. Let m = $X \times Y$, so there are m grid points in the sensor field. Let M = $\{m_1, m_2 \ldots, m_m\}$ be the set containing all the grid points and each of the points are represented by a location vector, $m_k = (x_k, y_k)$, where x_k and y_k are the coordinates for grid point m_k.

- **Sensor node**: Sensors, termed sensor nodes or nodes, are randomly distributed in the sensor field. Each sensor node has sensing capability as well as computing and communication capabilities to execute protocols and exchange messages. S is used to denote the set of sensor nodes deployed in the sensor field, where all the sensor nodes are homogeneous and have unique IDs. A node with id k is referred to as s_k ($s_k \in S$).

20

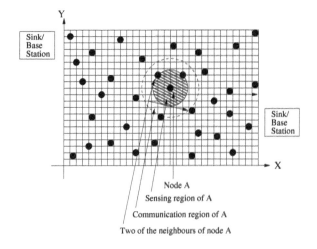

Figure 2.5: A Sensing Grid with Two Sinks.

Each sensor node is aware of its physical location information either through GPS or through location discovery algorithms (for example, [Hu and Evans, 2004]). Notation $s_k = (x_k, y_k)$ is used, where x_k and y_k are the coordinates for sensor node s_k.

- **Sensing and Transmission Range**: Since sensor nodes are homogeneous, all nodes are equipped with the same type of sensing and communication hardware. They have the same sensing range (t_s) and transmission or communication range (t_r).

- **Sensing region**: A node can sense a particular region of the sensor field within its sensing range. As is mentioned earlier, the sensing range of a sensor node is assumed to be uniform in all directions, so the sensing region of a node is circular.

- **Neighbour nodes**: Nodes within the transmission range of each other are called neighbours. As transmission ranges are fixed, each sensor node has a fixed set of neighbours. Communication between neighbouring nodes is bidirectional.

- **Sink/Base stations**: Sink or base stations are special nodes in the field to collect data from sensor nodes. Unlike sensor nodes, these have ample resources, such as sufficient memory capacity, processing power and unlimited energy supply. A sensor network can be a single-sink or multi-sink network.

- **Network topology**: Sensor network topology can be represented as a graph where nodes are sensors or sinks and edges are communication links. In such a network, each link represents a one-hop connection, and the neighbours are those within the one-hop communication distance of each other.

2.4 Summary

In this chapter, the typical sensor node architecture used in this thesis was described, and specific limitations of sensor networks were explained. The rest of the thesis addresses these limitations, and proposes solutions to overcome or mitigate those. Existing and future possible sensor network applications that put the work in this thesis into context have also been described.

Chapter 3

Energy Balanced Sensor Networks

3.1 Introduction

Sensor networks need to be able to dynamically restructure their network backbone and data paths in response to changing network conditions [Santi, 2005]. This is particularly important for energy efficiency because nodes have limited energy supply. Nodes are generally unattended, so that the energy supply is irreplaceable [Ganesan et al., 2004]. For these reasons, node organisation techniques should aim to prolong node lifetime. Mechanisms to best improve network lifetime must take into account more than individual nodes' energy consumption, since energy remaining after the network fails is wasted energy. Networks with no remaining energy are better than networks with some wasted energy.

If a node's battery is depleted, this will affect neighbours who rely on it for connection to the rest of the network. Node organisation techniques should consider overall network energy consumption and should delay node exhaustion. Ideally all nodes should become exhausted at the same time however, in reality, this is impossible due to the different node position and uneven traffic in the network. A node that is close to a base station has to perform more tasks than the nodes at the boundary region as it has to relay data from other nodes to the base stations.

Existing node organisation approaches emphasise network quality of services by providing complete coverage and connectivity. For example, by sharing all possible network information such as node coordinates, states and energy levels a network is formed providing complete coverage and connectivity [Heinzelman et al., 1999]. This requires exchanging a considerable amount of control information which is impracticable in a resource limited network. To reduce the information exchanged, a small group of nodes, called clusters, can be formed [Heinzelman et al., 2002; Taek et al., 2003], however periodic exchange of network related information even within a small group may be energy inefficient. Instead of continuous network monitoring, sensor networks can be formed adaptively where nodes are only activated when network quality degrades [Cerpa and Estrin, 2004]. These approaches cannot extend the network lifetime due to lack of energy conserve measures. For example, in such approaches, once a node is made active it remains active until it depletes its energy reserves [Cerpa and Estrin, 2004].

If a sensor network becomes less effective because of the exhaustion of important nodes, the quality of the network is degraded. To protect nodes from early exhaustion, energy consumption across the network should be even. Even energy consumption will protect nodes from exhaustion due to running out of energy, while their neighbours still have enough energy. The energy consumption of a node is directly proportional to the tasks performed by that node. It is preferred to share tasks among nodes such that energy usage is balanced. The task sharing mechanism itself needs to be efficient and should consider the sensing area and network conditions. That is, a dynamic network control protocol enabling the distribution of tasks according to current node capabilities is required.

This chapter proposes a method of managing self-configuring nodes such that the network operational lifetime is maximised, called Energy Balanced Clustering (EBC). Small groups of nodes are organised into clusters to share their energy levels. Within a cluster, nodes are organised as gateway and non-gateway nodes, where a gateway node can communicate with any other nodes (gateways or non-gateways) but a non-gateway can only communicate with gateways. Clusters are formed around gateway nodes, and neighbours of such a node become members of that cluster. Gateway nodes collect data from cluster members and forward to base stations. To maintain the network connectivity, clusters are overlapped so a cluster may contain multiple gateway nodes. To identify a node capability for becoming a gateway, EBC classifies nodes according to their residual energy levels. A node is considered eligible to be a gateway if it has sufficient energy to relay the others' data. When the residual energy of a gateway drops below a predefined level it voluntarily gives up the gateway job and thus extending its lifetime. This helps preserve network coverage and connectivity by preventing nodes from early exhaustion.

An analytical and experimental evaluation was performed to compare EBC with existing techniques such as All-Active [Cerpa and Estrin, 2002], LEACH [Heinzelman et al., 2002] and ASCENT [Cerpa and Estrin, 2004]. The analytical result shows that the lower bound of a node lifetime using EBC is at least around 15% higher than that of the existing techniques.

Since the energy balancing mechanism of EBC protects nodes from early exhaustion, this extends node lifetime. Extensive simulation confirmed that EBC has at least 20% more evenly distributed energy than networks using existing schemes. Better energy balancing was achieved because unlike existing techniques, EBC balances tasks among nodes. Energy balancing has a significant effect on network lifetime, which is demonstrated using three metrics, 1) the time taken for the first node to deplete its battery, 2) the time taken for the first network partition to occur, and 3) the time taken for 50% of deployed nodes to exhaust their energy supply. In all three cases, EBC outperformed existing techniques, and our result shows that EBC network lifetime is extended by at least 40% when measuring time for "first node to die" and by at least 10% when other two lifetime metrics were considered.

The rest of this chapter is organised as follows. Existing node organisation and node characterisation schemes are described in section 3.2. Section 3.3 provides details of the proposed energy based node classification technique. The proposed clustering technique is described in section 3.4. An analytical framework for identifying the lower bound of a node lifetime under various techniques is given in section 3.5. A detailed analytical comparison of the existing and proposed schemes is also presented in section 3.5. This is followed by simulation results and performance evaluation in section 3.6. Finally, comparative results are discussed and the conclusion is drawn in sections 3.7 and 3.8 respectively.

3.2 Related Work

Relevant solutions for topology control and network related issues in sensor networks are discussed in this section. A topology refers to either the shape of a network or a network layout, how different nodes are connected and how they communicate with each other [Subramanian and Katz, 2000]. The discussion starts with the most basic approach for sensor node organisation, and then improvements are demonstrated.

Sensor Protocols for Information via Negotiation (SPIN)

One basic approach to node organisation is collecting and sharing all network related information (such as node status and energy levels) to construct an overall view of the network. Such an approach is Sensor Protocols for Information via Negotiation (SPIN) [Heinzelman et al., 1999]. The method uses high-level data descriptors, called meta-data, to eliminate redundant network information. Based on meta-data contents, SPIN nodes organise themselves to provide the best coverage and connectivity. The experimental result shows that a SPIN network can deliver 60% more data than networks using conventional approaches such as flooding [Heinzelman et al., 1999]. However, exchanging a substantial amount of meta-data across the network is an energy consuming activity which can reduce the network operational lifetime.

Low Energy Adaptive Clustering Hierarchy (LEACH)

Clustering is often used to reduce control overhead by restricting network information exchange to within small groups of nodes. Low Energy Adaptive Clustering Hierarchy (LEACH) [Heinzelman et al., 2002] is a well known clustering approach, where nodes are organised around a cluster head selected from a subset of nodes. The base station selects cluster heads for a certain time period using a stochastic and rotation based selection policy. Intra-cluster network information (for example, node position, status and energy levels) is sent periodically to the base station to compute the cluster-head probability of each node. After each time round, LEACH adaptively elects "capable nodes" as cluster heads, and each node determines the cluster to which it belongs based on communication distances. The drawback of LEACH is related to the amount of information periodically exchanged even within a cluster which can affect node lifetime.

Radio Channel Based Clustering

Radio channel based clustering is another popular method, where a group of nodes tune their radio transmitter to a common frequency to form a cluster. One example of this type of clustering mechanisms is Dual Network Clustering (DNC) [Sohrabi et al., 2004]. The method proposes that each node should have two radios on board, and those radios create two distinct networks or channels in the sensor field. Radios on a node are tuned to a specific and known set of fixed channels. The first radio to wake up and detect a free channel becomes the cluster head for that channel, and nodes that wake up later on that channel become members of that cluster. Although the mechanism is simple, it lacks control over topology such as uncontrolled cluster membership determination. A similar approach is proposed by Sohrabi et al. [2004], called Rendezvous Clustering Algorithm (RCA), which tunes one of the two radios on a node to a fixed network signalling channel. A node uses this channel to advertise its presence to its neighbours and to gather advertisements from other nodes. Based on collected advertisements, a node becomes a member of a cluster. Although using separate control channels provides better control over the network, distributed time synchronisations and continuous link monitoring mechanisms are required to maintain those channels.

Passive Clustering

Instead of conventional clustering, Taek et al. [2003] propose a multi-level clustering technique to achieve scalability. This could be described as "passive clustering" [Taek et al., 2003], where clusters share some common nodes that are used as intermediaries for inter-cluster data communication. Common nodes eliminate the need for special type cluster head nodes. This flexibility also leads to substantially higher overheads. Every time the topology changes there will be two types of selection procedures triggered - one for cluster head and another for identifying common nodes agreed by neighbouring cluster heads.

Adaptive Self-Configuring sEnsor Networks Topologies (ASCENT)

Topology can be formed adaptively, where nodes join the network whenever necessary. For example, Adaptive Self-Configuring sEnsor Networks Topologies (ASCENT) [Cerpa and Estrin, 2004] activates nodes one by one to maintain network coverage and connectivity. In ASCENT, once a node is activated it stays awake throughout its lifetime and performs both sensing and multi-hop routing. The drawback of ASCENT is not being able to conserve node energy. Since the area of interests for sensing may not be fixed, an active node may no longer be needed for a while. In such an environment, an active ASCENT node will waste its limited energy reserves. ASCENT also does not guarantee maximum network operational lifetime because some nodes become exhausted by performing additional tasks, while some of their neighbours are idle.

Hierarchical Node Organisation

Other than clustering, hierarchical node organisation schemes can also be used. These schemes include the hub-spoke technique [Ma and Aylor, 2004], where a Resource Oriented Protocol (ROP) is used to build network topology. This protocol divides network operations into two phases. In the topology formation phase, nodes report their available resource characteristics and, based on this, optimal network architecture is built. ROP assumes there exist some nodes with limitless resources, and a top-down appointment process then builds the architecture with the minimum resource consumption of ordinary nodes. In the topology update phase, additional sensors are accepted into the network with an optimal balance of resources. The technique is manageable in such environments, where nodes at the top of the hierarchy can be attached to the mains power supply to be considered limitless resources. But this scheme may not be applicable in certain conditions where sensors are thrown in a hostile environment with fixed energy reserves.

A special type of flat hierarchical scheme uses a graph based method for node organisation [Cheng et al., 2003], where nodes and communication links are considered graph vertices and edges respectively. For a given set of sensors, transmission power is assigned to each sensor in such a way that the network formed contains only bidirectional links and is strongly connected. Like traditional hierarchical node organisation techniques, the graph based method has constraints on space and node membership. Hierarchy restructuring is also an energy costly task, so that it may not be feasible for a sensor network.

Summary

In summary, a basic network information sharing approach was initially suggested for organising sensor network topologies. Due to high energy overhead of network information sharing, different self-organising techniques have been proposed such as clustering [Heinzelman et al., 2002; Taek et al., 2003; Sohrabi et al., 2004], hierarchy [Cheng et al., 2003; Ma and Aylor, 2004] or adaptive topology [Cerpa and Estrin, 2002; 2004]. Although these approaches can reduce network control overhead, they produce uneven energy consumption of nodes by only considering individual node energy usage. Uneven node energy usage resulted in unevenly distributed node lifetime. As a result, the early exhaustion of an important node degrades the network quality of service such as coverage and connectivity.

3.3 Residual Energy Based Node Classification

Existing node organisation protocols only concentrated on local energy efficiency [Heinzelman et al., 2002; Taek et al., 2003; Cheng et al., 2003; Baek et al., 2004], where global energy consumption is important to minimise energy wastages. The method proposed in this chapter is organising nodes such that the global energy consumption is balanced over the network. This will extend the network operational lifetime by protecting nodes from early exhaustion. A residual energy based node classification technique is provided. The node classification helps to identify high energy nodes that may perform additional tasks other than sensing. Then nodes are organised based on their capabilities to share tasks of a low energy node by high energy neighbours.

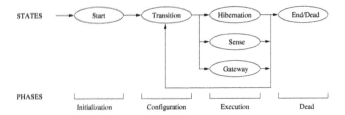

Figure 3.1: Sensor Node Life-Cycle.

In the proposed residual energy based node classification, nodes are classified as high and low energy nodes to share energy usage among them. The energy consumption of a node is directly proportional to the tasks performed, so that energy usage will be balanced if tasks are shared. It is assumed that tasks involved in a sensor lifetime need to be identified to enable task sharing among neighbouring nodes.

3.3.1 Tasks of a Sensor Node

Node lifecycle is defined as a set of different phases (such as Initialisation, Execution) and tasks (such as start, sense) involved in each phase are identified. This will help identify tasks that can be shared among neighbouring nodes during different phases of a node lifecycle. In the literature, node phases are demonstrated as either active or passive over the node life span [Chang and Tassiulas, 2004; Cerpa and Estrin, 2004]. Those phases are elaborated and differentiated into basic states. The transition criteria between those states are also identified.

Every node follows a specific pattern in its lifecycle. For example, nodes start by initialising and then, based on some parameters (such as energy level and query requests), they may sense and/or transmit data or hibernate. Finally, every node may become exhausted by finishing the energy reserve. Amongst these activities, sensor lives can be divided into four phases (see Figure 3.1) and explained below.

1. *Initialisation phase:* A sensor starts its lifecycle in an Initialisation phase, where it identifies neighbours and sets up network parameters (such as node position, sensing and transmission ranges). The Initialisation phase is represented by the Start state in Figure 3.1.

2. *Configuration phase:* Sensor nodes take various decisions during their lifetime such as, should the node be active or inactive. Such decisions are taken in the Configuration phase using available node and network information. The Configuration phase is represented by the Transition state in the diagram.

3. *Execution phase:* Each node enters the Execution phase by being inactive or active, as decided during the Configuration phase. In the inactive state, nodes do nothing other than listening for wake-up requests. This is represented by the Hibernating state in the figure. Nodes in the active state may be performing sensing and data transmission. Most generally nodes perform only sensing, and some will also be collecting data for forwarding to base stations. These are represented by the Sense state and Gateway state respectively in Figure 3.1.

4. *Dead phase:* After consuming their limited energy, nodes eventually become exhausted. Nodes may also be failed by external events such as natural disasters or human interventions. The End/Dead state is representing the Dead phase in Figure 3.1.

3.3.2 Node Classification

Nodes are classified based on their current energy levels to define capable nodes of performing tasks on behalf of their low energy neighbours. Initially it is assumed that all nodes possess the same energy reserves. As soon as a node starts performing activities, the node's energy level gradually decreases. Since tasks at different phases consume different amounts of energy, the residual energy of all nodes will differ at any given time. For example, compared to sensing a gateway node may consume more energy relaying other's data. Such additional tasks should be redistributed among nodes to balance the energy consumption. Distribution of tasks must be fair, ensuring that a node is not considered for additional tasks if it has only the minimum required energy to sense and transmit its data.

The node energy reserve is the only parameter that is variable and decreasing over time considering that nodes are having the same memory and processing powers. This leads to us characterising sensor nodes based on their residual energy levels. A similar approach is noticed in traditional distributed systems where processors are characterised by their process loads [Sinha, 1997]. For example, processors having loads below a certain threshold are called "under-loaded processors", and processors having loads above that threshold are considered "over-loaded processors". A similar approach is adopted by dividing sensors into two types shown in Figure 3.2 which are -

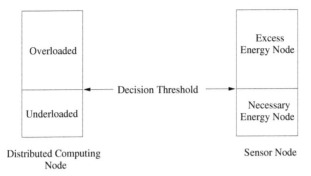

Figure 3.2: Typical Distributed and Sensor Node Characterisation.

- Excess Energy Node (EEN), and

- Necessary Energy Node (NEN).

Nodes having enough energy to perform additional tasks are called EEN, as opposed to nodes having sufficient energy only to perform its own sensing tasks, which are called NEN.

3.3.3 Determining Node Types (EEN/NEN)

The aim of this section is to analytically determine node types, EEN or NEN, based on some network assumptions. This will also help in determining node lifetimes analytically (see Section 3.5). Node types are calculated using the consumed energy or the residual energy level of a node. If the energy requirement for sending and receiving a packet is already known, the residual energy of a node can be computed by considering packet generation and packet arrival rates (alternatively, a node could just measure its battery). This will enable a node determining its type, EEN or NEN, by comparing its residual energy with a predefined threshold (E_{th}).

The residual energy level of a node is normalised to the maximum battery capacity and scaled to 100 [Hong et al., 2002]. The normalised energy level makes it easier to handle even heterogeneous nodes with different battery capacity. Based on the battery capacity, a minimum level of energy, denoted as E_{th}, is identified. The value of E_{th} is application depended and is considered the minimum required energy to perform a node's own tasks for a certain amount of time. Nodes having residual energy above E_{th} are called EEN (Excess

Energy Node), otherwise they are called NEN (Necessary Energy Node). A node will be considered exhausted when it finishes its energy reserves.

For simplicity it is assumed that -

- A node is either in the gateway state, called a gateway node, or in the sensing state, called a non-gateway node.

- Compared to the data transmission or reception, energy consumption while sensing is negligible [Min et al., 2002].

- Packet generation at a node is directly proportional to sensing tasks that it performs [Heinzelman et al., 2002].

- The query for sensing objects may be random so that each sensing node has packet streams with Poisson distribution [Hong et al., 2002].

A non-gateway node senses its sensing region and forwards sensed data to connected gateway nodes. If E_{tx} is the required energy for transmitting a single packet from one node to another, and λ_i is the packet generation rate at node i, the energy requirement of a non-gateway node for transmitting packets over time t is defined as follows.

$$E_{i(NG)}(t) = E_{tx} \times \lambda_i \times t \tag{3.1}$$

A Gateway node generates sensing data and is also responsible for receiving packets from neighbours to be forwarded to the next gateway. Since neighbours have independent packet streams with Poisson distribution, a gateway node also has a packet stream with a Poisson process. Let us assume that gateway j has n_j neighbours. Then the packet arrival rate at gateway j is $\sum_{k=1}^{n_j} \lambda_k$.

If the packet generation rate at Gateway j is λ_j, and the expected value of total packets at gateway j for duration t is $\overline{X_j}(t)$, the expected value of packets at gateway j over time t can be computed as follows.

$$\overline{X_j}(t) = \lambda_j \times t + \sum_{k=1}^{n_j} \lambda_k \times t \tag{3.2}$$

$$= t \left(\lambda_j + \sum_{k=1}^{n_j} \lambda_k \right) \tag{3.3}$$

32

Transmitting a data packet usually consumes more energy than receiving a data packet[12]. For simplicity, let us assume that the energy consumption to transmit (E_{tx}) a single data packet is twice the energy consumption of receiving (E_{rx}) a single data packet. If a node consumes C amount of energy for receiving a data packet, total consumed energy at gateway j over time t can be obtained as follows.

$$E_{j(G)}(t) = E_{rx} \times \sum_{k=1}^{n_j} \lambda_k \times t + E_{tx}\overline{X_j}(t) \tag{3.4}$$

$$= C \times \sum_{k=1}^{n_j} \lambda_k \times t + 2C \times t \left(\lambda_j + \sum_{k=1}^{n_j} \lambda_k \right) \tag{3.5}$$

$$= C \times t \left(2\lambda_j + 3 \sum_{k=1}^{n_j} \lambda_k \right) \tag{3.6}$$

The consumed energy of a node depends on the time it acts as a gateway or a non-gateway node. During the lifetime, if node i acts as a non-gateway for t_1 time and a gateway for t_2 time, the consumed energy can be computed using equation 3.1 and equation 3.6. If the total energy consumption of node i over time t (where, $t = t_1 + t_2$) is $E_i(t)$, it can be determined as follows.

$$E_i(t) = E_{i(NG)}(t_1) + E_{i(G)}(t_2) \tag{3.7}$$

A node can now calculate the residual energy using equation 3.7 to determine its node type. If the amount of initial energy is E, and the energy decision level is E_{th} [Energy Threshold], a node can decide its type, EEN or NEN, by comparing its residual energy level with E_{th}. Node type determination is shown in the following equation.

$$\delta = \frac{E - E_i(t)}{E} = \begin{cases} \delta > E_{th} & Type = EEN \\ \delta \leq E_{th} & Type = NEN \end{cases} \tag{3.8}$$

3.4 The Energy Balanced Clustering (EBC) Method

In this section, a clustering method, called Energy Balanced Clustering (EBC), is proposed to organise sensors according to their node types. This is an extension of conventional clustering

[1]Power usage of UC Mote: $E_{rx} = 2028$ nJ/bit and $E_{tx} = 4317$ nJ/bit [Hill et al., 2000]
[2]Power usage of MICA2 Mote: $E_{rx} = 10$ mA and $E_{tx} = 27$ mA (transmit with maximum power) [Crossbow, 2007b]

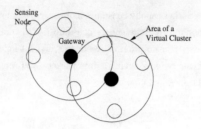

Figure 3.3: Clustering

approaches [Deng et al., 2005; Younis and Fahmy, 2004; Taek et al., 2003; Bandyopadhyay and Coyle, 2003] to deal with network energy balancing. Energy is balanced by choosing gateways or cluster heads only from EEN, and if a gateway becomes NEN, it reverts to being a non-gateway to preserve its energy. Should all the nodes in a cluster become NEN, they organise themselves as an All-Active network [Cerpa and Estrin, 2002] where all nodes act as gateways.

Whenever a node becomes a gateway and forms a cluster, neighbours of that gateway become automatically members of that cluster. In order to provide the required connectivity, gateways are chosen in such a way that there is always at least one gateway within the communication range of every gateway. As a result, clusters are overlapped and members of overlapping clusters may have multiple gateways to forward their data. The interconnection between gateways and overlapping cluster regions is illustrated in Figure 3.3.

3.4.1 Gateway Selection Algorithm

Since clusters are formed around gateways, the selection of gateways from EEN nodes forms the entire network. Whenever an EEN node enters the gateway state, it informs its neighbours using a gateway confirmation message. After receiving the confirmation message, nodes update their respective gateway tables for forwarding their data. To be able to forward the sensed data, every node needs to be connected to at least one gateway.

Gateways need to be connected because gateways only collect and forward data toward the base station using muti-hop communications. The intermediate nodes of a multi-hop path are also gateways. If an EEN node is connected with at least one other gateway, it is eligible to be a gateway. A predefined number G_{th} controls the number of gateways within the cluster. At most G_{th} gateways are allowed per cluster permitting redundant connectivity.

G_{th} is application dependent. If the application requires high Quality of Service (QoS), the value of G_{th} will be more than one. G_{th} tuning process is shown in Subsection 3.4.3.

Nodes initialise themselves as sense nodes, so that there are no gateways in the network initially. It is assumed that there are some fixed "initial gateways" such as sink or base stations to start the gateway selection procedure given in Algorithm 1.

A node can initiate the gateway selection procedure by simply broadcasting a gateway request message to its neighbours when it fails to communicate with existing gateways. Initially, nodes far from the initial gateways may start the selection procedure because they do not have any connectivity with a gateway. To minimise the overhead, a node that receives a gateway request message does not need to resend that message.

After receiving a gateway request message, a node determines its node type and the number of gateway neighbours to check its eligibility to be a gateway. The eligibility check is shown in Algorithm 1 at Line 1.2. Eligible nodes further verify whether the addition of another gateway will exceed the G_{th}. If it does, the eligible node refrains from becoming a gateway. Otherwise, it enters the transition state and participates in the gateway selection procedure. Nodes always save their previous state (such as sense or hibernating), to be able to revert should they not become a gateway (Lines 1.3 - 1.4 in the algorithm).

In the transition state, an eligible node announces its participation to become a gateway by broadcasting a message, called willingness message, to its neighbours. After sending the message, it waits for a predefined amount of time (t_p) to receive such messages from others. t_p is chosen as the round trip time to send a message and receive the reply from a neighbour. Within the waiting time, if the node does not receive any other gateway willingness messages, it assumes that there are no other gateway aspirants among its neighbours, and then it enters the gateway state by broadcasting a gateway confirmation message (Lines 1.18 - 1.21). After receiving a gateway confirmation message, neighbour nodes update their gateway tables.

Should a waiting eligible node receive willingness messages from other nodes (within its wait time t_p), this indicates that there are more than one eligible node. All eligible nodes go through a random back-off process to discourage multiple nodes from entering the gateway state. The random back-off is a technique used to avoid collision in medium access control [Stallings, 2007] and also used in sensor networks to avoid redundant coverage [Tian and Georganas, 2005]. This process is shown in Lines 1.7 - 1.16 of Algorithm 1, where each eligible node waits a random amount of time (t_s). The wait time t_s is chosen as round trip times between one and the number of eligible nodes. The eligible node that receives the lowest waiting time will get the chance to become a gateway by sending the gateway

---
Algorithm 1: Gateway Selcetion Algorithm

Assume:

Each node has a gateway information table to store at most G_{th} number of gateway info.

Let :

NType: type of node G_{No}: no of gateways

G_{th}: gateway threshold   State: state of the node

Msg: Control message   Table: gateway info

t_p: predefined wait time t_s: random wait time

1.1 *When gateway request message received*;

1.2 **if** *NType* $\neq$ *NEN AND* $G_{no} \neq 0$ *AND* $G_{no} \leq G_{th}$ **then**

1.3 $State_{prev} \leftarrow State_{current}$;

1.4 $State_{current} \leftarrow State_{transition}$;

1.5   Broadcast($Msg_{willingness}$);

1.6   Wait(t_p);

1.7   **if** $Msg_{received} == Msg_{willingness}$ **then**

1.8   Wait(t_s);

1.9   **if** $Msg_{received} == Msg_{confirmation}$ **then**

1.10   Update(Table);

1.11 $State_{current} \leftarrow State_{prev}$;

1.12   **end**

1.13   **else**

1.14   Broadcast($Msg_{confirmation}$);

1.15 $State_{current} \leftarrow State_{gateway}$;

1.16   **end**

1.17   **end**

1.18   **else**

1.19   Broadcast($Msg_{confirmation}$);

1.20 $State_{current} \leftarrow State_{gateway}$;

1.21   **end**

1.22 **end**

---

confirmation message. If an eligible node receives a gateway confirmation message within time t_s, it exits from the gateway selection procedure and reverts to its previous state.

3.4.2 Algorithm Complexity

To show the computational performance, the algorithmic complexity of EBC is identified. The performance is measured as the message and time complexity of the gateway selection algorithm shown in the following.

The message complexity is important for a sensor network protocol because energy consumption is directly proportional to messages sent and received by a sensor node. A node n_i sends gateway request messages to its neighbours whenever that node fails to communicate with its gateways. If there are average N neighbours, n_i has to send N request messages. In response, all the eligible neighbours participate in the gateway selection procedure by sending gateway willingness messages to their respective neighbours. In the best case scenario, there may have only one eligible node in the neighbour set of n_i to become a gateway. That node broadcasts a willingness message and a gateway confirmation message to its N neighbours. If each broadcast takes $O(N)$ messages, the message complexity of the proposed algorithm is also $O(N)$. In the worst case scenario, all N neighbours of node n_i may be eligible to become a gateway. In that case, each of those EEN nodes sends N willingness messages and only one of them sends another N gateway confirmation messages. With that, the message complexity becomes in the order of $O(N^2)$ for the worst case scenario.

The time complexity shows how fast the algorithm can organise nodes. The time complexity of EBC is constant in either case. For the best case, an eligible node only has to wait for a predefined time t_p which is the round trip time of a data packet. For the worst case, the wait time is $t_p + t_s$, where the maximum value of t_s can be N unit time.

3.4.3 Algorithm Parameters

The proposed clustering method has two important parameters, namely the energy threshold (E_{th}) and the gateway threshold (G_{th}). E_{th} controls each node's capability to become a gateway, and G_{th} controls the level of redundant connectivity between nodes and gateways. The values of both of the parameters depend on network topology and applications. For instance, E_{th} in a sparse network should be low enough to reduce node reorganisation. On the other hand, if fault tolerance and higher QoS is required, G_{th} should be higher to provide redundant connectivity.

37

Table 3.1: Network Parameters for Determining EBC Energy and Gateway Thresholds

Parameter	Value	
Initial node energy	100 unit	
Energy usage per data packet	Transmit	0.04
	Receive	0.02
Average number of neighbours per node	2 to 10	
Packet generation rate	Uniformly Random	

The energy threshold E_{th} balances energy usage over the network by preventing nodes below E_{th} performing additional tasks. If E_{th} is set too high, an EEN node will become a NEN after a short period of time because its energy level will decrease below the threshold quickly. When all nodes become NEN, the network acts like an All-Active network [Cerpa and Estrin, 2004], so that energy consumption will be uneven. If E_{th} is set too low, a gateway node will consume most of its energy reserves before becoming a NEN from an EEN. As a result, a NEN node will get less energy reserve to perform its own tasks and exhaust early.

To find the best value for E_{th}, experiments were performed to compute the standard deviation of energy using equation 3.8. E_{th} was varied from 0% to 50% with other parameters as shown in Table 3.1. The standard deviation of residual energy levels was measured when the first node became exhausted and results are shown in Figure 3.4. The figure shows that the standard deviation of residual energy was about 90% when E_{th} was 0%. At E_{th}=0%, an EEN node cannot share its tasks with others because it performs gateway task until it finishes its energy reserves. When E_{th} was increased to 10% from 0%, a significant change in standard energy deviation was noticed. The deviation decreased from 90% to 60% because an EEN node shared tasks with its neighbours. With the increase of the energy threshold value, the standard energy deviation reduced more up to $E_{th} = 30\%$ where the deviation was below 40%. After that, with the increase of the threshold value, the standard deviation of residual energy levels started increasing. Since the least standard deviation of energy was observed at $E_{th} = 30\%$, it was set to 30% for subsequent simulations (see Section 3.6).

The gateway threshold G_{th} represents the number of communication paths within a given cluster. If G_{th} is high, there will be redundant connectivity for a node to gateways. This will allow multiple nodes within a cluster consuming excess energy. For a sparse network, it may

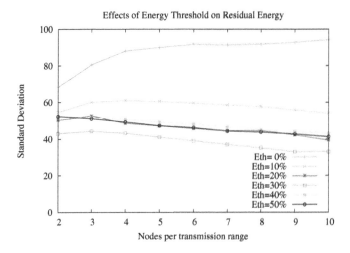

Figure 3.4: Standard Deviation of Remaining Energy for Various Energy Threshold Values.

not be possible to replace all those gateways when they become NEN. Other than that, a network with excessive gateways will work more like an All-Active network where all nodes are gateways [Cerpa and Estrin, 2004]. If G_{th} is low, there will be fewer options for a node to send data and that may cause network congestion and degraded QoS.

Another experiment was performed to find the best value of G_{th}. The same testbed described in section 3.6 was used and set E_{th} to 30%. By varying G_{th} from 2 to 5, the standard deviation of residual energy levels and the network lifetime to when the first node became exhausted were measured. Figure 3.5 shows that in a sparse network, the residual energy deviation among nodes is low. Since there were fewer neighbours to share the task of a low energy node, the network became All-Active and most of the nodes were acting as gateways. With the increase of the node density, the energy deviation was increasing but almost stabilised to a certain value for all G_{th} levels. Figure 3.5 also shows that the energy deviation is not affected by G_{th} when the nodes per transmission range is ≥ 5. A similar effect is noticed in Figure 3.6, where lifetime is proportional to the gateway threshold up to a certain node density, after which network lifetime becomes saturated. Interestingly, saturation points for standard energy deviation and network lifetime were almost the same

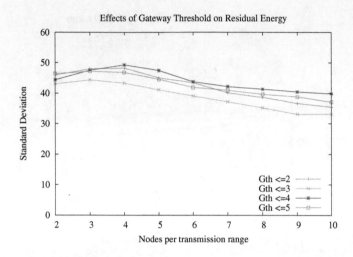

Figure 3.5: Standard Deviation of Remaining Energy for Various Gateway Threshold Values.

in the experiment because better energy balancing increases network lifetime. In Figure 3.5, the best energy balancing is found at $G_{th} = \leq 3$, and in Figure 3.6, the best network lifetime is found at the same threshold for all node densities. Experiments described in Sections 3.5 and 3.6 used $G_{th} \leq 3$ for measuring performances of EBC.

3.4.4 The Network Connectivity of EBC

This section shows that EBC can always provide connectivity to all deployed nodes because it forms a network based on connected gateways. An EEN node only becomes a gateway, if it is connected to another gateway. Since clusters are formed based on gateways, clusters are not mutually exclusive. That is, a cluster has intersecting member sets with neighbouring clusters. Most importantly, at least one gateway node belongs to one of those intersecting sets. If there is a gateway in one of the intersecting sets of a cluster, members of that cluster are connected to another cluster through that gateway. Since gateways are selected outwardly from the "initial gateways", all the clusters are connected to each other. Every deployed node is attached to a cluster, and connected clusters ensure that all nodes are reachable. To formally show such a claim, let us introduce the following parameters.

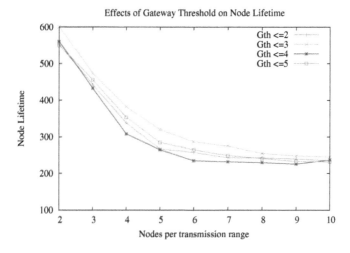

Figure 3.6: Network Lifetime for Various Gateway Threshold Values.

- S is the set of all sensor nodes in the network.

- N_i is the set of neighbouring nodes of node i.

- C_i is the set of cluster members of gateway i, and $C_i = N_i$.

- $f(N)$ is the gateway selection algorithm selecting gateways from set N as described in Subsection 3.4.1.

The gateway selection algorithm $f(N)$ forms a sequence of gateways because an EEN only becomes a gateway if it is connected to another gateway. If the communication range of a node is t_r, the average distance between two neighbouring gateways is $\frac{t_r}{2}$. That is, the gateway selection algorithm $f(N)$ ensures that there will be a gateway within half of the transmission range of another. Since $f(N)$ starts from the initial gateways, there will be a gateway sequence from initial gateways conforming to the following recursion rule.

Lemma 3.4.1 *If the distance between the initial gateway and two neighbouring gateways, say node i and node i+1, are d_i and d_{i+1} respectively, following properties are found:*

41

$$|d_{i+1} - d_i| \leq t_r \tag{3.9}$$

$$\Rightarrow d_{i+1} \leq d_i + t_r \tag{3.10}$$

Since clusters are formed around gateway nodes, according to Equation 3.10, two neighbouring clusters are connected to each other by their respective gateways. That is, $f(N)$ chooses an EEN node as a gateway from an existing cluster. If x_{i+1} is an EEN node belonging to a cluster C_i of neighbour set N_i, the gateway selection algorithm will select x_{i+1} to form a new cluster C_{i+1}. Then C_i and C_{i+1} are overlapped at least through gateways. This can be stated as follows.

$$f(N_i) = \{x_i | x_i \in C_i \wedge x_i \in C_{i-1}\} \tag{3.11}$$

$$f(N_{i+1}) = \{x_{i+1} | x_{i+1} \in C_{i+1} \wedge x_{i+1} \in C_i\} \tag{3.12}$$

This implies that two neighbouring clusters are not mutually exclusive, that is -

$$C_i \cap C_{i+1} \neq \phi \tag{3.13}$$

Equation 3.13 shows that two neighbouring clusters are overlapped, and Equation 3.12 shows that x_i and x_{i+1} are in the intersection set of C_i and C_{i+1}. That is -

$$\{x_i , x_{i+1}\} \in C_i \cap C_{i+1} \tag{3.14}$$

According to EBC, if any node fails to communicate with a gateway, it initiates a new cluster formation procedure to be associated with at least one cluster. Hence, the union of clusters is the super set of all deployed sensors, which is shown in the following equation.

$$C_0 \cup C_1 \cup C_2 \cup \ldots \ldots \cup C_i = S \tag{3.15}$$

Equation 3.14 states that a cluster is connected at least to another cluster. This ensures connectivity in the network. Equation 3.15 states that the algorithm covers all the deployed node set.

Table 3.2: Symbol Table for Identifying Node Lifetime.

Symbol	Denote
E	Initial energy in a sensor node
$E_i(T)$	Energy spent by the ith sensor over time T
$E_{i(NG)}$	Energy spent by the ith sensor as a Non Gateway node
$E_{i(G)}$	Energy spent by the ith sensor as a Gateway node
C	Energy needed to transmit or receive a single data packet
N	Average number of neighbours of the ith sensor
λ	Data packet generation rate
δ	Ratio of the residual energy and total energy

3.5   The Lower Bound of a Node Lifetime

This section provides an analytical evaluation of EBC and some well known schemes such as the All-Active approach [Cerpa and Estrin, 2002], LEACH [Heinzelman et al., 2002] and ASCENT [Cerpa and Estrin, 2004]. The evaluation is based on the lower boundary of node lifetime because this is also the lower boundary of the network lifetime. A relationship between node lifetimes versus average nodes per transmission range is identified. This will help us determine the lower boundary of node lifetime for different node organisation techniques.

3.5.1   Node Lifetime

In the following, the consumed energy of a node over a certain period of time is identified mathematically with some assumptions. Based on time to consume a certain amount of energy, node lifetime is identified. It is defined as the time it takes from entering the Start state to the End/Dead state (see Figure 3.1). In this chapter, a node is considered dead only when it finishes its energy reserves.

Let us consider that there are n nodes in a sensor field, and the average number of nodes per transmission range of a sensor node is N. Let E be the initial energy, λ be the packet generation rate at each node, and T be the time when first node becomes exhausted from the network. The boundary value of T is determined using equations described in Section 3.3.3. The symbols used for computations are given in Table 3.2.

Energy Balanced Clustering (EBC)

EBC protects a node from early exhaustion using an energy threshold E_{th}. EBC nodes are classified as EEN and NEN based on E_{th}. Each node starts as an EEN, and after consuming a certain amount of energy reserves it becomes a NEN. A node can be a gateway only if it is an EEN, otherwise it will be in a non-gateway state such as sensing. If a node spends all of its energy reserves above E_{th} as a gateway node and the rest as a non-gateway node, this is considered the earliest time that a node can be exhausted in EBC.

If a node is continuously sensing and/or forwarding data, the consumed energy of a node over time T is the sum of the energy consumed by that node as a non-gateway and a gateway as shown in equation 3.7. Let us now consider that a node acting as a gateway for t_1 time and as a non-gateway for t_2 time where $T = t_1 + t_2$. If T is the lower boundary of a node lifetime, a node n_i consumes $(100 - E_{th})\%$ of its initial energy reserves in t_1 time as a gateway and $E_{th}\%$ of initial energy reserves in t_2 time as a non-gateway.

If E is the initial energy reserves, and $E_{i(G)}(t_1)$ is the consumed energy by n_i as a gateway, using equation 3.6, t_1 is determined as follows.

$$\frac{(100 - E_{th})}{100}E = E_{i(G)}(t_1) \tag{3.16}$$

$$\Rightarrow \frac{(100 - E_{th})}{100}E = Ct_1\left(2\lambda + 3\sum_{k=1}^{N}\lambda\right) \tag{3.17}$$

$$\Rightarrow t_1 = \frac{(100 - E_{th})E}{100C\lambda(3N + 2)} \tag{3.18}$$

If $E_{i(NG)}(t_2)$ is the consumed energy over time t_2 for n_i, using equation 3.1, t_2 is determined as follows.

$$\frac{E_{th}}{100}E = E_{i(NG)}(t_2) \tag{3.19}$$

$$\Rightarrow \frac{E_{th}}{100}E = 2C\lambda t_2 \tag{3.20}$$

$$\Rightarrow t_2 = \frac{E_{th}E}{200C\lambda} \tag{3.21}$$

The lower boundary of an EBC node lifetime T is the sum of equations 3.18 and 3.21 and is given below.

44

$$T = t_1 + t_2 \tag{3.22}$$

$$= \frac{(100 - E_{th})E}{100C\lambda(3N + 2)} + \frac{E_{th}E}{200C\lambda} \tag{3.23}$$

$$= \frac{E}{100C\lambda}\left(\frac{100 + 3NE_{th} + E_{th}}{3N + 2}\right) \tag{3.24}$$

The All-Active Method

In the All-Active technique, a basic node organisation method is applied without any energy conserving measure - all nodes act as gateways. If an All-Active node i consumes $E_i(T)$ energy over time T, the consumed energy can be computed using equation 3.6 as follows.

$$E_i(T) = E_{i(G)}(T) \tag{3.25}$$

$$= C\lambda T(3N + 2) \tag{3.26}$$

If T_{all} is the time to exhaust an All-active node, according to equation 3.8 T_{all} can be computed as -

$$E = E_i(T_{all}) \tag{3.27}$$

$$T_{all} = \frac{E}{C\lambda(3N + 2)} \tag{3.28}$$

Low Energy Adaptive Clustering Hierarchy (LEACH)

LEACH [Heinzelman et al., 2002] periodically initiates a cluster head selection process, in which each node broadcasts their current status to base stations where it calculates the probability of each node to be a gateway. That is, after each round each node sends N packets to their neighbours. If the time for the ith node to exhaust under LEACH is T_{LEACH}, and the cluster head (or gateway) selection process rate is Δ, the energy consumed by a node participating in the gateway selection procedure during its lifetime will be $\frac{T_{LEACH}}{\Delta}NC$.

If a LEACH node spends its entire lifetime as a cluster head or gateway, using equation 3.6 the consumed energy over time T_{LEACH} can be determined as follows.

45

$$E = E_{i(G)}(T_{LEACH}) + \frac{T_{LEACH}}{\Delta} NC \tag{3.29}$$

$$\Rightarrow \quad E = C\lambda T_{LEACH}(3N+2) + \frac{T_{LEACH}}{\Delta} NC \tag{3.30}$$

$$\Rightarrow \quad T_{LEACH} = \frac{\Delta E}{C(3N\Delta\lambda + 2\Delta\lambda + N)} \tag{3.31}$$

If a LEACH node spends its entire lifetime as a cluster member or non-gateway node, using equation 3.1 the consumed energy over time T_{LEACH} can be determined as follows.

$$E = E_{i(NG)}(T_{LEACH}) + \frac{T_{LEACH}}{\Delta} NC \tag{3.32}$$

$$\Rightarrow \quad E = 2C\lambda T_{LEACH} + \frac{T_{LEACH}}{\Delta} NC \tag{3.33}$$

$$\Rightarrow \quad T_{LEACH} = \frac{\Delta E}{C(2\Delta\lambda + N)} \tag{3.34}$$

In LEACH, base stations select nodes as gateways or cluster heads based on parameters such as residual energy levels and distances between neighbours. Let us assume that the cluster head rotation is evenly distributed over the node lifetime. The lifetime T_{LEACH} is then approximated by adding equations 3.31 and 3.34 (actual lower bound of a LEACH lifetime may be less than the average because LEACH does not have any low energy node protection measure like energy threshold in EBC). T_{LEACH} is computed as follows.

$$T_{LEACH} = \frac{\Delta E(3N\Delta\lambda + 4\Delta\lambda + 2N)}{2C(3N\Delta\lambda + 2\Delta\lambda + N)(2\Delta\lambda + N)} \tag{3.35}$$

Adaptive Self-Configuring sEnsor Networks Topologies (ASCENT)

In ASCENT, once a node becomes active from inactive state, it remains active throughout its lifetime. ASCENT's active state is equivalent to the gateway state in EBC. If the ratio of active to total lifetime is x, the energy spent by an ASCENT node over time T is as follows.

$$E_i(T) = E_{i(G)}(xT) \tag{3.36}$$

$$= C\lambda xT(3N+2) \tag{3.37}$$

If an ASCENT node becomes exhausted at T_{ASCENT} time, the node lifetime can be computed as follows.

Table 3.3: Summary of the Lower Bound of a Node Lifetime.

Method	Node Lifetime
EBC	$\frac{E}{100C\lambda}\left(\frac{100+3NE_{th}+E_{th}}{3N+2}\right)$
The All-Active method	$\frac{E}{C\lambda(3N+2)}$
LEACH	$\frac{\Delta E(3N\Delta\lambda+4\Delta\lambda+2N)}{2C(3N\Delta\lambda+2\Delta\lambda+N)(2\Delta\lambda+N)}$
ASCENT	$\frac{E}{xC\lambda(3N+2)}$

$$E = E_i(T_{ASCENT}) \tag{3.38}$$

$$T_{ASCENT} = \frac{E}{xC\lambda(3N+2)} \tag{3.39}$$

3.5.2 Comparative Study

In what follows, EBC is compared against three well known techniques, namely All-Active [Cerpa and Estrin, 2002], LEACH [Heinzelman et al., 2002] and ASCENT [Cerpa and Estrin, 2004]. The analysis will provide a way of comparing node lifetime between all these approaches, and it will show the impact of energy balancing on node lifetime.

The lower boundary of node lifetime for various node organisation techniques is compared using the lifetime equations given in Table 3.3. To compute node lifetime, an arbitrary sensor field was considered where nodes were stochastically distributed. Nodes were assumed to be architecturally identical, having equal sensing and transmission ranges. Each node stacked with 100 unit of energy, and a single packet receiving consumed 0.02 units of power which is half of the required energy to transmit a data packet. In the algorithm parameter tuning (Subsection 3.4.3), the best value of E_{th} was found at 30% for our simulation testbed. The energy threshold E_{th} was set to 30%. The ratio of active to total time, x, and the cluster head selection period, Δ, are taken from [Cerpa and Estrin, 2004] and [Heinzelman et al., 2002] respectively. The ratio of active to total time (x) for ASCENT was set 0.4 [Cerpa and Estrin, 2004], and the cluster head selection period (Δ) for LEACH was set 20 unit times [Heinzelman et al., 2002]. With these fixed parameters, the density of sensor nodes was increased gradually to vary the number of nodes per transmission range from 2 to 10.

Table 3.4: Network Parameters for Analysing Node Organisation Schemes

Parameter	Value		
Number of nodes (S)	Varied from 100 to 500		
Average number of neighbours per node	2 to 10		
Initial node energy (E)	100 unit power		
Data transmission cost (E_t)	0.04 unit power		
Data receiving cost (E_r)	0.02 unit power		
Data generation rate (λ)	low	5	
	moderate	10	
	high	20	
Energy threshold (E_{th}) for EBC	30%		
Gateway selection period (Δ) for LEACH	20 unit time		
Ratio of active time to total time (x) For ASCENT	0.4		

The lower boundary of node lifetime was calculated using equations described for three different network properties, where lifetime was considered the time to exhaust the first node. Network conditions were varied by changing packet generation rates, where the packet generation rate was considered low when 5 packets were generated per unit time ($\lambda = 5$), moderate when 10 packets were generated per unit time ($\lambda = 10$), and high when 20 packets were generated per unit time ($\lambda = 20$).

Figure 3.7 shows the lower bound of node lifetime when packet generation rate is low. The lifetime equation of EBC (equation 3.24) shows that node density has a minimum impact on EBC lifetime because more neighbours per node implies better energy sharing. LEACH lifetime equation shows a similar effect (equation 3.35), and it is affected by the gateway selection rate (Δ) as well. Figure 3.7 shows that EBC and LEACH lifetime are almost stable with the increase of the number of nodes per transmission range. The lifetime equations of ASCENT (equation 3.39) and the All-Active method (equation 3.28) show that their lifetime are inversely proportionate to the node density. This is because, higher number of neighbours implies that a gateway may have to relay higher numbers of data packets. Figure 3.7 shows that with the increase of the number of nodes per transmission range, ASCENT and All-Active lifetimes are decreasing. For example, the lifetime of an EBC node varies from 387 to

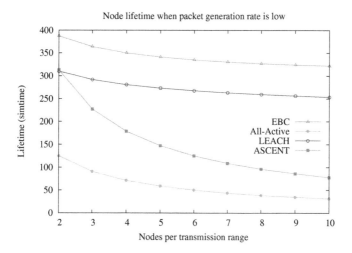

Figure 3.7: Lower Bound of a Node Lifetime when Packet Generation Rate (λ) is Low.

321 simulation times (simtimes) for various node density, while an ASCENT node lifetime varies from 312 to 80 simtimes for the same node density range.

Figure 3.7 reveals that EBC outperforms LEACH by 15%, ASCENT by 55% and the All-Active by 70%. Because of the energy threshold (E_{th}) based node exhaustion protection, EBC nodes avoided early exhaustion. Although LEACH periodically rotates the cluster head among neighbours, it cannot prevent a node being a cluster head while it has low energy reserves. The All-Active method does not have any energy preserving measures, so the lower boundary of a node lifetime is the least for this method. ASCENT controls network topology by keeping a subset of nodes inactive. It gradually activates those nodes whenever a node fails to communicate with its active neighbours. By keeping a subset of deployed nodes inactive ASCENT performed 50% better than the All-Active method.

Figures 3.8 and 3.9 show node lifetime when the packet generation rate are increased to 10 and 20 respectively from 5 per unit time. Results follow a similar trend to the one in Figure 3.7. However, with the increase of the packet generation rate, lifetimes for all methods are also reduced. EBC still outperformed other techniques with the same percentage that it maintained when the packet generation rate was low (Figure 3.7).

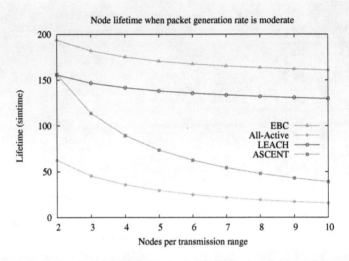

Figure 3.8: Lower Bound of a Node Lifetime when Packet Generation Rate (λ) is Moderate.

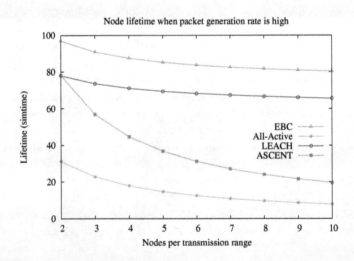

Figure 3.9: Lower Bound of a Node Lifetime when Packet Generation Rate (λ) is High.

3.6 Performance Analysis

In addition to exploration of the lower boundary of node lifetime discussed in Section 3.5, experimental evaluation of various schemes has been performed to validate analytical results of EBC. Two other prominent node organisation schemes, namely LEACH [Heinzelman et al., 2002] and ASCENT [Cerpa and Estrin, 2004] (see Section 3.2), have also been implemented for comparing against EBC. Since the All-Active method [Cerpa and Estrin, 2002] is the basic approach to node organisation, this is considered as the base line for comparisons.

The simulation environment consisted of sensor nodes randomly distributed and nodes were assumed to be architecturally identical. Each node had the same memory, energy and processing powers. Nodes were also having the same communication and sensing ranges, and the node communication was bidirectional. The number of deployed nodes varied from 100 to 500 to vary the network node density. For the sake of experiment result discussion, a network is referred as *sparse* when the average nodes per transmission range was ≤ 5, otherwise the network is called *dense*.

The number of generated data packets was uniformly distributed to the nodes. To collect data from deployed sensors, there were five sink or base stations. It is assumed that sink or base stations were machines connected to the main power supply. Data packets were to be routed to the sink node through multi-hop data communication using the shortest path routing algorithm.

The specification of the network environment was the same as mentioned in section 3.5 and is also given in Table 3.5.

To measure the performance of various node organisation techniques the standard deviation of residual energy levels and network lifetime are used as metrics. The standard node energy deviation shows how balanced the network is, while the network lifetime shows how long each method can keep the network operational. Three different network lifetimes are measured to compare techniques from various points of view. Definitions of those three network lifetimes are given below.

1. Time for exhausting the first node in the network.

2. Time until the first network cut or partition occurs.

3. Time for exhausting half of the deployed nodes.

Table 3.5: Simulation Environment for Implementing Node Organisation Schemes

Parameter	Value
Number of nodes (S)	Varied from 100 to 500
Number of nodes per transmission range (t_r)	2 to 10
Initial node energy (E)	100 unit power
Data transmission cost (E_t)	0.04 unit power
Data receiving cost (E_r)	0.02 unit power
Data transmission range (t_r)	4 unit distance
Energy threshold (E_{th})	30%
Gateway threshold (G_{th})	≤ 3
Gateway selection rate for LEACH (Δ)	20 unit time
Node active to inactive time ratio for ASCENT (x)	0.4
Sensing rate	Uniformly random
Data generation rate	Uniformly random

For each of those cases, the residual energy levels of sensor nodes were recorded to calculate the standard deviation of remaining energy and network lifetime.

3.6.1 Lifetime 1: When the First Node becomes Exhausted

To compare various node organisation techniques, the standard deviation of residual energy levels and network lifetime were measured when first node became exhausted. Since nodes forward data to the base stations through multi-hop data communication, nodes close to a base station relay more data than nodes far from base stations. These are the most important nodes for maintaining connectivity between base stations and the rest of the network. Such nodes will exhaust earlier due to performing more tasks than others. A network starts becoming operationally ineffective when nodes are exhausting so that the time for exhausting the first node is considered as a network lifetime.

The standard deviation of remaining energy when the first node dies is shown in Figure 3.10. The first node exhausted by relaying more data packets than others is one of the most important nodes, being close to the base station. For an ideal condition, the standard deviation of remaining energy levels should be zero at any moment where tasks are evenly

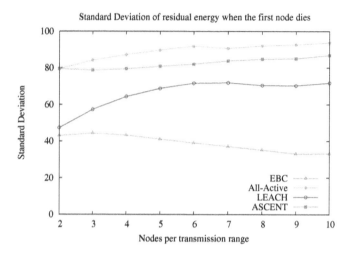

Figure 3.10: Standard Deviation of Remaining Energies when First Node becomes Exhausted.

distributed. In reality, nodes are randomly distributed and nodes in different positions have different numbers of tasks to perform. Neither the All-Active nor ASCENT have any energy or task balancing measure in their node organisation schemes but EBC redistributes tasks whenever the energy level drops below a certain threshold. LEACH also periodically rotates the responsibilities of nodes which balances the energy usage. Due to energy balancing measures, EBC and LEACH have less energy wastages compared to the All-Active and ASCENT. LEACH does not have any explicit node protection measure like E_{th} in EBC, so it cannot prevent a low energy node being a cluster head while its neighbours still have enough energy reserves. For this reason, the standard deviation of residual energy levels for LEACH was 75% more than EBC when first node became exhausted. Figure 3.10 shows that EBC has an energy deviation of about 40% that is, on average, all other nodes still have 40% of their energy reserves remaining when the first node exhausted. The result also shows that energy deviations of the All-Active and ASCENT are about 90%, and LEACH displays about 70% residual energy deviation.

Figure 3.11 shows the time to exhaust the first node as a function of nodes per transmission range. The figure clearly shows that EBC outperforms existing techniques. EBC

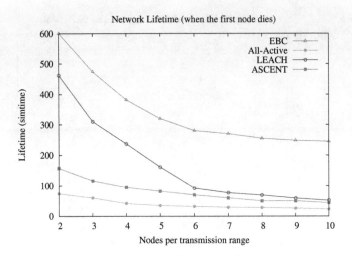

Network Lifetime (when the first node dies)

Figure 3.11: Network Lifetime when First Node becomes Exhausted.

classifies nodes as EEN and NEN based on their residual energy levels. EEN nodes are considered high energy nodes, and only an EEN can become a gateway. Once the energy level of a gateway node drops below E_{th}, it voluntarily leaves the gateway state thus extending its lifetime. Such a technique is absent in existing node organisation methods. The result also shows that in a sparse network, an EBC node lifetime is about 600 simtimes which is about 100 simtimes more than a LEACH node lifetime. LEACH periodically rotates cluster heads among neighbours where the cluster head selection procedure depends on broadcasting node current status to base stations. Periodic broadcasting has an impact on node lifetime and LEACH also does not protect a low energy node being a cluster head. However, at low network density, a LEACH node still can survive about 250 simtimes more than an ASCENT node. ASCENT forms the network adaptively, that is, it keeps nodes in an inactive state and activates one by one when the network QoS degrades. Since an ASCENT node has less number of active neighbours than others, it survives 50 simtimes longer than an All-Active node when the network is sparse. The All-Active method is a basic node organisation technique where all nodes act as gateways. The result shows that at low network density its lifetime is only 80 simtimes, and this is the least among all the compared techniques.

At high network density, network lifetimes for all methods reduced from their respective lifetimes at low node density. The lifetime reduces because of the increasing number of neighbours. A higher number of neighbours imply that a gateway node has to relay more data packets. Interestingly, network lifetime for EBC became stabilised when the number of nodes per transmission range increased to ≥ 5. EBC controls the network connectivity using a gateway threshold G_{th}, that is, EBC permits maximum G_{th} number of gateways per cluster. In this simulation, G_{th} was set to 3, and the network became saturated when the number of nodes per transmission range became ≥ 5. The same threshold was used for LEACH as well to control redundant connectivity, so that it also showed a similar behaviour to EBC. At high node density, Figure 3.11 also shows that an EBC node has a network lifetime about 250 simtimes which is at least 150 simtimes longer than other techniques.

3.6.2 Lifetime 2: When the First Cut occurs

When a node becomes isolated due to the exhaustion of all of its neighbours, it is called cut or network cut. The time to occur the first cut (that is when first isolated node is found) is measured. This is an important performance metric because partitioning can make a network ineffective. The standard deviation of residual energy levels and network lifetime were observed when the first cut occurred and results are described below.

The standard deviation of residual energy when the first cut occurs is shown in Figure 3.12. The result shows that the standard energy deviation of LEACH matches with EBC when the number of nodes per transmission range was 2. At an extremely low node density, LEACH rotates the cluster head job among all the neighbours, whereas EBC waits for a gateway to become NEN from EEN to rotate the gateway task. With the increase of the number of neighbours per node, LEACH fails to rotate the cluster head job among all nodes due to random placement of nodes. Although the gateway task is rotated among a subset of neighbours, LEACH periodically finds new gateway eligible nodes using broadcasting. The periodic broadcasting is an energy costly event. EBC is advantageous over LEACH because it invokes the gateway selection procedure only when an existing gateway becomes NEN. The figure shows that at high node density EBC is able to decrease the energy deviation to 25% while LEACH standard energy deviation increases to 60% from 40%. ASCENT and the All-Active methods do not rotate the cluster head or gateway jobs, so nodes have about 80% energy left while their neighbours are failing.

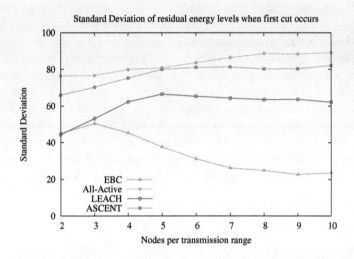

Figure 3.12: *Standard Deviation of Remaining Energies when First Cut occurs.*

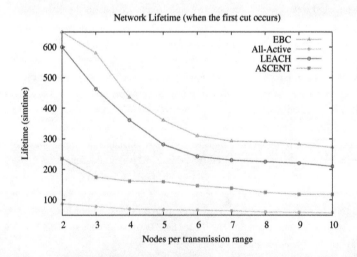

Figure 3.13: *Network Lifetime when First Cut occurs.*

Figure 3.13 shows the time taken before at least one node is isolated from the network for various node densities. The differences between lifetimes of EBC and LEACH become narrow when lifetime is considered the first cut to occur. LEACH lifetime improves about 200 simtimes than the first node to exhaust lifetime (Figure 3.11) because LEACH gets sufficient time to rotate cluster head job among neighbours. However, the figure shows that EBC lifetime is still at least 25% higher than LEACH lifetime because of the energy based node protection measure. ASCENT also shows a noticeable improvement from the lifetime when first node to exhaust was considered, however, ASCENT lifetime is about 400 simtimes less than LEACH and EBC at low network density. At high node density, the differences between lifetimes reduce but still ASCENT lifetime is 100 and 150 simtimes less than LEACH and EBC respectively. The All-Active method performed badly and has a lifetime less than 100 simtimes due to lack of any energy conserving measures.

3.6.3   Lifetime 3: When 50% of Total Nodes become Exhausted

The time for exhaustion of 50% of total nodes is considered because some of the existing work such as [Cerpa and Estrin, 2002; 2004] use similar metrics as network lifetime. The network may not be effective up to that point, however the experiment is included for the sake of completeness.

Standard deviation of remaining energy between nodes when half of the nodes have died is shown in Figure 3.14. Due to the energy balancing measure of EBC and the cluster head rotation policy of LEACH, the standard energy deviation curves are steady for these two approaches. The figure shows that EBC has the least energy wastage compared to other approaches when half of the deployed nodes are exhausted. At low node density, the standard deviation of residual energy levels for EBC is about 40%, while LEACH has 60%, the All-active method has about 75% and ASCENT has 80%. When the node density was increased, unlike other approaches the standard deviation for EBC was gradually decreasing. The result shows that the standard deviation decreases to about 25%, while LEACH standard deviation increases to 70%. The All-active and ASCENT both have about 85% energy deviation at high node density.

Figure 3.15 illustrates the time taken for 50% of nodes to die, while node density is varied. The time differences between the first node to exhaust and 50% of nodes to exhaust shows an important characteristic for various techniques. Ideally, all nodes should become exhausted at the same time however, in reality, it is not possible due to different responsibilities and

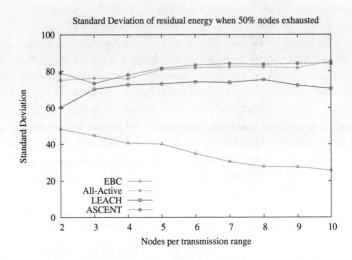

Figure 3.14: Standard Deviation of Residual Energies when 50% of Total Nodes Exhausted.

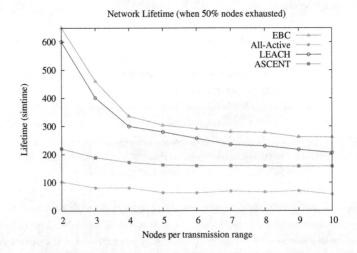

Figure 3.15: Network Lifetime when 50% of Total Nodes Exhausted.

tasks that nodes perform such as a node closer to the base station has to relay more data packets than others. On average the lifetime increased 10% with EBC from first node to exhaust to 50% nodes to exhaust. It is 35% for LEACH, 40% for ASCENT and 44% for the All-Active method. That is, EBC has the least time difference between exhausting the first node to 50% of nodes. This implies that EBC is able to operate closer to the ideal condition compared to existing techniques. Figure 3.15 also shows that EBC able to extend the network lifetime by 10% more than LEACH in all network densities. It also outperforms ASCENT and the All-Active method by about 400 and 500 simtimes respectively when the network is sparse. At high node density, lifetime differences among compared schemes reduce but EBC still outperforms those approaches by about 100 and 200 simtimes respectively.

3.7 Discussion

In this section, the implication of analytical and simulation results is discussed. In section 3.5, the lower bound of a node lifetime of an EBC network was analytically determined and compared against existing node organisation approaches, namely the All-Active [Cerpa and Estrin, 2002], LEACH [Heinzelman et al., 2002] and ASCENT [Cerpa and Estrin, 2004]. Section 3.6 shows the experimental results of those methods for three different network lifetime definitions. The lifetimes are defined as - time to exhaust the first node, time to occur the first network cut and time to exhaust 50% of deployed nodes. The standard deviation of residual energy levels and network lifetime are considered as performance criteria, and results are observed for above mentioned node organisation approaches. The summary of the experimental results are also shown in Tables 3.6 and 3.7.

Table 3.6: Average Network Standard Deviation of Residual Energies (in %)

	First node to die		First cut to occur		50% node to exhaust	
Approach	Sparse	Dense	Sparse	Dense	Sparse	Dense
ASCENT	80%	83%	72%	80%	82%	83%
All-Active	85%	90%	79%	83%	79%	82%
LEACH	55%	65%	55%	62%	62%	65%
EBC	41%	37%	40%	30%	42%	29%

Section 3.5 identifies the lower boundary of a node lifetime where it is considered the time when the network effectiveness starts deteriorating. A mathematical analysis for different network traffic and node density was performed. The lifetime equations (see Table 3.3) show that EBC and LEACH lifetimes have less impact with the increasing number of nodes per transmission range because both techniques change the cluster heads with the changing network environments. ASCENT and the All-Active node lifetimes are inversely proportional to increasing node density because increase of neighbours implies that their fixed gateways have to relay more data packets. The analytical results also show that EBC can extend node lifetime at least 15% more than any of those existing techniques. EBC is advantageous over other techniques because of its energy threshold based node exhaustion protection technique.

Table 3.7: Average Network Lifetime (in simtime)

Approach	First node to die		First cut to occur		50% node to exhaust	
	Sparse	Dense	Sparse	Dense	Sparse	Dense
ASCENT	125	70	190	140	190	170
All-Active	50	10	60	30	90	90
LEACH	300	75	450	250	450	260
EBC	450	250	500	320	500	300

Section 3.6 shows the performance analysis of various techniques using simulation experiments. Table 3.6 summarises that EBC can balance energy better than other techniques in all cases by enabling task sharing. This implies that an EBC network has less wasted energy when the network becomes ineffective. LEACH periodically rotates the gateway based on some parameters including residual energy levels. This also balances energy among the neighbours as shown in Table 3.6. On average LEACH has about 20% more wasted energies than EBC because LEACH fails to protect nodes from early exhaustion. ASCENT adaptively forms the network by activating nodes in case of network congestion or node failures. Since ASCENT allows a node to become exhausted while their neighbours have sufficient energy, it has on average 80% standard energy deviations for all three compared lifetimes. The All-Active method does not have any energy conserving measures, hence the amount of wasted energy is the highest, about 90%, for each compared lifetimes.

Energy balancing can extend network lifetime. For example, EBC has the least wasted energy and it also has a network lifetime longer than any other techniques as shown in Tables 3.6 and 3.7. The result shows that the average lifetime is higher for a sparse network than a dense network. Since the packet generation rate at each node is uniformly random, an increase of number of neighbours uniformly increases the number of forwarding packets by a gateway. However, due to connectivity restrictions (G_{th}), network lifetime gradually stabilises at a minimum value with the increasing node density. LEACH, similar to EBC, rotates the energy consuming tasks among the neighbours, so that its network lifetime is noticed close to EBC's. Table 3.7 also shows that the other methods cannot perform well because of their inefficient energy management schemes (see Table 3.6).

The simulation result validates the analytical outcome. In Section 3.5, Figure 3.7 shows that when network lifetime was defined as first node to die, EBC has average network lifetimes of 375 and 300 simtimes for sparse and dense networks respectively,. The simulation result (Figure 3.11) also shows that EBC lifetimes are 450 and 250 simtimes for sparse and dense networks for sparse and dense networks respectively, which are close to the analytical results. A little deviation is noticed because a fixed packet generation rate was considered for mathematical analysis, whereas the packet generation rate was uniformly random when simulation was performed.

3.8 Conclusion

A high variance in node energy consumption can cause an early network partition. To counter this, an energy balanced sensor node organisation technique, called Energy Balanced Clustering (EBC), is proposed in this chapter. Balancing loads with fairness is very common in typical distributed systems preventing nodes from overloading. A similar approach is taken by exploiting node self-organising capability to share tasks among neighbours. To balance tasks among high and low energy neighbours, sensor nodes are classified based on residual energy levels, and nodes are organised into clusters based on node types. EBC can prevent nodes from early exhaustion by reducing energy consuming tasks performed by a node having residual energy below a threshold. The lower bound of network lifetime was analytically computed for EBC and existing techniques (namely All-Active [Cerpa and Estrin, 2002], LEACH [Heinzelman et al., 2002] and ASCENT [Cerpa and Estrin, 2004]), and our result shows that EBC has a network lifetime at least 15% longer than those compared techniques. It was found from the experimental performance evaluation that when measuring the time to exhaust the first node, EBC can prolong network lifetime by at least 40% compared to existing techniques. The experimental results also show that EBC can extend network effectiveness at least 10% more than existing techniques when effectiveness was defined as the time till the network partition or as the exhaustion of half of the deployed nodes.

In this chapter, entire deployed node set was considered necessary to form a network. Some of those nodes may share coverage region with their neighbours. These nodes can cause redundant energy consuming activities which can shorten network lifetime. Redundant nodes can be identified and deactivated from the network to improve overall energy efficiency. Such nodes may be used to replace failed nodes to stretch the network operational lifetime more. The next few chapters investigate how redundant nodes can be used to deal with the node failures.

Chapter 4

Identification and Deactivation of Redundant Nodes

4.1 Introduction

The operational lifetime of a sensor network can be extended by eliminating redundant energy consumption. Sensor nodes are becoming small in size and low in cost, and such low cost miniature sensors can be redundantly deployed to make sensor network fault-tolerant [Zou and Chakrabarty, 2005]. Redundant nodes may consume additional energy by performing unnecessary repetitious sensing and thus affect network operational lifetime. This chapter examines maximising network lifetime by identifying and deactivating redundant nodes.

Network coverage and connectivity are the two most important requirements for a sensor network. Network coverage relates to the ability to sense throughout the sensor field, and connectivity is the ability to route data across a network [Megerian et al., 2005]. Since sensors are randomly distributed, a redundant deployment of sensors is a common approach to meet these requirements. As a result, network operational lifetime is less than optimal because of the energy consumption by redundant nodes. For this reason, those redundant nodes should be deactivated in such a way that the network requirements are preserved by the remaining active node set. A process to solve the coverage and connectivity preserving redundancy elimination problem has several constraints. First, it should be distributed because sensors are distributed in the network. Second, the solution should be scalable to cope with a large number of sensors. Finally, the method should be able to identify the maximum set of redundant nodes with the minimum computational overhead.

Most of the existing active node set optimisation techniques have a focus on providing either network connectivity or coverage. For example, a connected dominating node set is identified by disabling unnecessary nodes to build a communication backbone [Schurgers et al., 2002]. On the other hand, the problem of sensing coverage is investigated more extensively. Such as using global network information, a minimum set of active nodes is found to provide complete coverage [Chakrabarty et al., 2002]. However, network coverage and connectivity are both required for a sensor network to be functionally effective. A relatively new area of research attempts to provide both requirements, while redundant nodes are identified. Initially two separate methods are proposed for checking the coverage and connectivity [Zou and Chakrabarty, 2005], where the computational complexity increases exponentially due to separate complex methods. Zhang and Hou [2004] showed that complete coverage can ensure complete connectivity under some constraints, which integrates coverage and connectivity checking in a common framework [Xing et al., 2005]. Those integrated frameworks are also computationally intensive due to their used complex geometrical computations such as Voronoi polygon [Carbunar et al., 2006]. Limitation of these approaches relates to their inability to identify all the existing redundant nodes due to their imprecise redundancy computation process [Xing et al., 2005].

To identify all possible redundant nodes, a method is proposed that exploits the local information such as coordinates of both the sensor and sensor field. Using the field local information, it is assumed that a sensor field is a sensor grid, and the field is divided into finite grid points. Using the node local information, the node sensing region of a sensor is approximated by a subset of grid points. By examining the coverage degree of those points, redundant nodes are detected while network requirements are preserved.

In this chapter, a redundancy calculation method is proposed, called the Self Calculated Redundancy Check (SCRC) method, detecting maximum possible redundant nodes with minimum computational overhead. SCRC computes node redundancy by calculating the coverage information of a set of grid points, called sensing points. It uses the distance between a sensing point and a node to identify the coverage information of each point. If the distance between a sensing point and a node is within the sensing range of a node, that point is considered covered. To calculate the point coverage information, a node only needs to compare the distances between a point belonging to its sensing region and its neighbours. Probable node redundancy is identified by aggregating the coverage information of all the points inside a node's sensing region. Possibly redundant nodes may have overlapping regions with each other, so that SCRC also performs a random-backoff check to consider the coverage

64

and connectivity effects of a redundant node. This helps to avoid any coverage or connectivity holes due to deactivation of a node. In SCRC, each node checks its own redundancy, hence the method is distributed. It is scalable because only neighbour information of a node is involved in the computation process. Algorithm analysis shows that the time, message and space complexity of SCRC is linear and in the order of the number of neighbours of a node.

Using expected value optimisation technique, the redundant node behaviour for random distribution of deployed nodes was analysed. The experimental result of SCRC and other existing techniques, namely Sponsored Area Scheme (SAS) [Tian and Georganas, 2003], Coverage-Centric Active Nodes Selection (CCANS) [Zou and Chakrabarty, 2005] and Coverage Configuration Protocol (CCP) [Xing et al., 2005] shows that SCRC is more consistent with the analytical result compared to others. The result also shows that SCRC identifies at least 5-10% more redundant nodes than CCANS, CCP or SAS because of its distance based accurate node redundancy calculation. The computational overhead analysis showed that SCRC needs linear node organisation time like SAS, however SAS identifies at least 10% less redundant nodes than SCRC. The other two techniques require polynomial time to detect a redundant node.

The rest of this chapter is organised as follows. Related redundant node identification techniques are discussed in Section 4.2. Section 4.3 formulates the problem as a function of coverage and connectivity over a sensor field. Section 4.4 introduces the conceptual model for the proposed Self Calculated Redundancy Check (SCRC) method. An analytical framework characterising the "best" possible solutions under various node distributions is shown in Section 4.5. This is followed by simulation results and performance evaluation in Section 4.6. Finally, after discussing the results in Section 4.7, Section 4.8 concludes the chapter.

4.2 Related Work

The problem of identifying redundant sensor nodes has been studied examining a number of aspects for example, identifying redundant nodes while providing connectivity, coverage or both. In the following, identifying a connected minimum node set to provide network connectivity is discussed first. Then the problem of identifying a minimum active node set providing complete coverage is discussed. Finally, schemes identifying an optimum node set while providing both coverage and connectivity is discussed.

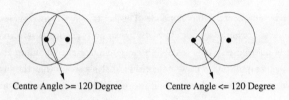

Centre Angle >= 120 Degree   Centre Angle <= 120 Degree

Figure 4.1: The Relationship between the Centre Angle and the Intersecting Regions.

Minimum Connected Dominating Set (MCDS)

A connected minimum node set can provide complete network connectivity. To find a virtual connected backbone, dominating set based routing algorithms are used. Routing based on a Connected Dominating Set (CDS) is a well known approach, where the routing search space is reduced to the nodes in the set. A set is dominating if all the nodes in the system are either in the set or neighbours of nodes in the set [Alzoubi et al., 2002; Sivakumar et al., 1998]. CDS algorithms form virtual communication backbones by connected routing nodes [Das and Bharghavan, 1997]. For example, Wu [2002] proposes a localised algorithm to form CDS by marking a node non-redundant when it has two neighbours not connected to each other. Since finding the Minimum CDS (MCDS) is an NP-hard problem [Guha, 1998], the algorithm uses shortest distance based heuristics to find a pseudo-optimal solution. Such approaches can dynamically construct network communication backbones, however do not address network coverage.

Sponsored Area Scheme (SAS)

Another important challenge is providing the coverage with a minimum active node set. One of the earliest coverage-centric sensor node redundancy calculation techniques is the Sponsored Area Scheme (SAS) [Tian and Georganas, 2002; 2003]. This method depends on a local geometric calculation of overlapping sensing regions to identify redundant nodes. A SAS node turns itself off when each of its coverage sectors is already "sponsored" or covered by other nodes. The sponsored area of a node is calculated using the centre angle of intersecting circular sensing regions [Tian and Georganas, 2003]. A centre angle is created at each node's centre by two intersecting points as shown in Figure 4.1. For simplicity, SAS considers neighbours having centre angles ranging from $120° - 180°$. By considering fewer neighbours, SAS identifies those redundant nodes with a reduced computational overhead.

Jiang and Dou [2004] identified several limitations of SAS. For example, the area of sponsored region is always smaller than the area of the intersection. Due to unconsidered overlapping areas, the technique cannot identify all possible redundant nodes.

k-Coverage Preserving Technique

Another well known area of research involves preserving a certain number of coverage degree of a sensing region. For example, Huang and Tseng [2003]; Huang et al. [2006] propose a perimeter coverage checking algorithm determining the k coverage of a region where a region is k-covered if it is covered by k nodes. Their method proves that an area is k-covered when each sensor in that region is k-perimeter-covered. A node is only considered redundant if its sensing region is at least $k + 1$-perimeter-covered. The determination of perimeter coverage requires that each sensor communicates with all neighbours twice. If N is the number of neighbours, the computational complexity of this approach is $O(NlogN)$. The coverage information is then used to determine each node redundancy and inactive schedule periods for redundant sensors. To avoid any coverage holes, a possibly redundant sensor asks all of its neighbours to re-evaluate the coverage of their perimeter without considering that node. This requires a sensor running the perimeter coverage N times, and the complexity of the protocol increases to $O(N^2logN)$.

Coverage-Centric Active Nodes Selection (CCANS)

Identifying and deactivating redundant nodes, while preserving network coverage and connectivity, is a relatively new area of research. An example of such a technique is the Coverage-Centric Active Nodes Selection (CCANS) [Zou and Chakrabarty, 2004; 2005]. This method proposes a distributed approach to identify redundant nodes using CDS information. CCANS is a sensing ratio based technique, where the coverage ratio is the ratio of all CDS nodes that can cover a region and the coverage provided by a single node situated at that region. CCANS is a two stage algorithm where each node evaluates its coverage ratio in stage 1, and the nodes check the connectivity in stage 2. A token based approach is used to calculate potentially redundant nodes by calculating the sensing ratio. If the sensing ratio of a node region is greater than a predefined threshold, the node is marked as 'unset'. Each neighbour of an 'unset' node recalculates its redundancy except for the fact that one of its neighbours is now in the 'unset' state and sends the result to the 'unset' node. If the node is still potentially redundant, it enters into the inactive state.

The computational complexity of CCANS is in the order of the square of the number of neighbours. CCANS also does not consider the coverage hole problem and may leave some regions uncovered. It was identified in our experimental analysis that CCANS cannot identify all possible potentially redundant nodes due to its token based serial redundancy checking approach.

Coverage Connectivity Protocol (CCP)

Zhang and Hou [2004] show that implying k-coverage also ensures k-connectivity when the transmission range of a sensor node is at least twice of the sensing range. Using a similar proposition, a well known k-coverage and connectivity preserving solution is proposed in [Wang et al., 2003; Xing et al., 2005]. Wang et. al., propose a redundancy identification technique, called Coverage Connectivity Protocol (CCP) which can provide different degrees of coverage and meanwhile maintain communication connectivity. CCP partitioned the sensor field into a collection of coverage patches, each of them bounded by arcs of sensing circles and/or the boundary of the sensor field, and all points in each coverage patch have the same coverage degree. The redundancy is measured by examining the coverage degree of those patches. In CCP, if a node is inside a k+1-covered sensing patch, it is deactivated. CCP can maintain the coverage and connectivity when transmission range is at least twice of sensing ranges. If communication ranges are less than twice of sensing ranges, CCP is integrated with SPAN[1] [Chen et al., 2002] to provide both sensing coverage and communication connectivity.

The limitation of CCP is its higher complexity. The computational complexity for the redundant eligibility algorithm of CCP is $O(N^3)$ where N is the number of nodes in the sensing neighbour set. Another limitation of CCP is that it is not able to optimise the active node set because it considers the active node set optimisation as reducing coverage degrees of sensing patches instead of observing node sensing regions.

Geometric Computation Approach

Geometrical computations can be used for identifying redundant nodes, whilst coverage and connectivity are preserved. Carbunar et al. [2004; 2006] detected redundant nodes using the localised information of a sensor field. The necessary and sufficient conditions for a sensor to be redundant are derived using Voronoi polygon and Delaunay triangulation. A

---

[1]SPAN is a distributed coordination technique for multi-hop ad hoc wireless networks that reduces energy consumption without significantly reducing the capacity or connectivity of the network [Chen et al., 2002].

sensor s calculates the redundancy by creating a Voronoi diagram of the Voronoi neighbours of s when s is excluded. The 2 Voronoi Vertices (2-VV) of a sensor s are the Voronoi vertices of the 2-Voronoi diagram of s, and a 2-Voronoi Intersection Point (2-VIP) of s is the intersection between an edge of the 2-Voronoi diagram and the coverage circumcircle of s. If all the 2-VVs and 2-VIPs of s are covered by the Voronoi neighbours of s, sensor s is redundant. Since each node can calculate their own 2-VV and 2-VIPs, the technique is distributed and the complexity of locally determining redundancy is $O(NlogN)$. However, creating a Voronoi diagram needs global sensor field information, and which is not entirely localised because Voronoi polygons of nodes resides at the boundary of a sensor field cannot be created locally [Zhang et al., 2006].

Summary

Since coverage and connectivity are equally important for a sensor network to keep the network operationally effective, any sensor node set optimisation technique should preserve both. In earlier active node set research, network connectivity and coverage are addressed individually [Wu, 2002; Tian and Georganas, 2002]. A combined effort of coverage and connectivity checking is proposed in [Zou and Chakrabarty, 2005] where the computational complexity of this technique is high because two separate methods are used to check the coverage and connectivity. Coverage and connectivity are integrated in a common framework in [Xing et al., 2005; Carbunar et al., 2006], which simplifies the redundant node identification problem more. These techniques still prove energy costly due to their complex computational processes, and they cannot identify all possible redundant nodes due to their imprecise node redundancy calculations.

4.3 Problem Formulation

In this section, the problem of identifying redundant nodes while preserving network requirements - complete sensing coverage and node connectivity, is formalised. Ideally, a network that provides a higher degree of coverage and connectivity can guarantee a higher Quality of Service. In reality, sensors are resource limited, especially energy, and the redundant deployment of nodes can cause redundant energy consuming tasks such as sensing an object by multiple nodes. To conserve energy, redundant nodes should be eliminated from the network. Redundant nodes should be identified in such a way that the network Quality of Service is preserved. For this reason, the redundant node problem is regarded as temporarily deactivat-

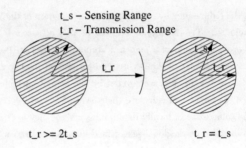

Figure 4.2: Ensuring Coverage ensures Connectivity (with some Constraints).

ing the maximum possible set of redundant nodes, while the network remains operationally effective. In other words, in the following, the node redundancy problem is formalised as an active node set optimisation problem with coverage and connectivity constraints, and to simplify that, coverage is related to connectivity.

Active Node Set Optimisation

Rather than having a dense deployment of nodes, it is sufficient to have a sparse but uniform distribution of active nodes providing required network coverage and connectivity. To minimise active nodes, redundant nodes should be deactivated where a node redundancy depends on the coverage degree of its sensing region. Since the degree of coverage of a region depends on the presence of active nodes, redundancy depends on the node density in that particular region. To control redundancy, active node density should be minimised. Formally, the problem is stated as follows.

- *Objective :* Minimise the density of active nodes.

- *Subject to :*

    1. Maintain the same coverage and,

    2. Maintain the same connectivity of the original set of nodes.

Relationship between Coverage and Connectivity

There is a relationship between coverage and connectivity - Xing et al. [2005] show that ensuring coverage can ensure connectivity under some constraints. Coverage is one of the fundamental problems relating to the provision of specified quality surveillance [Meguerdichian et al., 2001], and connectivity ensures that all nodes are reachable from any other nodes or base stations [Tian and Georganas, 2005]. The relationship between the coverage and connectivity is important because devising algorithms to fulfil both conditions is, in general, more difficult than fulfilling only one of them. If one condition (coverage) implies another (connectivity), the problem of maintaining both conditions is simplified.

Zhang and Hou [2004] show that a complete coverage of a convex region can infer connectivity provided that the transmission range of a sensor node is at least twice the sensing range as shown in Figure 4.2. If the sensing range and the transmission range are denoted as t_s and t_r respectively, the relationship between the coverage and connectivity can be stated as follows.

Lemma 4.3.1 *Assuming the number of sensors in any finite sensing region is finite, the condition of $t_r \geq 2t_s$ is both necessary and sufficient to ensure that complete coverage of a convex region implies connectivity [Zhang and Hou, 2004].*

Zou and Chakrabarty [2005] show that coverage and connectivity can still be preserved for a heterogeneous sensor network. Since they propose separate coverage and connectivity checking methods, the technique can maintain network coverage and connectivity even for varied sensing and communication ranges.

These simplifying assumptions give us the flexibility to concentrate only on ensuring coverage. Since the aim of this research is to identify redundant nodes, they will be identified for both $t_r = 2t_s$ and $t_r = t_s$ while preserving network coverage.

4.4 Self Calculated Redundancy Check (SCRC) Method

Existing coverage and connectivity preserved redundant node elimination techniques exploit the geometric properties of either the node sensing region [Carbunar et al., 2006] or the sensor field [Xing et al., 2005; Zou and Chakrabarty, 2005]. Instead, the advantages of both are used to maximise the identifiable redundant nodes set. Using the local information, the sensor field is divided into grid points, and the sensing region of a sensor node is approximated

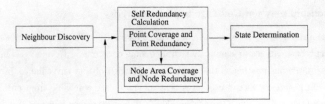

Figure 4.3: The Proposed Redundant Node Detection Method.

using those points. The coverage information of points is used to identify and deactivate a redundant sensor.

A node's redundancy is identified by checking only redundant coverage because complete coverage ensures complete connectivity (under some constraints) [Zhang and Hou, 2004; Zou and Chakrabarty, 2005]. It is assumed that a node's sensing region is uniform in all directions and is circular. The radius of a circular sensing region is the sensing range (t_s) of a sensor node, and the centre of the circle is the location of the sensor. A sensor's sensing region may overlap other sensors' regions due to random distribution of nodes. If a sensor sensing region is completely overlapped, that sensor is treated as redundant.

4.4.1 Detecting Redundant Nodes

This section describes the proposed distributed redundancy identification scheme based on available network information such as field and node coordinates. A node is redundant when its sensing region is completely covered by neighbours so the sensing region and neighbours are identified. Using these information, intersections between neighbour sensing regions are computed to determine node redundancy. The process is illustrated in Figure 4.3.

The proposed method starts with a neighbour discovery phase to identify the neighbour node set. After that a novel technique, named Self Calculated Redundancy Check (SCRC), detects node coverage redundancy by calculating overlapping sensing regions. This method completes with a state determination phase to avoid any possible coverage holes. In this phase, each potentially redundant node checks whether it is required.

Neighbour Discovery

Neighbours are identified to calculate redundant node sensing regions. Each node has a specific neighbour set, and a node sensing region can overlap with only its neighbour's sensing

72

Algorithm 2: Neighbour and Neighbour Position Discovery

   Notation:

        MSG is the Control message

        Neigh[i] is the neighbour information table

        Id is the node ID

        (x, y) is the node coordinate

        state is the node current state

2.1 Initialize Neigh[i] $\leftarrow \phi$;

2.2 Initialize $MSG_i \leftarrow \{\ Id_i,\ (x_i, y_i),\ state_i\ \}$;

2.3 Broadcast MSG_i;

2.4 **while** $TRUE$ **do**

2.5   Receive MSG_j from neighbours;

2.6   Store neighbour information - Neigh[j] $\leftarrow \{\ Id_j,\ (x_j, y_j),\ state_j\ \}$;

2.7 **end**
---

regions. To detect node redundancy, overlapping regions need to be identified, and to identify overlapping regions, neighbour information is needed. The neighbour discovery procedure is given in Algorithm 2.

Every node starts its life-cycle with an initialisation phase where it sets network parameters and collects neighbour information [Sakib et al., 2005]. In this phase, each node broadcasts its coordinate and state information to the nodes within its transmission range as shown in Lines 2.2 and 2.3 in Algorithm 2. After receiving the broadcast message, the nodes store their neighbour information in a table, called the neighbour information table (Line 2.6). At the subsequent configuration phase, each node chooses to become active (for example, gateway or sense node) or inactive (for example, hibernating node) based on these information as shown in Figure 3.1, Chapter 3.

Self Calculated Redundancy Check (SCRC)

A node calculates its redundancy by checking how much of its sensing region overlapped with its neighbours. To check coverage, the Self Calculated Redundancy Check (SCRC) technique is proposed which calculates node redundancy based on distances between sensing points and neighbouring nodes. The steps of SCRC are described below, and the method is defined in Algorithm 3.

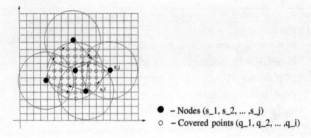

● – Nodes (s_1, s_2, ... ,s_j)
○ – Covered points (q_1, q_2, ... ,q_i)

Figure 4.4: Coverage Calculation: a Function of Distance from the Neighbouring Nodes.

- *Discretised Sensing Region -*

  It is assumed that a sensor field is a plane, and the sensing region of a sensor is a circle with the radius equivalent to the sensing range of that sensor. Chakrabarty et al. [2002] show that a sensor field can be assumed as a grid if field location is available, so here a sensor field is represented by a finite set of grid points, called sensing points. Since a sensor covers a certain circular region, the sensing region of a sensor node is a subset of that finite point set. This helps to quantify each node's coverage by the coverage information of those sensing points as shown below.

- *Point Coverage -*

  If a sensing point q_i belongs to the sensing point set of a node s_i, q_i is called covered by s_i. Point coverage is calculated using the distance between a sensing point and a sensor node. For example, if the distance between q_i and s_i is less than or equal to the node sensing range t_s, q_i belongs to the sensing point set of s_i and hence, is covered. Figure 4.4 shows how each sensing point is called covered if that point is within the coverage range of at least one sensor node.

- *Redundant Coverage of a Point -*

  A point is redundantly covered when it is within the sensing range of more than some predefined number of nodes. Redundant coverage of a point is calculated using the sensing point coverage given above. The coverage degree of a point q_i is the number of sensors that cover q_i, and this is used to define the redundant coverage of a point. Sometimes sensing applications require a high degree of redundancy to fulfil the specific

Algorithm 3: SCRC - Self Calculated Redundancy Check

    Notation:

             $N_i(s)$ is the set of neighbours for node i

             $Cov_i(p)$ is the set of points covered by node i

             t_s is the sensing range

             RP[i] is the redundant point checking table

             Flag is a Boolean variable generating {TRUE,FALSE}

    Result :

             Returning the Boolean value **Flag** denoting node redundancy. If the value is FALSE, the node is redundant, otherwise non-redundant.

3.1 **for** $N_i(s)$ - *all sensors in the neighbour table* **do**

3.2   **for** $Cov_i(p)$ - *all points in the coverage point set* **do**

3.3   Calculate the distance between p_i and s_i ;

3.4   **if** *the distance is less than the t_s* **then**

3.5   RP[i] ← TRUE;

3.6   **end**

3.7   **else**

3.8   RP[i] ← FALSE;

3.9   **end**

3.10   **end**

3.11 **end**

3.12 Initialize Flag ← TRUE;

3.13 **for** *all points belongs to* $Cov(p_i)$ **do**

3.14   **if** *RP[i] == FALSE* **then**

3.15   Flag ← FALSE ;

3.16   **end**

3.17 **end**

3.18 Return($Flag$)

quality of surveillance. If a higher quality of surveillance is required, the coverage degree of each point also needs to be higher. The minimal coverage degree is one to maintain the network coverage and connectivity. If the coverage degree of a sensing point is greater than a required coverage degree, the point is redundantly covered. Let us assume that the required redundancy is ν - point q_i is redundantly covered when it is within the sensing range of more than ν nodes.

- *Node Region Coverage/Redundancy -*

  A node's sensing region is redundantly covered when all the sensing points inside that sensing region are redundantly covered. The redundancy computation process is shown in Algorithm 3. To calculate coverage redundancy, each node identifies the coverage points that belong to their sensing region by comparing distances between each sensing point and the sensing range. Each node can calculate point coverage and point redundancy by comparing distances between a sensing point and its neighbours. This is shown from Lines 3.2 to 3.10 in the algorithm. Using the coverage effects of each sensing point, a node decides its redundancy as shown in Lines 3.13 - 3.17 in Algorithm 3. The redundancy computation detail is also given in Subsection 4.4.2.

  If all the sensing points belonging to a node's sensing region are redundantly covered, that node may not be needed. Such nodes are called "potentially redundant" because multiple potentially redundant nodes can overlap with each other, and further network hole checking is required before deactivating appropriate redundant nodes. On the other hand, if at least one sensing point from a node sensing region is found to be non-redundantly covered, that node is non-redundant.

State Determination

To avoid any coverage and/or connectivity holes, potentially redundant nodes from the same neighbour set do not simultaneously enter the sleeping state. Since potentially redundant nodes may have overlapping sensing regions, simultaneous deactivation of all of them could leave regions uncovered. A random back-off method is used where redundant nodes are found that can be deactivated without creating any holes. Random back-off is a simple contention avoidance technique, widely used for medium access control in distributed systems [Stallings, 2007]. A similar approach is used here to prevent simultaneous deactivation of multiple potentially redundant nodes from the same region, as illustrated in Algorithm 4.

Algorithm 4: State Determination Algorithm

    Notation:

              SCRC() is the Self Calculated Redundancy Check method

              N is the number of neighbours

              MSG_w is the message to show intention to go to the hibernation

              MSG_c is the confirmation message to go to the hibernation state

              r_t is the round trip time

              w_p is the predefined wait time equivalent to r_t

              w_r is the random wait time

4.1 Broadcast the MSG_w among the neighbours;

4.2 Wait for predefined w_p time;

4.3 **if** *MSG_w is received from other neighbours* **then**

4.4   Wait for w_r time ($1\ r_t \geq w_r \leq N\ r_t$);

4.5   **if** *if MSG_c received from neighbour i* **then**

4.6   Update neighbour table by marking i as inactive;

4.7   Execute **SCRC()**;

4.8   **end**

4.9   **else**

4.10   Broadcast MSG_c to the neighbours;

4.11   Change the node state to Inactive;

4.12   **end**

4.13 **end**

4.14 **else**

4.15   Broadcast MSG_c to the neighbours;

4.16   Change the node state to Inactive;

4.17 **end**

After calculating the probable redundancy, each potentially redundant node sends messages, called willingness messages, to their neighbours as shown at Line 4.1 in the algorithm. After that, it waits for a predefined w_p amount of time to receive such messages from its neighbours. w_p is carefully chosen allowing a node sufficient time to receive other willingness messages from neighbours, so that it is set greater than the one hop round trip time. If a potentially redundant node receives willingness messages within the waiting time w_p, it implies that there are multiple potentially redundant nodes from the same neighbour set. Then it waits another random amount of time w_r, chosen between one round trip time to the number of neighbours round trip times (shown at Line 4.4). If a potentially redundant node receives any confirmation messages within the w_r time, it refrains from entering the inactive state. Otherwise, it sends a redundancy confirmation message and goes to the inactive or sleeping state.

If a potentially redundant node does not receive any willingness messages within the wait time w_p, it assumes that there are no other redundant nodes within its neighbour set. Hence, it can enter the inactive state and sends a redundancy confirmation message to its neighbours which is shown in Lines 4.14 - 4.17 in Algorithm 4. After receiving a redundancy confirmation message, each node updates its neighbour table and recalculates node redundancy.

4.4.2 The SCRC Computation Detail

In this section, the computation detail of the proposed redundancy identification method is described. Since redundantly covered sensing points reside in intersecting node sensing regions, the identification of those regions is given. The union of intersecting regions of a node contains all the redundantly covered sensing points and thus decides node redundancy. In the following, coverage and redundancy definitions are summarised from the previous subsection, then the point redundancy calculation is given by showing that redundantly covered points reside in the intersecting sensing regions. The symbols used for the computation are summarised in Table 4.1.

Assumptions and Definitions

Let us assume that $Q = \{q_0, q_i, \ldots, q_m\}$ is the sensor field, and $S = \{s_0, s_1, \ldots, s_n\}$ is the set of deployed sensors. Each node $(s_i | s_i \in S)$ is represented by a set of points $(K_i | K_i \subset Q)$ where $K_i = \{q_{i_0}, q_{i_1}, \ldots, q_{i_j}\}$. Let us also assume that the sensing region of a node s_i is a circle represented by κ_i. If the coverage degree requirement for each point is ν, the point

Table 4.1: Symbol Table for SCRC Computation.

Symbol	Denote
S	The set of sensors
n	Number of sensors in set S
s_i	i th Sensor
κ_i	A circle with radius t_s and centre at s_i
K_i	Set of points belongs to the sensing region of s_i
Q	The sensor field
q_i	a point belongs to sensor field Q
t_s	Sensing range of a sensor
t_r	Transmission range of a sensor
ν	Required coverage degree
$N(s_i)$	The neighbour set of node s_i

coverage, region coverage, region redundancy and node redundancy are defined as follows.

Definition *ν-Coverage of a point* - if any point $(q_i|q_i \in Q)$ in the sensor field is within the coverage range of at least ν nodes, q_i is called ν-covered.

Definition *ν-Coverage of a region* - if all the points q_i inside a node region $(\kappa_i|\kappa_i \subseteq Q)$ are covered by at least ν nodes, κ_i is called ν-covered.

Definition *ν-Redundancy of a point* - if any point $(q_i|q_i \in Q)$ in the sensor field is covered by at least $\nu + 1$ nodes, q_i is called $(\nu$-$)$redundant or redundantly covered.

Definition *Node redundancy* - a node is called redundant *iff* all the points $(K_i|K_i \subset Q)$ of its sensing region κ_i are ν-redundant.

Node Redundancy Calculation

A node is redundant if its entire sensing region is intersected by ν neighbours. Using neighbour coordinates, a node calculates how much of its region is covered based on distances between sensing points and neighbours.

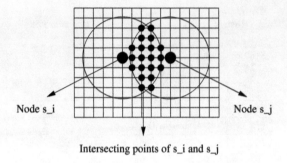

Node s_i   Node s_j

Intersecting points of s_i and s_j

Figure 4.5: Redundant Sensing Points in the Intersecting Region.

Points in the intersecting region have distances less than or equal to the sensing range from any neighbour nodes. Since the coordinates of neighbours and their coverage ranges are known, a node can calculate intersecting regions covered by its neighbours. If a point $q \in K_i$ (set of points belongs to sensing region of node s_i) also belongs to K_j, point q is in the intersecting region of both s_i and s_j as shown in Figure 4.5. If the coordinate of q and s_j are (x_q, y_q) and (x_j, y_j) respectively, the Euclidian distance between q and s_j is calculated by the following equation.

$$\|q - s_j\| = \delta = \sqrt{(x_p - x_j)^2 + (y_p - y_j)^2} \tag{4.1}$$

Since q is in the intersecting region of s_i and s_j's sensing regions, the distance δ between q and s_j is also less than or equal to the sensing range t_s. Formally, the condition is stated as follows.

$$\|q - s_j\| = \delta \leq t_s \tag{4.2}$$

A node is redundant if, and only if, all the points inside its node sensing region are otherwise covered by at least ν neighbours. This implies that redundantly covered sensing points of a node reside in the intersecting regions of at least $\nu + 1$ nodes. For simplicity, let us consider when ν is 1, then node redundancy is redefined as follows. *A node i is redundant if, and only if, each sensing point belonging to K_i is also covered by at least one of the neighbours of i.* The redundancy determination is then equivalent to checking whether the sensing point subset K_i of i is a subset of the union of intersecting regions between node

i and its neighbours' sensing regions. If the neighbour node set of a node s_i is $N(s_i)$, the redundancy condition for s_i can be stated as follows.

$$K_i \subseteq \bigcup_{j \in N(s_i)} K_j \tag{4.3}$$

$$\Rightarrow K_i \subseteq \bigcup_{j \in N(s_i)} (K_j \cap K_i) \tag{4.4}$$

All the sensing points of a node residing in the intersecting regions are identified using equation 4.2 as shown in Algorithm 3 at Line 3.3. Then the node redundancy is calculated based on those intersecting sensing points using equation 4.4 as shown in the algorithm from Lines 3.13 to 3.16.

4.4.3 Complexity Analysis and Comparison

Required time, space (or memory) and number of messages to organise nodes are important performance criteria for a resource limited sensor network. The time, space and message complexity of SCRC are identified and compared against three well known existing redundant node elimination techniques, namely Sponsored Area Scheme (SAS) [Tian and Georganas, 2003], Coverage-Centric Active Nodes Selection (CCANS) [Zou and Chakrabarty, 2005] and Coverage Configuration Protocol (CCP) [Xing et al., 2005].

Complexity is identified based on some assumptions. Let λ be the node density, and each node has an average of λ neighbours. Let us also assume that a single broadcast process takes $O(\lambda)$ time as shown in [Zou and Chakrabarty, 2005]. The organising time is denoted as the time taken to identify a node as a redundant node. Space complexity is the required memory to hold information that is needed to calculate node redundancy. The number of messages involved in the redundancy identification method is the message complexity. The organising time, space and message complexity for SCRC along with other existing techniques are derived in the following.

Complexity of Self Calculated Redundancy Check (SCRC)

SCRC performs three steps to identify a redundant node as described in Figure 4.3. First, each node discovers neighbours by receiving neighbour announcement messages. Second, it calculates redundancy using SCRC by identifying intersecting sensing regions. Finally, if a node finds itself potentially redundant, it enters the state determination phase. A potentially redundant node sends a willingness message to its neighbours and waits for a predefined time w_p. Within the wait time, if any other willingness messages are received, a node waits for another random amount of time w_r to confirm its redundancy.

To identify node redundancy, a SCRC node requires time to discover neighbours, to check point redundancy and to determine the state of a potentially redundant node. According to Algorithm 2, the neighbour discovery step consists of one broadcast of a neighbour announcement message, hence takes $O(\lambda)$ time. Since set K_i is the point approximation of a sensor s_i, coverage checking takes $|K_i|$ time. The state determination (Algorithm 4) takes at most two broadcasts and two waiting times, that is approximately $(\lambda + w_p + \lambda + w_r)$ time. Therefore, time complexity for the proposed technique is $(3\lambda + |K_i| + w_p + w_r)$ which is in the order of the node density, that is $O(\lambda)$.

Assume there is no packet loss and that each node sends exactly one neighbour announcement, one willingness and one redundancy confirmation message. Each node also receives at most one neighbour announcement, one redundancy willingness and another redundancy confirmation message from each neighbour. If there are λ neighbours per node, each node receives at most 3λ messages from its neighbours. This implies that the message complexity is also in the order of λ, that is $O(\lambda)$.

A SCRC node needs to store its neighbour IDs, coordinate values and state information. Hence, the space complexity is in the order of the number of neighbours which is $O(\lambda)$.

Complexity of Sponsored Area Scheme (SAS)

In SAS [Tian and Georganas, 2003], each node goes through three steps similar to a SCRC node which are neighbour discovery, redundancy calculation and state determination. For the computational simplicity, SAS does not consider neighbours with centre angles less than $120°$, so that on average the technique leaves half of the neighbours out of the consideration. As a result, the average node organisation time of SAS is less than SCRC but complexity is still in the order of the number of neighbours, that is $O(\lambda)$. In SAS, message communication is restricted to neighbours, so the complexity is also in the order of λ. Since a SAS node has to store all neighbour information, space complexity is the same as SCRC which is the order of λ or $O(\lambda)$.

Table 4.2: Summary of Complexity Analysis for Various Redundant Node Elimination Techniques .

Complexity is measured in terms of node density λ			
Approach	Time	Space	Message
SAS	$O(\lambda)$	$O(\lambda)$	$O(\lambda)$
CCANS	$O(\lambda^2)$	$O(\lambda)$	$O(\lambda)$
CCP	$O(\lambda^3)$	$O(\lambda)$	$O(\lambda)$
SCRC	$O(\lambda)$	$O(\lambda)$	$O(\lambda)$

Complexity of Coverage-Centric Active Nodes Selection (CCANS)

CCANS [Zou and Chakrabarty, 2005], described in Section 4.2, is a token based algorithm. The node holding the token calculates its redundancy, after which it passes the token to the next neighbour. Token based computation introduces a time complexity in the quadratic order of the number of neighbours because each node has to wait for the token from one of its neighbours. Zou and Chakrabarty [2005] give the complexity as $O(\lambda^2 + \lambda)$ which is equivalent to $O(\lambda^2)$. The required space and message communication are restricted to the neighbours, so that complexities are linear and in the order of the node density, that is $O(\lambda)$.

Complexity of Coverage Configuration Protocol (CCP)

CCP [Xing et al., 2005] divides the sensor field into patches and identifies the coverage degree of those patches with a view to reducing the degree to an acceptable level. A node turns itself off to reduce the coverage degree of a patch. To maintain the required coverage degree, neighbour collaboration is performed before sending a node to the sleeping state. If a node finds its sensing region is in a redundantly covered patch, it declares itself as eligible to be redundant. The eligibility algorithm has a reported computational complexity of $O(\lambda^3)$, where λ is the node density [Xing et al., 2005], so the time complexity is also considered $O(\lambda^3)$. The space and message complexity are the same as other techniques, that is in the order of λ. The complexity of CCP also depends on an external algorithm (for example, SPAN [Chen et al., 2002]), as CCP uses that algorithm to check required connectivity.

Table 4.2 summarises the time, space and message complexity for various approaches.

Table 4.3: Symbol Table for Analysing the Redundant Node Identification Model

Symbol	Denote
H	The optimisation function, minimising active nodes
χ	Coverage quantifier for points in the sensor field
β_i	A binary variable, Quantifying i-th point
$RP[i]$	Point redundancy check vector
α_i	A binary variable, Quantifying i-th sensor
λ	Node density of the sensor field
l	Width and length of the sensor field

The table shows that SCRC has linear time, space and message complexity, and only SAS has the same complexity. However, as SAS does not consider entire overlapping neighbours, it cannot identify all the possibly redundant nodes from the network. Although CCANS and CCP have linear space and message complexity, CCANS has a quadratic time complexity, and CCP has a cubic computational complexity.

4.5 Analysis of the Redundant Node Identification Model

In this section, possible redundant nodes are identified mathematically which will help to analytically compare performances of redundant node identification techniques (see Section 4.6). An expected value optimisation technique is used to identify the possible number of redundant nodes. The technique assumes node location probabilistically using two different node distributions, namely uniform and Poisson. The mathematical basis for the model is described, and the model for those two node distributions are analysed. In addition to Table 4.1, symbols used in this section are depicted in Table 4.3.

4.5.1 Mathematical Building Blocks

The redundant node elimination problem is defined as a function that identifies the minimum number of active nodes required to maintain network coverage and connectivity. Instead of complete deployed sensor set, a subset of active nodes may be sufficient to maintain the network requirements. If S is the sensor set, the coverage- and connectivity-centric problem

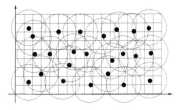

Figure 4.6: n Circles (κ), Centred by n Sensors in the Sensor Field.

is to find a minimal subset of non-redundant nodes, say S' ($S' \subseteq S$), that covers the sensor field. That is only nodes in S' are required to maintain the same coverage and connectivity provided by S. In the following, the active node set minimisation function is formulated based on some assumptions, and then the expected value optimisation technique is used to solve the function.

Assume that Q be a sensor field, and Q is approximated by a finite point set $\{q_1, q_2, ..., q_m\}$, called the sensing point set. Let the cardinality of set S be n (that is $|S| = n$), and Q is covered by the node set S. A node sensing region is a circle, so that Q can be treated as the union of the n circles ($\kappa = \{\kappa_1, \kappa_2, ..., \kappa_n\}$) (see Figure 4.6). Since κ_i is a subset of Q, the coverage information of a subset of sensing points that belongs of κ_i can measure the redundancy of each κ_i. To compute the coverage of sensing points, a coverage detection function χ is considered. By applying χ, each sensing point is described in terms of coverage.

The active node set optimisation task is denoted as a function H identifying the minimum possible number of active nodes by minimising the density of κ with coverage and connectivity constraints. That is function H identifies the number of circles (κ) that satisfies the coverage function χ. If q is a sensing point in κ_i, function H is given as follows.

$$H(\kappa) = \sum_{i=1}^{n} \int_{\kappa_i} \chi(q) dq \qquad (4.5)$$

The objective function, $\min_\kappa H(\kappa)$, is finding the minimum number of circles κ needed to cover the sensor field, where the process of minimisation of active nodes is the process of elimination of redundantly covered circles (κ).

4.5.2 Expected Value Optimisation Technique

In this section, the expected value optimisation technique is used to solve equation 4.5 because probabilistic methods are specific and optimised for particular problems consisting random variables [Huyse, 2001]. The technique depends on a set of values, called *mass*, and a *probability* function computing the probability of an event occurring over the mass [Johnson, 2003]. This technique is applied to identify the maximum possible number of redundant nodes using the deployed node set (as the mass) and the probability of a node to be redundantly covered. In the following, the required active node set is formulated as an expected value function, and then node distribution models are used to evaluate the function.

The sensing region of a sensor is approximated by a set of sensing points which enables to define the node redundancy by considering the coverage of those points. It is assumed that the sensor field is a grid having a finite set of sensing points and the sensing region of a node is a subset of the sensor field. Using equation 4.1, the sensing point subset for a sensor s_i is obtained by checking whether a point is within the sensing range of s_i. That is each of the circles κ_i, representing sensor s_i, is approximated by a set of points K_i where $K_i = \{q_1, q_2, ..., q_m\}$.

Since nodes are capable of on-board computation, they can calculate the coverage information of points belonging to their sensing regions. Using neighbour coordinates, nodes check whether those points are ν-redundant or not where a point is redundantly covered if it is at least $\nu + 1$-covered. To define q_i in terms of coverage, a binary variable β_i is associated with each point $q_i \in K_i$. If c_i is the coverage degree of point q_i, β_i defines q_i as redundantly covered when c_i is greater than ν, otherwise non-redundant. Then point coverage can be defined as follows.

$$\beta_i = \left\{ \begin{array}{ll} True & if \ c_i \geq \nu \\ False & Otherwise \end{array} \right. \tag{4.6}$$

Each κ_i is identified redundantly or non-redundantly covered by using the stored point coverage information. If all the points inside K_i, the point approximation of κ_i, are ν-redundant, the product of β_i is True. This implies that K_i or κ_i is redundantly covered. If any point fails to be ν-redundant, the product of β_i is False, and κ_i is needed. The optimisation function described in equation 4.5 is then redefined from κ_i to K_i as follows.

$$H(K) \;=\; \sum_{i=1}^{n} \prod_{K_i} \beta_i \tag{4.7}$$

In order to find the active node set, binary variable $\alpha_i (1 \leq i \leq n)$ is associated with each sensor s_i where α_i is the quantitative redundancy measurement of s_i. Node s_i discovers its redundancy by accumulating the point coverage effects using equation 4.7. If s_i is needed, α_i will be True, otherwise False. The definition of α is given below.

$$\alpha_i = \begin{cases} True & if\ s_i = ACTIVE \\ False & Otherwise \end{cases} \tag{4.8}$$

Since K_i represents the i-th sensor node, S can be used instead of K in equation 4.7. This leads us to find the minimum number of sensor nodes covering the sensor field. By accumulating the sensing point quantifier β_i, the node quantifier α_i is found, and the sum of α_i gives us the required number of active nodes. The expected value operation is shown in the following.

$$H(\kappa) \;=\; \sum_{i=1}^{n} \prod_{\kappa_i} \beta_i \tag{4.9}$$

$$\Rightarrow H_\kappa(S) \;=\; \sum_{i=1}^{n} \prod_{s_i} \beta_i \tag{4.10}$$

$$\cong\; \min\left(\sum_{i=1}^{n} \prod_{s_i} \beta_i \right) \tag{4.11}$$

$$=\; E_{(S)}\left(\sum_{i=1}^{n} \alpha_i \right) \tag{4.12}$$

4.5.3 Redundancy Distribution Models

In this section, the expected number of redundant nodes is derived using equation 4.12. Since nodes are randomly distributed, there is a relationship between the overlapping coverage of a region and the node distribution. A probability distribution function is used to find the probability of a node present in a specific region. This enables identification of overlapped node regions which include redundant nodes.

The overlapping coverage of a sensing region depends on how nodes are distributed. Two most common and important node distribution techniques, namely uniformly random and

Poisson distribution, are considered to predict the presence of a node in a region. Nodes can be deployed with a predefined pattern having constant probability to cover a particular sensing region which is modelled by uniformly random node distribution [Meguerdichian et al., 2001]. A node deployment can also be random where overlapping coverage of a sensing region is independent to occur. In such deployment related problems, Poisson point process is used to model node distribution schemes [Du and Lin, 2005; Meguerdichian et al., 2001]. Both distribution models are analysed, and the probability of a node sensing region being redundantly covered is identified.

Uniformly Random Node Distribution

The probability of a node being redundant is identified by identifying the probability of its sensing region being redundantly covered when nodes are distributed uniformly randomly. Node redundancy probability is used to identify the expected number of redundant nodes present in a given network.

The probability of a sensing point being covered by a node is constant when nodes are uniformly distributed. The probability of a sensing point q_i covered by randomly deployed node s_i is the ratio of areas of the sensing region of s_i and the sensor field. It is assumed that the sensor field Q is a square region having length and width of l, and it is divided into a $l \times l$ grid. If the sensing range of a sensor node is t_s, the probability equation of q_i being covered by s_i is given as follows.

$$P(q_i \in s_i) = \frac{\pi t_s^2}{l^2} \qquad (4.13)$$

Since nodes are uniformly distributed, equation 4.13 is also the probability of a region equivalent to a node sensing region being covered by a node [Lazos and Poovendran, 2006]. If the area covered by a sensor s_i is A_i, equation 4.13 gives us the probability of covering an area equivalent to $A_i \subseteq Q$. The probability of a region A_i being covered by node s_i is stated as follows.

$$P(A_i = s_i) = \frac{\pi t_s^2}{l^2} \qquad (4.14)$$

The probability of a sensing region being covered by multiple nodes also depends on node density, so equation 4.14 is redefined using the node density of sensor field. Density is the ratio of areas of all sensor nodes and the sensor field. If λ is the density of sensor nodes, it is calculated by the following equation:

$$\lambda = \frac{n\pi t_s^2}{l^2} \tag{4.15}$$

Then the probability of a region, equivalent to a node sensing region being covered by a node becomes the ratio of the node density and the number of deployed nodes. Equation 4.14 is modified as follows.

$$
\begin{aligned}
P(q_i \in s_i) &= P(A_i = s_i) & (4.16) \\
&= \frac{\lambda}{n} & (4.17)
\end{aligned}
$$

Since equation 4.17 gives the probability of a point q_i being covered by a sensor s_i, the probability of q_i not covered by s_i is derived as follows.

$$
\begin{aligned}
P(q_i \notin s_i) &= 1 - P(q_i \in s_i) & (4.18) \\
&= 1 - \frac{\lambda}{n} & (4.19) \\
&= \frac{n - \lambda}{n} & (4.20)
\end{aligned}
$$

The probability of a sensing point being covered by ν nodes is identified as the product of the probability of ν nodes that cover the point and the probability of rest of the nodes that do not cover that point. Nodes are uniformly randomly distributed and there are n nodes thrown with an equal probability, so the probability of first ν nodes ($s_1, ..., s_\nu$) covering q_i is computed as follows.

$$
\begin{aligned}
P(q_i = \nu) &= P(q_i \in s_1, ..., q_i \in s_\nu, q_i \notin s_{\nu+1}..., q_i \notin s_n) & (4.21) \\
&= P(q_i \in s_1)...P(q_i \in s_\nu)P(q_i \notin s_{\nu+1})...P(q_i \notin s_n) & (4.22) \\
&= P(q_i \in s_i)^\nu P(q_i \notin s_i)^{n-\nu} & (4.23)
\end{aligned}
$$

Since there are $\binom{n}{\nu}$ possible choices to ν cover the point q_i, the probability that point q_i will be ν-covered from n deployed nodes is computed as follows.

$$
P(q_i = \nu) = \binom{n}{\nu}P(q_i \in s_i)^\nu P(q_i \notin s_i)^{n-\nu} \tag{4.24}
$$

This is also the probability that an area $A_i \subseteq Q$ will be ν-covered as well [Lazos and Poovendran, 2006]. The probability of A_i being ν covered when there are n nodes, is stated as follows.

$$P(A_i = \nu) \; = \; P(q_i = \nu) \tag{4.25}$$
$$= \; \binom{n}{\nu} P(q_i \in s_i)^{\nu} P(q_i \notin s_i)^{n-\nu} \tag{4.26}$$

Once the probability of a ν-covered sensing area is found, the probability of a sensing area being redundantly covered can be derived. Redundancy probability function is given below.

$$P(A_i > \nu) \; = \; 1 - \sum_{i=0}^{\nu} P(A_i = i) \tag{4.27}$$
$$\Rightarrow P(s_i > \nu) \; = \; 1 - \sum_{i=0}^{\nu-1} \binom{n}{\nu} P(q_i \in s_i)^{i} P(q_i \notin s_i)^{n-i} \tag{4.28}$$
$$= \; 1 - \sum_{i=0}^{\nu-1} \binom{n}{\nu} \left(\frac{\lambda}{n}\right)^{i} \left(\frac{n-\lambda}{n}\right)^{n-i} \tag{4.29}$$

Using equation 4.29, the probability distribution of redundant nodes was calculated for various deployed node number and node coverage density. The value of ν was set to 1, and the transmission range of a sensor node t_r was set to 8 units. With node density ranging from 1 to 10, n was varied from 50 to 300.

Results were calculated for two cases when the transmission range t_r of a node was equal to the sensing range t_s, and when t_r was twice of t_s. Figure 4.7 shows that the probability of a node being redundant increases when node density is also increased for both of the cases. When $t_r = t_s$, it reaches to the maximum after adding certain number of nodes. For example, when the number of deployed nodes was 50, the node redundancy probability was about 0.45 at node density 2, and the probability increases to about 0.99 at node density ≥ 5. When the sensor field becomes completely covered, adding new nodes only increases node redundancy probability. The figure also shows that the node redundancy probability linearly increases when $t_r = 2t_s$ but the increase rate is moderate compared to the case where $t_r = t_s$. This is because smaller t_s denotes smaller sensing regions and less overlapping regions between neighbours.

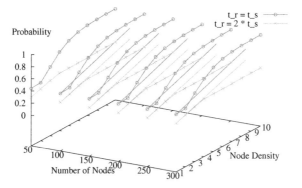

Probability distribution of redundant nodes for Uniformly Randomly Node Distributtion

Figure 4.7: Probability Distribution of Redundant Nodes when the Node Distribution is Uniformly Random.

The required minimum number of active nodes is the integration of the probability of a node not being redundant over the sensor field. The probability function given in equation 4.29 can predict the minimum number of required active nodes using equation 4.12. If S is the sensor set in the sensor field Q, and α_i is the binary variable quantifying i-th sensor depending on $P(s_i > \nu)$, equation 4.12 becomes as follows.

$$H_\kappa(S) \quad = \quad E_{(S)}\left(\sum_{i=1}^{n}\alpha_i\right) \qquad (4.30)$$

$$= \quad \int_S (1 - P(s_i > \nu))ds \qquad (4.31)$$

If $H'_\kappa(S)$ is the function identifying maximum possible number of redundant nodes, $H'_\kappa(S)$ is derived as follows.

$$H'_\kappa(S) \quad = \quad \int_S P(s_i > \nu)ds \qquad (4.32)$$

Using Fubini's theorem [Haaser, 1991], the expected number of potentially redundant

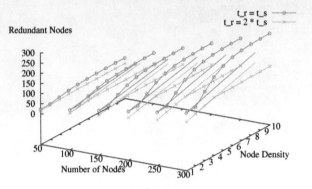

Figure 4.8: Expected Number of Potentially Redundant Nodes when the Node Distribution is Uniformly Random.

nodes is calculated where the redundancy probability for each of the sensor is given in equation 4.29.

$$H'_{\kappa}(S) = \int_S P(s_i > \nu)ds \tag{4.33}$$

$$= |S| \left(1 - \sum_{i=0}^{\nu-1} \binom{n}{\nu} \left(\frac{\lambda}{n} \right)^i \left(\frac{n-\lambda}{n} \right)^{n-i} \right) \tag{4.34}$$

$$= n \left(1 - \sum_{i=0}^{\nu-1} \binom{n}{\nu} \left(\frac{\lambda}{n} \right)^i \left(\frac{n-\lambda}{n} \right)^{n-i} \right) \tag{4.35}$$

Under various node density, the expected number of potentially redundant nodes is shown in Figure 4.8. The graph shows that in both cases the number of potentially redundant nodes linearly increases when the number of deployed nodes increases. The number of potential redundant nodes increases more quickly when $t_r = t_s$ than $t_r = 2t_s$ because of the higher redundancy probability. The figure also shows that node density has a significant impact on the number of potentially redundant nodes. When $t_r = t_s$, the number of potentially redundant nodes is about 70% of deployed nodes at low network density and it reaches to about 99% of deployed nodes at high network density. On the other hand, when $t_r = 2t_s$, about 40% of deployed nodes was found potentially redundant at low network density and about 90% of deployed nodes as potentially redundant at high network density. This is because once the network is completely covered, deploying additional nodes increses the number of potentially redundant nodes.

Poisson Node Distribution

The probability function for a node being ν-covered is derived when node distribution is Poisson. If nodes are deployed following a Poisson point process and λ is the node density, the probability of a node being ν-covered is derived using a similar formula presented at [Hall, 1988]. The equation is stated below:

$$P(s_i = \nu) = \exp^{-\lambda} \left(\sum_{i=0}^{\nu-1} \frac{\lambda^i}{i!} \right) \tag{4.36}$$

When n nodes are deployed using Poisson distribution, the probability that a node is ν-redundant is computed as follows.

$$P(s_i > \nu) = 1 - P(s_i = \nu) \tag{4.37}$$
$$= 1 - \exp^{-\lambda} \left(\sum_{i=0}^{\nu-1} \frac{\lambda^i}{i!} \right) \tag{4.38}$$

The probability of a node being redundant was computed for Poisson node distribution when transmission range (t_r) was the same as sensing range (t_s) and $t_r = 2t_s$. Other parameters were the same as those were for redundancy probability computation when nodes were uniformly distributed. Figure 4.9 shows that for both cases, probability increases more quickly with increasing node density than their respective results obtained for the uniformly random node distribution (Figure 4.7). For example, when the number of deployed nodes was 50 and node density was 4, the node redundancy probability was about 0.9 at $t_r = t_s$ which is about 20% more than the corresponding node redundancy probability when nodes were distributed uniformly randomly. This is because nodes are usually deployed as clusters in Poisson distribution so a node's sensing region has higher probability to be overlapped by its neighbours' sensing regions. The figure also shows that when $t_r = 2t_s$, the node redundancy probability is gradually increasing with the increasing node density, however when $t_r = t_s$, the probability reaches to the maximum value after a certain node density.

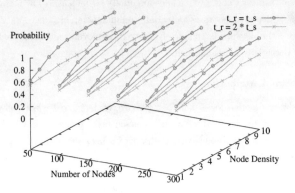

Figure 4.9: Probability Distribution of Redundant Nodes when the Node Distribution is Poisson.

For the Poisson node distribution, the probability distribution function in equation 4.35 is replaced to calculate the expected number of active nodes. The equation is derived as follows.

$$H'_\kappa(S) = |S|(P(s_i \geq \nu)) \tag{4.39}$$

$$= n\left(1 - \exp^{-\lambda}\left(\sum_{i=0}^{\nu-1}\frac{\lambda^i}{i!}\right)\right) \tag{4.40}$$

The expected number of potentially redundant nodes under various node density is shown in Figure 4.10. Result follows a similar trend as shown in Figure 4.9, and it shows that with the increase of the node density, the number of redundant nodes increases for both cases. An important observation from the figure is when $t_r = t_s$, the number of potentially redundant nodes reaches to a saturation point after a certain number of node density. For example, when the number of deployed nodes was 300 and node density was ≥ 4, about 99% of deployed nodes were found potentially redundant. Due to higher node redundancy probability, the number of potentially redundant nodes quickly reaches to the saturation when $t_r = t_s$ than

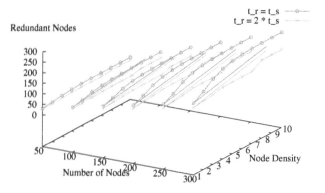

Figure 4.10: Expected Number of Redundant Nodes when the Node Distribution is Poisson.

$t_r = 2t_s$.

4.6 Performance Evaluation

In this section, the performance of SCRC is evaluated experimentally. An extensive simulation was performed to identify the performance of SCRC, and results are compared against existing schemes such as Sponsored Area Scheme (SAS) [Tian and Georganas, 2003], Coverage-Centric Active Nodes Selection (CCANS) [Zou and Chakrabarty, 2005] and Coverage Configuration Protocol (CCP) [Xing et al., 2005]. The experiment was performed under uniformly random and Poission node distributions and a comparative study of experimental results is given below.

Simulation Environment

To perform the simulation, the sensor field was considered as a (50 × 50) grid with spacing of 1 units between grid points. A similar consideration was used in [Tian and Georganas, 2003] and [Zou and Chakrabarty, 2005]. For node deployment, two different node distribution schemes - uniformly random and Poisson distributions, were used. To vary node density,

Table 4.4: Simulation Environment for Implementing Redundant Node Elimination Techniques

Parameter	Value
Sensor field area (Q)	50×50 grid
Number of nodes (S)	Varied from 50 to 300
Data transmission range (t_r)	8 unit distance
Node sensing range (t_s)	8 or 4 unit distance

the number of nodes varied from 50 to 300. All the deployed nodes were architecturally identical. Nodes could communicate with each other, if they were within their transmission ranges. Transmission range t_r was fixed for all nodes, and it was set to 8 grid units. Sensing range t_s was variable to detect redundant node behaviour when $t_r = t_s$ in one case and $t_r = 2t_s$ in another. Network parameters for the simulation is given in Table 4.4.

Compared Schemes

Various redundant node identification schemes were implemented to compare their performances against SCRC. As a baseline, a brute force algorithm was implemented to find the actual number of potentially redundant nodes present in the simulation testbed. The expected number of redundant nodes was analytically identified in Section 4.5. Both the baseline and the analytical results are compared to the number of redundant nodes identified by different redundant node identification schemes. The Sponsored Area Scheme (SAS) [Tian and Georganas, 2005], Coverage-Centric Active Nodes Selection (CCANS) [Zou and Chakrabarty, 2005] and Coverage and Configuration Protocol (CCP) [Xing et al., 2005] were implemented and compared to SCRC. Details of the existing schemes are given in Sections 4.2 and 4.4.3.

Performance Metrics

To compare the performances of various redundant node identification schemes, the number of potentially redundant nodes and the number of nodes actually deactivated by compared schemes were measured. Since the aim of this research is to identify and deactivate redundant nodes, these two metrics are used as the performance criteria. Section 4.4.3 shows that the algorithm complexity of all techniques are the same, except for time complexity. Therefore, the average simulation time to detect a redundant node was also measured.

For each experiment, nodes were deployed using either uniformly-random or Poisson distribution to observe how different schemes behave under different node distributions. Node density also has an effect on redundant nodes, so the simulation was performed under various network density. For the sake of result discussion, a network is referred to as *sparse* when the number of deployed nodes is ≤ 150, otherwise it is called *dense*. To observe the effect of various sensing ranges, the simulation was performed for two cases - when sensing range is equal to transmission range and when sensing range is half of transmission range. Each experiment recorded the above mentioned metrics for comparison.

4.6.1   Case 1: Transmission Range (t_r) = Sensing Range (t_s)

Nodes with a large sensing range have a higher probability to be redundant. This is because the sensing range of a node is the radius of the circular sensing region, and a larger node sensing region has higher probability to be redundantly covered by neighbours' sensing regions. In this experiment, sensing range t_s was made the same as transmission range t_r. For two different node distributions, namely uniformly random and Poisson distribution, the following results were observed.

Uniformly Random Distribution

Figure 4.11 shows the number of potentially redundant nodes under different node density. The analytical, actual and simulation results are plotted together and the behaviour of SCRC is consistent with analytical outcomes. The sensor field became completely covered after a certain number of nodes are deployed. Figure 4.11 shows that SCRC identifies about 70% of deployed nodes as potentially redundant when the network is sparse. It identifies almost 95% of nodes as potentially redundant when the number of deployed nodes is ≥ 150.

The results also show that CCANS and SAS identify about 5% less potentially redundant nodes than SCRC. CCANS identifies redundant nodes using a sequential coverage checking which may leave some potentially redundant nodes unconsidered. On the other hand, SAS considers only a subset of neighbours to check its redundancy, so SAS identifies fewer potentially redundant nodes than SCRC. The deviation of CCP from analytical and actual results is noticeable. CCP cannot identify all possible redundant nodes because it reduces the coverage degree of sensing patches instead of considering node sensing regions. It identifies about 50% less potentially redundant nodes than SCRC.

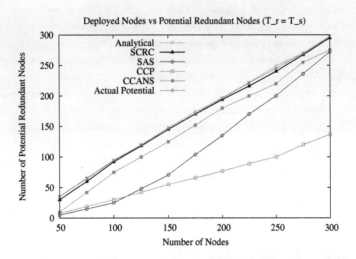

Figure 4.11: Potentially Redundant Nodes when $t_r = t_s$ and the Distribution is Uniform.

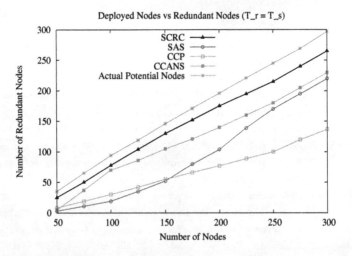

Figure 4.12: Actual Redundant Nodes when $t_r = t_s$ and the Distribution is Uniform.

The deactivation of all the potentially redundant nodes can create coverage and connectivity holes. Innocuous redundant nodes, called actual redundant nodes, are identified from the set of potentially redundant nodes to avoid network holes. Since the analytical result does not consider the coverage hole problem, it is not included in Figure 4.12. The actual number of potentially redundant nodes is shown for comparison with the number of actual redundant nodes. Figure 4.11 shows that sensor field becomes completely covered after deploying 150 nodes. As a result, the number of actual redundant nodes for all techniques are close to their respective potential redundant nodes when the deployed node number is ≥ 150. SCRC identifies almost all the detected potentially redundant nodes as redundant up to 150 deployed nodes. After that, it leaves about 10% potentially redundant nodes without deactivating to maintain required network coverage. Similar scenario is also observed for other techniques, except CCP. It deactivates all the potentially redundant nodes that it detected because CCP identifies only those nodes as potentially redundant which reduce the coverage degree of a sensing patch. Figure 4.12 shows that SCRC identifies about 40% more redundant nodes than CCP. SCRC also outperforms SAS and CCANS by identifying 10% more actual redundant nodes because of its distance based precise redundant node detection scheme.

Node organisation time is the redundant node identifying time. Figure 4.13 presents the node organising time as the ratio of simulation seconds (simtimes) and the number of redundant nodes. The figure shows that SCRC takes the least time up to the number of deployed nodes reaches 150. Figures 4.11 and 4.12 show that up until that point, it identified at least 10% more redundant nodes than any other techniques and identified all the potentially redundant nodes as redundant. This implies that there were no overlapping between potentially redundant nodes so SCRC takes less time in the state determination phase (see Algorithm 4). When the number of deployed nodes becomes greater than 150, SCRC leaves about 40 potentially redundant nodes as active to maintain complete coverage. Determining the state of those nodes takes more time and, as a result, SCRC node organisation time increases to about 10 simtimes more than SAS. At high node density, SAS takes less organising time per redundant node than SCRC because SAS identifies 10% less potentially redundant nodes than SCRC and, as a result, SAS spent less time determining the state of potentially redundant nodes. When the network is sparse, CCANS takes less time to identify a redundant node than SAS because it identified more redundant nodes compared to SAS. When the number of deployed nodes increased, CCANS takes four times more organising time than SAS. This is because CCANS goes through a serialised algorithm to find appropriate redun-

Simtimes per redundant node (Transmission Range = Coverage Range)

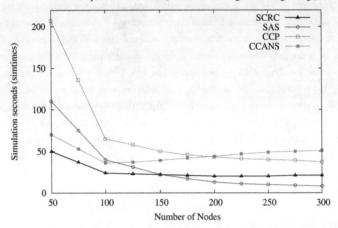

Figure 4.13: Organising Time per Node when $t_r = t_s$ and the Distribution is Uniform.

dant nodes from the potentially redundant nodes to ensure network connectivity. A similar result is also noticed for CCP which has a cubic computational complexity. Another observation is that the differences between times per detected redundant node for all techniques are less when the network is dense. At high node density, the number of redundant nodes is significantly increased, and this reduces the detection time per redundant node.

Poisson Distribution

To observe the effect of node distribution, the experiment was repeated using Poisson node distribution instead of uniformly random. In this experiment, all other parameters were the same as stated above, and following results were observed.

Figure 4.14 shows the potentially redundant nodes identified by different schemes when Poisson node distribution was used. Nodes are usually distributed as clusters with independent overlapping probability in a Poisson node distribution. In such a network, the possibility of covering the same sensing area by multiple nodes is higher than a network of uniform node distribution. The effect of node distribution was also noticed in the experiment as the expected number of potentially redundant nodes reached more quickly 99% of deployed nodes

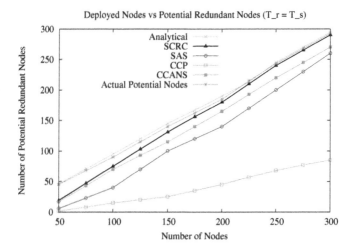

Figure 4.14: Potentially Redundant Nodes when $t_r = t_s$ and the Distribution is Poisson.

than in the uniformly distributed node network. There is a little deviation between SCRC and analytical results at low node density, as in reality, nodes have less overlap between sensing regions when the density is low. With the increase of node density, the sensor field became completely covered and SCRC became consistent with the expected number of potentially redundant nodes. Figure 4.14 shows that SAS and CCANS also follow the same trend as SCRC, however they identify 5-10% less potential nodes than SCRC. Because of their imprecise coverage calculation methods, they cannot identify all the potentially redundant nodes. CCP performed badly and identified only 40% of analytically expected outcomes as potentially redundant. To identify a node redundancy, CCP calculates the redundancy of the sensor field whereas all other techniques check the redundancy of a node region.

Figure 4.15 shows the number of actual redundant nodes that have been deactivated by different techniques. Actual potentially redundant nodes are also shown in the figure to show the differences between potential and redundant nodes. When the node distribution is Poisson, the node density is uneven throughout the sensor field. This decreases the probability of overlapping between potentially redundant nodes' sensing regions. As a result, it has been noticed from Figure 4.14 and Figure 4.15 that the differences between numbers of identified

101

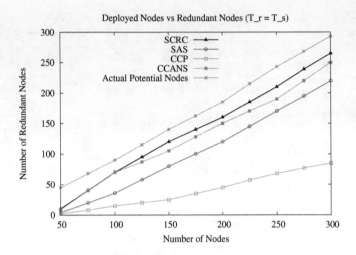

Figure 4.15: Actual Redundant Nodes when $t_r = t_s$ and the Distribution is Poisson.

potentially redundant nodes by different schemes and their respective numbers of deactivated redundant nodes are insignificant. Figure 4.15 also shows that SCRC identifies more actual redundant nodes as it identifies more potentially redundant nodes than others. SCRC identifies about 40% more redundant nodes than CCP, and it also outperforms CCANS and SAS by identifying about 5-10% more redundant nodes than those.

Figure 4.16 shows the average time to detect a redundant node. SAS takes about 8 simtimes to detect and deactivate a redundant node and outperforms others including SCRC. Previous results (Figure 4.14 and 4.15) show that it identifies about 10% less redundant nodes than SCRC. SAS does not consider all the overlapping regions created by neighbours, so it cannot detect all the potentially redundant nodes. A smaller number of potentially redundant nodes results in less possibility of having overlapping between two neighbouring redundant nodes and thus SAS takes less time to determine the state of a potentially redundant node. The average time to organise nodes for CCANS is quadratic due to their token based serial approach. CCP takes less time than CCANS when node density is high but it identifies almost 40% less redundant nodes than CCANS. Both techniques take almost double the time than SCRC which takes about 20 simtimes to detect a redundant node.

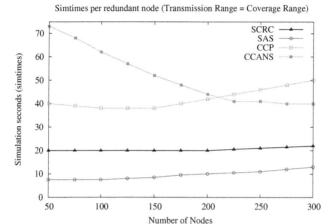

Figure 4.16: Organising Time per Redundant Node when $t_r = t_s$ and the Distribution is Poisson.

4.6.2 Case 2: Transmission Range $(t_r) = 2 \times$ Sensing Range (t_s)

A smaller sensing range denotes a smaller sensing region for a sensor node, so the probability of a node's sensing region being redundantly covered with neighbours' sensing regions is less. To observe the effect of smaller sensing range, t_s was made half of t_r in this case. Other parameters remained the same as those stated above. This experiment is important as Zhang and Hou [2004] show that having complete coverage ensures complete connectivity when sensing range is less than or equal to half of transmission range. As before, nodes were distributed using uniformly random and Poisson node distributions. The proposed and existing schemes were implemented on top of the deployed sensor nodes, and the results are given below.

Uniformly Random Distribution

Figure 4.17 shows the number of potentially redundant nodes when nodes are uniformly randomly distributed. The number of potentially redundant nodes is noticed less than in case 1. Because of the reduced sensing range, intersecting regions between neighbours are

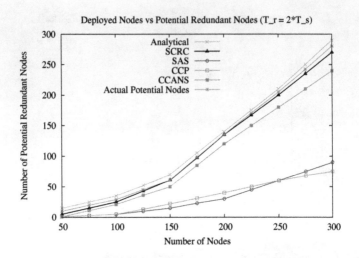

Figure 4.17: *Potentially Redundant Nodes when* $t_r = 2t_s$ *and the Distribution is Uniform.*

also reduced which reduces the number of potentially redundant nodes. The analytical result showed that the number of potentially redundant nodes drops 10% from case 1 and the actual number of redundant nodes also shows a similar result. The figure shows that SCRC is consistent with analytical and actual results by performing closely to them. CCANS follows SCRC closely but identifies about 5% less number of potentially redundant nodes than SCRC. SAS identifies about 40% less potentially redundant nodes than the expected number of potentially redundant nodes. SAS considers only those neighbours having $\geq 120°$ centre angles, and reduced sensing range limits the considered neighbours. The result also shows that CCP performs similarly to SAS. CCP considers the coverage degree of a sensing patch to reduce the redundancy, and the redundant coverage probability is drastically reduced when sensing range is reduced.

Figure 4.18 shows the actual number of redundant nodes that have been deactivated. The actual number of redundant nodes and potentially redundant nodes for all schemes are the same at low node density. With the increased number of deployed nodes, the number of redundant nodes reduces from their corresponding potential redundant nodes, except for CCP. CCP deactivates all the potentially redundant nodes. The differences between poten-

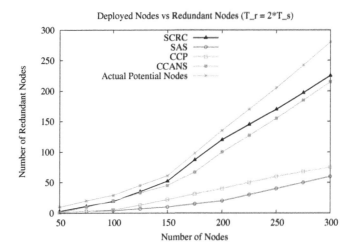

Figure 4.18: Actual Redundant Nodes when $t_r = 2t_s$ and the Distribution is Uniform.

tially redundant nodes and actual redundant nodes for other approaches are smaller, even when the node density is increased. This is because the smaller sensing range reduces the probability of overlapping between potentially redundant nodes. The result also shows that SCRC can deactivate about 40% more redundant nodes than SAS or CCP and about 10% more than CCANS.

The organisation time or simulation time per redundant node for each scheme is shown in Figure 4.19. Result shows that all the techniques require a significant time per detected redundant node at low network density. The organising time for each scheme is almost doubled the organising time those methods took at the same network density when $t_r = t_s$. Although each node performed the same procedure it previously performed at $t_r = t_s$, the detection time increased because shorter sensing range reduces the number of redundant nodes. Once the network becomes completely covered, the detection time for each technique was reduced because after that, deploying new nodes increased the number of redundant nodes. Figure 4.19 shows that SAS takes less time to identify and deactivate redundant nodes due to the fact that it identifies fewer potentially as well as actual redundant nodes than SCRC. CCANS takes almost 250 simtimes when the network is sparse, however the organisation

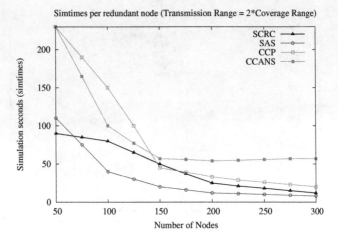

Figure 4.19: *Organising Time per Redundant Node when $t_r = 2t_s$ and the Distribution is Uniform.*

time per redundant node reduces to about 60 simtimes when the network is dense. The organisation time for CCANS is still about three times higher than other techniques because of its serialised token based redundancy calculation.

Poisson Distribution

Figure 4.20 shows the number of potentially redundant nodes identified by various techniques when the node distribution is Poisson and $t_r = 2t_s$. The figure shows that SCRC is consistent with the actual number of redundant nodes. For example, when the network is sparse, there are about 43% of deployed nodes which have the potential to be redundant in the simulation testbed, and SCRC identifies about 41% of deployed nodes potentially redundant. When the node density increased, SCRC identifies about 90% of deployed nodes potentially redundant, which is about 1% fewer than the actual redundant nodes. The figure also shows that at low node density, CCP is hardly able to identify any potentially redundant nodes because of the low coverage degree of sensing patches. When the node density increases, it identifies about 30% of deployed nodes as potentially redundant which is about $\frac{1}{3}$ of SCRC's identification rate. SAS does not perform well either because by considering only a subset of neighbours, it

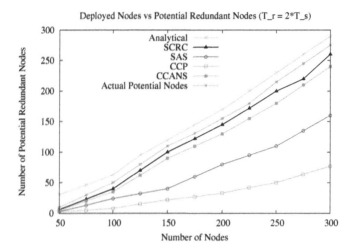

Figure 4.20: Potentially Redundant Nodes when $t_r = 2t_s$ and the Distribution is Poisson.

identifies 50% of expected possibly redundant nodes as potential to be redundant. CCANS performs similarly to SCRC by identifying about 80% of expected potentially redundant nodes as potential, and this is about 5% less than SCRC. CCANS used sequential token based redundancy computation and sequential computation may have left some potential redundant nodes unconsidered.

Figure 4.21 shows the number of redundant nodes identified after considering coverage and connectivity. SCRC identifies the maximum number of redundant nodes among compared techniques and is close to the actual number of potentially redundant nodes in the network. The figure shows that 43% of deployed nodes have the potential to be redundant at low network density, and SCRC deactivates about 95% of them. When the network is dense, there are about 90% of deployed nodes which have the potential to be redundant, and SCRC identifies about 70% of deployed nodes as actual redundant nodes. The rest are left as active to avoid possible coverage holes. Although CCANS performs closely to SCRC, it identifies about 5% less redundant nodes than SCRC. SAS identifies about 40% less redundant nodes than SCRC, and CCP is outperformed by SCRC by about 70% because their redundancy calculation techniques could not identify all potentially redundant nodes.

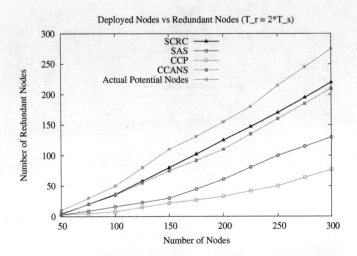

Figure 4.21: Actual Redundant Nodes when $t_r = 2t_s$ and the Distribution is Poisson.

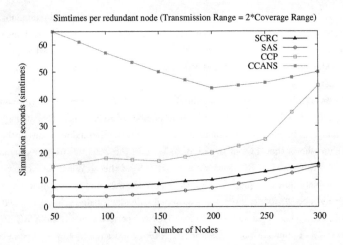

Figure 4.22: Organising Time per Redundant Node when $t_r = 2t_s$ and the Distribution is Poisson.

Figure 4.22 shows that the organising time per redundant node for SCRC and SAS are close to each other. The time difference between these two techniques is almost the same for all network densities, except for an extremely high network density. When the network is sparse, SAS and SCRC take 4 and 8 simtimes per redundant node respectively. The time difference reduces to 1 simtime when the number of deployed nodes increases to 275 - 300, as the figure shows that those methods take 14 and 15 simtimes respectively at that period. The detection time for SAS increases because of the increasing number of overlapped potentially redundant nodes at high node density. When the network is sparse, CCP takes three times more simtimes than SAS to identify and deactivate redundant nodes. The organising times for CCP show a sharp increase rate with the increase of the node density, and it reaches from 15 to 45 simtimes when the number of deployed nodes increases to 300. This is because CCP's computational complexity increases on a cubic order of the average number of neighbours per node. CCANS has a higher organising time per redundant node at low network density which is about 65 simtimes. With the increase of deployed nodes, the ratio of organising time and redundant nodes decreases up to a certain number of deployed nodes because the number of redundant nodes is also increased. After that, the organising time per detected node shows a polynomial increase due to their token based serial algorithm.

4.7   Discussion

In this section, the implication of experimental results are discussed for both uniformly random and Poisson node distributions. Simulations were performed for two different sensing ranges to identify redundant nodes for different network conditions. The possible number of redundant nodes were calculated analytically from Section 4.5. This gives us the expected number of redundant nodes for our simulation testbed. A brute force algorithm was also performed to identify the actual number of redundant nodes in the simulation testbed. These two results are used to compare redundant node identifying techniques, namely SCRC, SAS, CCP and CCANS. The summary of the experimental performance analysis of various redundant node identification techniques are given in Tables 4.5 and 4.6. In the summary table, a network is denoted sparse when the number of deployed nodes is ≤ 150, otherwise dense.

When the node distribution is uniform, intersections between neighbours' sensing regions have equal probability to occur. The sensor field becomes completely covered after a certain number of nodes are deployed and, after that, deploying additional nodes increases potentially redundant nodes. Since the network is completely covered, those potentially redundant nodes

Table 4.5: Summary of Simulation Results of Redundant Node Elimination Techniques - Case: 1.

Percentage of Identified Redundant Nodes when $t_r = t_s$				
	Uniform Distribution		Poisson Distribution	
Approach	Sparse	Dense	Sparse	Dense
SCRC	70%	90%	60%	90%
CCANS	50%	82%	56%	85%
CCP	20%	50%	15%	30%
SAS	15%	80%	30%	80%

have higher probability of being redundant. For this reason, the number of actual redundant nodes should be close to the number of potential redundant nodes at high network density. Figure 4.11 shows that at high network density, about 99% of deployed nodes are potentially redundant when $t_r = t_s$. Table 4.5 reveals that SCRC identifies 90% of deployed nodes as redundant when the network is dense. Similarly, Figure 4.17 shows that at high network density almost 90% of deployed nodes are potentially redundant when $t_r = 2t_s$ and SCRC identifies about 85% of deployed nodes as redundant (Table 4.6). The experimental results show that SCRC is consistent with analytical results for both cases. Other techniques cannot exactly follow the analytical results due to their imprecise coverage calculation methods. For example, CCANS nodes calculate their coverage ratio serially, and serial redundancy computation may leave some potentially redundant nodes unconsidered.

When the node distribution follows a Poisson distribution, nodes are often distributed in clusters so, in such a network, the number of redundant nodes should be close to the number of potentially redundant nodes for all network densities. At low network densities, about 80% and 60% of deployed nodes were potentially redundant for $t_r = t_s$ and $t_r = 2t_s$ respectively. SCRC identified about 80% of them as redundant for both cases. When the network was dense, about 99% and 85% of deployed nodes had the potential to be redundant for $t_r = t_s$ and $t_r = 2t_s$ respectively. The experimental result shows that SCRC identified about 90% of them as redundant for both cases. The results also demonstrated that SCRC outperforms existing techniques because it uses precise distance based redundancy computation.

The algorithm analysis shows that complexity varies only for computational time, so the

Table 4.6: Summary of Simulation Results of Redundant Node Elimination Techniques - Case: 2.

Percentage of Identified Redundant Nodes when $t_r = 2 \times t_s$				
	Uniform Distribution		Poisson Distribution	
Approach	Sparse	Dense	Sparse	Dense
SCRC	30%	85%	40%	70%
CCANS	30%	80%	36%	65%
CCP	10%	40%	10%	30%
SAS	10%	40%	15%	45%

simulation time taken per redundant node was also observed. The result shows that SCRC takes almost a constant time for various node densities due to its distributed algorithm. This also implies that SCRC is scalable. Although the number of identified redundant nodes by CCANS was close to SCRC's, CCANS had a detection time in the order of square of the number of neighbours. The results also show that CCP has node organisation time similar to CCANS. SAS takes the least time to organise, however this technique does not identify all possible redundant nodes.

Section 4.4.3 presents the complexity analysis of various techniques, where SCRC and SAS show the least complexity in terms of time, space and message passing. However, the limitation of SAS is not being able to identify all possible redundant nodes which is also noticed from experimental results. SCRC outperforms SAS by identifying maximum possible number of redundant nodes with the same order of complexity of SAS. On the other hand, CCANS and CCP have higher computational complexity than SCRC and SAS.

4.8 Conclusion

The redundant node deployment can cause redundant energy consuming activities and thus affect the sensor network operational lifetime. To extend network lifetime, redundant nodes are identified and deactivated. Redundant nodes and their activities are eliminated by using sensor and sensor field local information. A method, called Self Calculated Redundancy Check (SCRC), is proposed to identify redundant nodes in a distributed manner. SCRC considers the sensor field as a finite set of sensing points, and assumes that a sensor node covers a fixed subset of those points. Each SCRC node calculates the coverage information of a subset of sensing points and decides possible node redundancy based on those. Since there may be overlapping sensing regions between multiple potentially redundant nodes, a random back-off technique is proposed to identify actual redundant nodes. Complexity analysis shows that SCRC has a linear combinatorial complexity by having time, message and space complexity in the order of node density λ, that is $O(\lambda)$. A statistical analysis was also performed for calculating the expected number of redundant nodes under two different node distributions, uniform and Poisson. The analytical result validates the proposed method because an extensive experiment showed that SCRC was consistent with the analytical outcome. Existing techniques such as SAS [Tian and Georganas, 2003], CCANS [Zou and Chakrabarty, 2005] and CCP [Xing et al., 2005] were also implemented and the result shows that SCRC identifies at least 5-10% more redundant nodes than those techniques.

In this chapter, potentially redundant nodes and deactivated actual redundant nodes have been identified to extend network operational lifetime. If deactivated redundant nodes are properly reused, network lifetime can be extended more. In the next two chapters, further work is done examining the reactivation of redundant nodes to recover network holes that occur due to active node failures.

Chapter 5

Failed Node Detection

5.1 Introduction

Sensors are redundantly deployed to meet coverage and connectivity requirements, and a sensor network identifies and deactivates redundant nodes to reduce energy wastage. In such a network, only a subset of nodes remains active and provide complete network coverage. In such networks, if an active node fails, it creates a coverage and/or connectivity hole. This may also affect the network lifetime because neighbours of a failed node have to perform additional tasks, such as sensing and data communication on behalf of the failed node. To maintain the network effectiveness, failed nodes should be properly identified and be replaced by deactivated redundant nodes.

A node is considered to have failed when it becomes disconnected from its neighbours (although it may be still fully functional). Protocols devised for detecting failed sensor nodes need to be energy efficient by having low overheads because a sensor network has limited resources, especially energy. To minimise the control overhead, existing network mechanisms (such as data packet transmissions between neighbours) can be used for failure identification, instead of continuous explicit node monitoring techniques (for example, probing [Zhuang et al., 2005]). A proper identification of failed nodes needs synchronisation of failure detectors to validate a failure assumption. The distributed clocking mechanism to synchronise failure detectors consumes significant energy, so failure detection method should be asynchronous. The method should also be *complete* by identifying all failed nodes and *accurate* by avoiding false positives.

Traditional failure detection mechanisms for distributed systems do not consider computational overheads because nodes are considered limitless resources. For example, with active or passive failure detection methods, a node periodically sends probe packets to its neighbours and waits for acknowledgements [Hayashibara et al., 2002]. In such techniques, packets can be lost during transmission, and as a result, a live node can be considered as failed. Although wrong suspicions are avoided by synchronisation between failure detectors, detection schemes rely on the global clocking mechanism to synchronise detectors [Renesse et al., 1998; Gupta et al., 2001]. In distributed systems, a considerable amount of control overheads is involved to maintain a global clock. To avoid clocking, asynchronous failure detection systems allow detectors to suspect a node mistakenly [Chandra and Toueg, 1996], and a different mechanism such as the consensus method [Fetzer, 2003] is proposed to correct false positives. Other than that, failure detection mechanisms for distributed systems are based on fixed network topologies [Chandra and Toueg, 1996]. Methods devised for fixed networks may not be applicable to dynamic networks such as sensor networks.

To detect a failed node, the data packets sent and received are monitored instead of separate probe or acknowledgement packets. The numbers of sent and received messages are compared, and in case of discrepancy node failure is assumed. To validate the assumption, a consensus mechanism is proposed among failure detectors selected dynamically. The self-organising capability of a sensor network is used to choose failure detectors from the deployed nodes. This also suits the dynamic structure of a sensor network.

The proposed method, called Asynchronous Failed Sensor node Detection (AFSD) aims at minimising energy and control overheads, while detecting all the failed nodes. Sensors are organised into clusters, and separate detection protocols are assigned to gateways (or cluster heads) and non-gateways (or cluster members). Each gateway node detects failed neighbours by tracking the data packet exchange with them, and similarly each non-gateway node tracks its gateways. To keep track of messages sent to and received from neighbours, a node running AFSD maintains a counter for each of its neighbours. These counters are called *failure counters*, and AFSD modifies the failure counter in such a way that, for a live node, the value of the counter is bounded and tends to zero. The value of the failure counter for a failed node is unbounded and tends to infinity. For a failed node, eventually the value will cross a predefined threshold at a live node, and that failed node becomes suspected. A node can fail to communicate with some of its neighbours while it still has connectivity with others. To avoid such false positives, a consensus is sought among the gateways from the same cluster before declaring a node as failed. The method analysis shows that AFSD is accurate and complete. The complexity analysis shows that the control, energy, and time overheads of AFSD are linear, in the order of number of neighbours and gateways.

114

Extensive simulation was performed to compare the performance of AFSD to other existing methods such as Keep-Alive Sharing Negative (KASN) [Zhuang et al., 2005], the Cluster method [Ranganathan et al., 2001] and Clustering with Backpointers (CB) [Tai et al., 2004]. The experimental results show that AFSD is consistent with the analytical result obtained from the complexity analysis, and that it is at least three times more energy efficient than any of those existing methods. AFSD reduces the control overhead by monitoring the data communication between neighbours instead of periodic probing. The result also shows that the average time for AFSD to detect a failed node is at least as good as other existing methods when the packet generation rate is high. However, existing methods are faster than AFSD when the packet generation rate is low.

The rest of the chapter is organised as follows. Failure detection schemes in traditional distributed systems and sensor networks are described in Section 5.2. The model of the proposed AFSD method is given in Section 5.3. Details of AFSD scheme is given in Section 5.4. The completeness and accuracy of AFSD is showed in Section 5.5. AFSD and some existing methods are analysed in Section 5.6 and 5.7. Finally, results are discussed in Section 5.8 and this chapter is concluded with future directions in Section 5.9.

5.2   Related Work

In this section, synchronous and asynchronous failure detection methods in traditional distributed systems are discussed and analysed. Node failure is also noticed in sensor networks where failure detection is addressed to be a means towards reliability.

5.2.1   Failure Detection in Synchronous Distributed Systems

Failure detection techniques for synchronous distributed systems have received considerable attention. In such systems, failure detection is comparatively easy, because timing is used to validate failure assumptions. For example, "Keep-Alive" algorithms [Coulouris et al., 2005] are widely used to detect failures in synchronous systems where globally synchronised nodes periodically probe each other to detect a failed node. Zhuang et al. [2005; 2003] identify two different approaches for Keep-Alive algorithms - gossiping and probing. In a gossip approach, a node periodically sends "I'm alive" messages to its neighbours [Renesse et al., 1998]. If a node fails to receive such a message from a neighbour, it considers that neighbour as failed. The drawback of this technique is high control message overhead and bandwidth requirements due to periodic flooding of live nodes. In a probe based approach [Stoica et al.,

2001], a node sends a particular neighbour an "are you alive?" message, to which a live neighbour replies with a positive message. If a node fails to reply, it is considered failed. Although the control overhead is less in the probing technique compared to the gossiping, it is still considered high, especially for a resource limited network.

To minimise the control overhead for Keep-Alive algorithms, sharing failure information among live nodes is investigated in [Han and Shin, 1997] to avoid redundant node probing. There are two types of (failure information) sharing mechanisms - positive and negative information sharing [Gupta et al., 2001]. In a Keep-Alive Sharing Positive (KASP) method [Zhuang et al., 2005], the failure detector always announces the information of a live node. In Keep-Alive Sharing Negative (KASN) method [Zhuang et al., 2005], a failure detector announces If a node has failed. KASP control overhead is much higher than KASN, because KASP periodically broadcasts messages when a node is alive.

5.2.2 Failure Detection in Asynchronous Distributed Systems

Failure detection is comparatively complex in an asynchronous environment due to lack of timing mechanisms [Fetzer, 2001; 2003]. To alleviate the problem, asynchronous failure detection schemes allow detectors to suspect a node mistakenly as failed for example, unreliable failure detectors [Chandra and Toueg, 1991]. Chandra and Toueg [1991] divide failure detectors into different classes, and the unreliable failure detector is in the weakest failure detection class [Chandra and Toueg, 1996]. The unreliable failure detectors are allowed to suspect a live node as failed, and wrong failure suspicions are corrected by a consensus among all the failure detectors [Chandra et al., 1992]. Each consensus participating node sends its observation for the suspected failed node, and eventually a common decision is made based on those observations. Chandra et al. [1992] theoretically prove that weakest failure detectors can solve the consensus problem in asynchronous failure detection systems [Chandra and Toueg, 1996]. Since sensor networks are a special type of asynchronous systems, the proposed theoretical basis can be used in such a network with energy efficiency measures.

Implementing a failure detection module in each node is inefficient, instead, clusters are formed where a cluster head monitors a group of nodes [Fox et al., 1997; Burns et al., 1999]. This reduces the control overhead for detecting a failed node. Cluster heads can implement any kind of keep-alive algorithms [Coulouris et al., 2005] to check their member nodes, and they are responsible for monitoring their own vicinity. For example, Ranganathan et al. [2001] propose to cluster distributed nodes in small groups, where the cluster head uses a gossip based Keep-Alive algorithm to identify failed nodes within the cluster. The drawbacks of such a technique include the overhead for gossiping and the vulnerability of a cluster head in a promiscuous system, for example, in sensor networks.

The failed node detection overhead for a Clustering method can be reduced by sharing failure information. Such as in the Clustering with Backpointers (CB) [Tai et al., 2004] nodes maintain a list of neighbours to inform about a failed node. Failure detectors are implemented in a distributed manner and a cluster-based communication architecture is used. The method uses intra-cluster Keep-Alive message diffusions to detect a failed node. Cluster heads forward a failure report across clusters through the upper layer of the communication hierarchy. By propagating failure information, CB reduces the control overhead because an already informed node does not need to further query a failed node. However, in addition to Keep-Alive messages, creating backpointers imposes additional overhead in such techniques such as every time the network topology changes, failure detectors need to rediscover their backpointers.

5.2.3 Failure Detection in Sensor Networks

Failure detection techniques in sensor networks are often linked to other research problems. For example, detecting failures is important in data aggregation where messages from a faulty sensor can produce misleading data. Krishnamachari and Iyengar [2004] propose a solution to the fault-event disambiguation problem in sensor networks. The method uses a Bayesian algorithm to correct the sensed event from a sensing region where 5-10% faulty nodes are allowed, but does not identify individual sensor node failures.

Reliability is another area where failure detection is needed. Creating an end to end reliable communication path is an important challenge. To maintain reliability, failed nodes should be replaced. Such a technique is proposed in the event-to-sink reliable transport protocol [Akan and Akyildiz, 2005], where a relationship between the message reporting frequency and reliability is established. This technique increases node density whenever network reliability decreases. The problem of this protocol is identifying the exact location of reinforcement, which requires the detection of failed nodes.

Failure of a group of nodes can partition the network. For example, Shrivastava et al. [2005] focus on identifying sensor network partitions by monitoring the status of a subset of deployed nodes. In this centralised approach, the base station monitors node failures to identify an ϵ-cut [1] in the network. Nodes to be monitored are identified by using the node local information and the minimum link separator [2] computation. The algorithm does not scale well in such a network because the computational complexity increases exponentially with the increase of node density due to periodical node monitoring.

5.2.4 Summary

In summary, synchronous failure detection methods are not feasible in sensor networks due to lack of global clocking mechanisms and high control overheads. The theoretical basis for asynchronous failure detection methods can be used in sensor networks. However, existing asynchronous methods (for example, the Cluster method [Ranganathan et al., 2001]) are related to distributed systems with fixed network architecture, and node resources are considered limitless. Although failure detection is essential for data aggregation and reliability, none of the existing methods explicitly identify failed nodes in sensor networks.

5.3 The Proposed Failure Detection Model

The aim of this section is to find failed sensors in an asynchronous manner. Operations in a synchronous system are coordinated by a centrally controlled fixed-rate clocking signal [Li and Rus, 2004]. In contrast, asynchronous systems have no global clocks, instead, they operate under distributed control with concurrent components communicating and synchronising locally [Arjomandi et al., 1983]. A sensor network is considered to be asynchronous system, where nodes can use their local clocks for internal synchronisation.

Node Failures and Failure Patterns

If a node is unreachable from any other nodes, the node is considered failed. A node can be disconnected from its neighbours due to software problems, hardware malfunction, link failure, external hindrances or depleted battery. Once a node fails, it is considered unrecoverable. The self-organising capability of a sensor network includes a mechanism to adopt

---

[1] An ϵ-cut, for any $0 < \epsilon < 1$, is a linear separation of ϵ nodes from the base station [Shrivastava et al., 2005].

[2] Given two disjoint simple polygonal curves, γ_1 and γ_2, in the plane, a separator is a polygonal curve that partitions the plane into two parts such that γ_1 and γ_1 lie on opposite sides of the separator. A minimum link separator for γ_1 and γ_1 is such a separator with the minimum number of vertices [Shrivastava et al., 2005].

new nodes (see Chapter 3), so that a node recovered from a temporary failure is viewed as a new node with different energy capacity.

Each node maintains a neighbour list, and nodes continuously update their neighbour list with the current neighbour status. Let us assume that a sensor network consists of a set S of n nodes, defined as $S = \{s_1, s_2, s_3, \ldots, s_n\}$. A failure pattern $Failed$ is also considered where $Failed_t(S)$ denotes a set of nodes that have failed during time t. The function $Failed$ is also defined for each node belonging to S. $Neighbour(s_i)$ (where $Neighbour(s_i) \subseteq S$) denotes the neighbour set of node s_i, and $Failed_t(s_i)$ represents the subset of failed nodes that belong to $Neighbour(s_i)$. A neighbour can fail at any time, and neighbour lists are updated incrementally. Then the failure pattern at node s_i can be stated as follows.

$$\forall t \ Failed_t(s_i) \subseteq Failed_{t+1}(s_i) \tag{5.1}$$

Similarly, another function $Alive(S)$, where $Alive_t(S) \subseteq S$, produces a set of live nodes at time t in the network. The set of live nodes within the communication range of a node s_i is $Alive_t(s_i)$ and is formally defined as follows.

$$\forall t \ Alive_t(s_i) = Neighbour(s_i) - Failed_t(s_i) \tag{5.2}$$

Failure Detectors

Nodes perform different tasks at different states (such as gateway state or non-gateway state as described in Chapter 3) over their lifetimes, and the failure detection module needs a different detection scheme for each state (see Subsection 5.4.2). The module has access to local failure patterns, that is to $Failed(s_i)$ and to $Alive(s_i)$, to synchronise failed node assumptions locally. When a failure is detected, the detector subsequently registers it in the neighbour list maintained within the node.

5.4 Asynchronous Failed Sensor node Detection (AFSD) Method

Existing failure detection methods for distributed systems focus on detection of failed nodes without considering control or energy overheads [Zhuang et al., 2005]. This makes those methods unsuitable for resource limited sensor networks. In this section, a method is proposed called Asynchronous Failed Sensor node Detection (AFSD), to identify failed nodes in an energy efficient manner. AFSD does not require any global timing mechanism, unlike conventional failure detectors [Larrea et al., 2004; Chandra and Toueg, 1996; Guerraoui et al., 1995]. It uses the data packets exchanged between neighbours to suspect a failure and then confirms the failure using a consensus procedure among gateway nodes.

5.4.1 Properties of AFSD

To keep track of neighbours, every node maintains a failure counter for each of its neighbours. An AFSD node modifies the failure counter whenever a message is sent to or received from a neighbour. AFSD maintains the failure counter in such a way that the value of the failure counter is always bounded for a live node, and the value is unbounded for a failed node. AFSD produces a list $(s_1, d_1), (s_2, d_2), \ldots, (s_k, d_k)$ at each sensor node s, where $\{s_1, s_2, \ldots, s_k\}$ are neighbours of s, and $\{d_1, d_2, \ldots, d_k\}$ are failure counters attached to corresponding neighbours. These integers are used to track messages sent to, and received from, each of those neighbours. When a message m is sent from s to s_j, AFSD modifies the corresponding integer variable d_j. When s receives any message or acknowledgement from a neighbour s_j, AFSD also updates the corresponding variable d_j. Counter is modified such that d_j for a live node s_j will eventually be zero, and for a failed node it will be increasing to infinity. When the value of a counter d_j reaches a predefined threshold c_{max}, node s suspects that node s_j has failed. The value of c_{max} is chosen based on the packet loss rate of a particular network. If the loss rate is high, c_{max} is also set high to give failure detectors sufficient time to establish a well-founded suspicion.

Let us assume that each sensor s_i maintains a vector F containing the list of s_i's neighbours as well as the corresponding failure counters. $F_{s_i}(t)$ at node s_i can be assumed as the result of AFSD at time t. That is, the vector is holding the neighbour failure counter values. The failure counter value at node s_i of neighbour s_j is defined as:

$$F_{s_i}(t)[s_j] = d_j \tag{5.3}$$

To suspect a node, the value of failure counters are compared to c_{max}. If the value of d_j reaches c_{max}, node s_j is marked as suspected to be failed, otherwise s_j is alive. The failed and live node properties are stated as follows.

1. At each live sensor node, the value of the failure counter of every failed neighbour is unbounded. For a given time t, $\forall s_i \in Alive(S)$, we have:

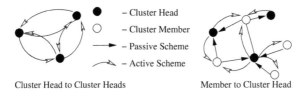

Figure 5.1: Detection Protocols Used in the Proposed Method.

$$if \ \forall s_j \in Failed(S) \cap Neighbour(s_i) \ then \ F_{s_i}(t)[s_j] > c_{max} \qquad (5.4)$$

2. At each live sensor node, the value of the failure counter of every live neighbour is bounded. For a given time t, $\forall s_i \in Alive(S)$, we have:

$$if \ \forall s_j \in Alive(S) \cap Neighbour(s_i) \ then \ 0 \leq F_{s_i}(t)[s_j] \leq c_{max} \qquad (5.5)$$

5.4.2 Failure Detection Protocols

Failure detection protocols for gateways (or cluster heads) and non-gateways (or cluster members) are defined in this section. Failure detection schemes follow various protocols and are broadly classified as either active or passive [Zhuang et al., 2005]. In an active approach, a node periodically sends explicit messages such as keep-alive packets to detect a failed node. Explicit messages in fact can be data packets sent between nodes. A passive approach uses only data packets to convey aliveness information. AFSD uses both approaches as shown in Figure 5.1. Since non-gateway nodes are attached to gateways, an active detection scheme is used at gateways to monitor the cluster members. Non-gateway nodes are only allowed to communicate with gateways, so that they can use their data packets and acknowledgements as aliveness notification.

Failure Detection by Gateways

Gateway nodes, communicating with non-gateway members and other gateways, use an active failure detection approach. A gateway collects data from its cluster members and forwards data toward base stations using multi-hop data communications. Intermediate nodes of a multi-hop path are also gateways. Since gateway nodes may not have to send data regularly, the Gateway-to-Non-gateway failure detection protocol is an active approach. A gateway node uses implicit messages to monitor its gateway members using received data packets. It only sends explicit keep-alive messages to its members, if nothing is sent or received for a certain period of time t_{max}. The value of t_{max} depends on the packet arrival rate at a live node. If the data communication is regular, t_{max} can be set to a minimum value.

A gateway node does not send any data packets to its non-gateway neighbours, instead, it only receives data from them and received packets are acknowledged. If a non-gateway fails to send data packets for t_{max} time, only then a gateway probes that node. For a successful packet transmission (that is, packet receiving and acknowledging), the failure counter value should be unchanged. In order to keep the failure counter value positive, it is incremented when a data packet is received and decremented when the corresponding acknowledgement is sent. In a gateway node, the counter value of a non-gateway node will be increasing only when the gateway node starts probing. The Gateway-to-Non-gateway failure detection scheme is described as follows.

1. Upon receiving a message from a member s_j at time t, Gateway s_i increments the corresponding failure counter $F_{s_i}(t)[s_j]$ by one. After sending an acknowledgement, s_i decrements the failure counter $F_{s_i}(t)[s_j]$ by one.

2. If nothing is received at gateway s_i from a member s_j for a certain period of time t_{max}, s_i sends a probe message and increments the failure counter $F_{s_i}(t)[s_j]$ by one and waits for the probe acknowledgement ack_j.

The Gateway-to-Gateway failure checking also needs to be an active approach because data communication between gateways depends on data received from non-gateway nodes. The failure detection scheme is optimised, that is, data packets replace explicit detection messages. In contrast to Gateway-to-Non-Gateway protocol, here the failure counter value of a gateway node can be increased either by repetitive sending of a failed data packet or by probe packets. The Gateway-to-Gateway Protocol is as follows.

1. After sending a message from a gateway s_i to another gateway s_h at time t, s_i increments the corresponding failure counter $F_{s_i}(t)[s_h]$ by one. After receiving the acknowledgement, it decrements $F_{s_i}(t)[s_h]$ by one.

2. If nothing is received at gateway s_i from gateway s_h for a certain period of time t_{max},

122

Algorithm 5: Failure Counter Modification - Gateway Side Algorithm

Notation:

msg - the data/control message

t, t' - storing current and previous time respectively

TD[i] is the time keeper

$Cluster_{Head}(s)$ - checks whether s is a cluster head.

5.1 **while** $TRUE$ **do**

5.2   **if** msg_j *received from node* s_j **then**

5.3 $t \leftarrow msg_j(\text{time})$;

5.4 $t' = \text{TD[j]}$;

5.5 $\text{TD[j]} = t$;

5.6   **if** $s_j \in Cluster_{Head}(s_i)$ **then**

5.7 $F_{s_i}(t)[s_j] \leftarrow F_{s_i}(t')[s_j]$ - 1;

5.8   send acknowledgement ack_j ;

5.9   **end**

5.10   **else**

5.11 $F_{s_i}(t)[s_j] \leftarrow F_{s_i}(t')[s_j] + 1$;

5.12   send acknowledgement ack_j ;

5.13   **end**

5.14   **end**

5.15   **if** msg_k *is sent to node* s_k **then**

5.16   **if** $s_k \in Cluster_{HEAD}(s_i)$ **then**

5.17 $F_{s_i}(t)[s_j] \leftarrow F_{s_i}(t')[s_j] + 1$;

5.18   **end**

5.19   **else**

5.20 $F_{s_i}(t)[s_j] \leftarrow F_{s_i}(t')[s_j]$ - 1;

5.21   **end**

5.22   **end**

5.23   **for** *all entries in* $TD[i]$ **do**

5.24   **if** $(current_{time}$ - $TD[i]) \geq t_{max}$ **then**

5.25   send a probe $msg_i(probe)$;

5.26 $F_{s_i}(t)[s_j] \leftarrow F_{s_i}(t')[s_j] + 1$;

5.27   **end**

5.28   **end**

5.29 **end**

s_i sends a probe message and increments the failure counter $F_{s_i}(t)[s_h]$ by one. Then it waits for the probe acknowledgement ack_j.

The various steps of the failure detection scheme for a gateway node are shown in Algorithm 5. At gateway s_i, if a packet is received from another gateway, s_i decrements the corresponding failure counter by one, where the received message is considered to be an implicit keep-alive message. This is shown in the algorithm, Lines 5.6 - 5.9. If the received message is from a cluster member node, s_i increments the corresponding failure counter (see Lines 5.10 to 5.13). To keep the counter value between zero and c_{max}, s_i modifies the failure counter inversely for acknowledgement messages, that is, if the acknowledgement recipient is a member node, it decrements the failure counter by one. Otherwise, it increments the failure counter by one which is shown in Lines 5.15 - 5.21.

If a gateway node s_i fails to receive any messages from a neighbour for t_{max} time after receiving the last message, s_i voluntarily sends a probe packet to that member and increments the corresponding failure counter by one. This is shown in Lines 5.23 to 5.28 of Algorithm 5.

The protocol ensures that failure counters for any live sensor node will eventually become zero. However, if a node fails, the corresponding failure counter will be gradually increasing. There is a failure counter threshold c_{max}, where the value of the c_{max} can be decided on the packet loss ratio of the network. If the packet loss ratio is high, c_{max} should also be high. Otherwise, it can be set to a minimum value. When a failure counter value for a neighbour reaches the threshold c_{max}, the cluster head initiates a consensus procedure among gateway nodes in its neighbour list to find out if others are also suspecting the node in question. The consensus procedure is given in Subsection 5.4.3.

Failure Detection by Non-gateways

A different protocol is proposed for the non-gateway side because tasks performed by a gateway and a non-gateway node are not the same. Non-gateway nodes communicate only with gateways that forward data to a base station. Nodes are regularly sensing and sending sensed data, so the non-gateway to gateway failure detection scheme can be passive to minimise failure detection control overhead. The non-gateway failure detection protocol is described below.

1. Non-gateway nodes only monitor their gateways.

2. Whenever a non-gateway node s_m sends data to a gateway s_i at time t, it increments the

124

Algorithm 6: Failure Counter Modification - Non-gateway Side Algorithm

---

      Notation:

             msg is the data/control message

             ack is the acknowledgement

             t, t' are storing current and previous time of the last received message

             TD[i] is the time keeper

6.1 **while** $TRUE$ **do**

6.2   **if** msg_j *received from node* s_j **then**

6.3 $t \leftarrow msg_j(\text{time})$;

6.4   store the time of last received message;

6.5 $t' = \text{TD}[j]$;

6.6 $\text{TD}[j] = t$;

6.7 $F_{s_i}(t)[s_j] \leftarrow F_{s_i}(t')[s_j]$ - 1;

6.8   send acknowledgement ack_j ;

6.9   **end**

6.10   **if** msg_k *is sent to node* s_k **then**

6.11 $F_{s_i}(t)[s_j] \leftarrow F_{s_i}(t')[s_j]$ + 1;

6.12   **end**

6.13   **for** *all entries in* $TD[i]$ **do**

6.14   **if** $(t - TD[i]) \geq t_{max}$ **then**

6.15   send a probe $msg_i(probe)$;

6.16 $F_{s_i}(t)[s_j] \leftarrow F_{s_i}(t')[s_j]$ + 1;

6.17   **end**

6.18   **end**

6.19 **end**

---

corresponding failure counter $F_{s_m}(t)[s_i]$ by one. Upon receiving an acknowledgement, s_m decrements the failure counter $F_{s_m}(t)[s_i]$ by one.

Identifying a failed gateway is important because a non-gateway node forwards the data to attached gateways only. If a non-gateway node is unable to communicate with its gateways, it can initiate a new gateway selection procedure (see Chapter 3). Since the gateway selection request message implicitly piggybacks gateway failure information, non-gateway nodes do not need to inform gateway failures to others. The non-gateway side failure detection is shown in Algorithm 6.

The non-gateway node or the cluster member decrements the corresponding failure counters whenever it receives a message or an acknowledgement from a gateway node. This is shown in Lines 6.2 - 6.9 in the algorithm. If a non-gateway sends any message to a gateway, it increments the corresponding failure counter (Lines 6.10-6.12). A non-gateway can probe a gateway to check the aliveness by repeatedly sending its previous message if it does not receive any requests or acknowledgements from a gateway (Lines 6.13-6.17). For a failed gateway, the failure counter will be increasing and will eventually cross the threshold.

5.4.3 Informing/Confirming Failures

After suspecting a node as failed, a gateway initiates a consensus procedure to avoid false positives. Using the failure counter, a gateway can only suspect a node but cannot declare failures for certainly because the suspected node can temporarily be unreachable from that gateway only. The gateway that suspects a node sends a message to other gateways within its communication range. All the gateways that receive this message further probe the suspected node before declaring it as failed.

In a cluster based node organisation, gateways are responsible for monitoring cluster members for any possible node failures. To share failure information, a gateway node announces a node failure after the consensus has been reached. The consensus procedure is described below.

Dolev et al. [1987] show that consensus may not be achieved in an asynchronous system where nodes can crash. However, Chandra and Toueg [1996] prove that a class of failure detectors that satisfy weak accuracy can solve the consensus problem. The condition, called weak accuracy, allows failure detectors to suspect nodes mistakenly. In the consensus, all live nodes agree to a final decision on a suspected node. A similar mechanism is proposed for sensor networks here. In a self-configuring sensor network, nodes are organised as overlapping

Algorithm 7: Solving Consensus

Notation:

msg is the data/control message

7.1 **for** *All nodes in the* $Neighbour(s_i)$ **do**

7.2   **if** $F(s_i, t)[s_j] \geq c_{max}$ **then**

7.3   Send $msg_{Suspect}(s_j)$;

7.4   Wait w_p time for the reply ;

7.5   **if** msg_{reply} *received* **then**

7.6 $F_{s_i}(t)[s_j] \leftarrow 0$;

7.7   **end**

7.8   **else**

7.9   Delete s_j from the $F_{s_i}(t)$;

7.10   Confirm failure of s_j ;

7.11   Broadcast $msg_{failed}(s_j)$;

7.12   **end**

7.13   **end**

7.14 **end**

7.15 **if** $msg_{Suspect}(s_j)$ *received from* s_k **then**

7.16   Check $F_{s_i}(t)$;

7.17   **if** $s_j \in Neighbour(s_i)$ **then**

7.18   **if** $F_{s_i}(t)[s_j] \geq c_{max}$ **then**

7.19   Do nothing ;

7.20   **end**

7.21   **else**

7.22   Send a probe message to s_j ;

7.23   wait for the reply ;

7.24   **if** *probe reply received* **then**

7.25   Send msg_{reply} to s_k

7.26   **end**

7.27   **end**

7.28   **end**

7.29 **end**

7.30 **if** $msg_{failed}(s_j)$ *received* **then**

7.31   **if** $s_j \in Neighbour(s_i)$ **then**

7.32   Delete s_j from the $F_{s_i}(t)$; 127

7.33   **end**

7.34 **end**

clusters, and a cluster member can be attached to multiple cluster heads or gateways. In such a network, instead of seeking consensus from all the deployed nodes, only gateways connected to the suspected node can participate in the consensus procedure to minimise the control and energy overhead.

The consensus problem is about agreeing on a common decision after one or more of gateways has proposed what that decision should be [Fischer, 1983]. In the AFSD method, gateway nodes propose a possible state of a suspected node, and they reach a unanimous and irrevocable decision based on their proposed state values. In other words, gateways may erroneously add nodes to their suspect list, and there is a time after which that gateway avoids false positives by consulting with other live gateways. Informing failures by solving the consensus problem is described in Algorithm 7.

If a gateway encounters an unreachable node, it announces this to its neighbour gateways, as shown in Line 7.3 in the algorithm, then it waits for a predefined time w_p to receive messages from others as shown at Line 7.4. w_p is set large enough to give gateways sufficient time to send back a reply message. Since gateways can further probe the suspected node, w_p is at least three round trip times long.

If a gateway receives a suspect message, it checks the suspected node to see whether it is alive. If the suspected node is in the neighbour list, it sends a probe message to the suspected node, and if the suspected node responds, it sends a dispute message to the consensus originator. Otherwise, it refrains from sending any reply (or can send a negative reply). This is shown in Lines 7.15 to 7.28 in the algorithm.

The failure decision depends on the responses of gateways. If the originator does not receive any messages from other gateways within the w_p time, it assumes that all the gateways agree with the suspicion and declares it by broadcasting the failure confirmation message (Lines 7.8 - 7.12). Nodes that received the confirmation message update their neighbour table as shown in Lines 7.30 to 7.33 in the algorithm. If the consensus originator receives any dispute messages, it refrains from announcing the failure and resets its failure counter.

5.5 Proof of Completeness and Accuracy of AFSD

Chandra and Toueg [1996] identify two performance criteria for failure detectors in distributed systems, which are *Completeness* and *Accuracy*. In this section, definitions of completeness and accuracy are redefined for sensor networks, and the completeness and accuracy of AFSD are proved.

128

Definition *of Completeness.* There is a time after which every failed sensor node is permanently detected by other neighbour nodes that are alive.

Definition *of Accuracy.* There is a time after which a live node is suspected by no other live nodes.

5.5.1 Achieving Completeness

The Completeness of a failure detector ensures that all the failed neighbours will be detected by that failure detector. The completeness of AFSD is shown in the following.

Theorem 5.5.1 *AFSD method satisfies the Completeness.*

Proof Let s_j be a sensor node that has failed. Suppose, there is a time t after which some live neighbours of s_j suspect s_j. We have to show that there is a time after which every live neighbour node detects s_j as failed.

The first property of AFSD (in Equation 5.4) describes that the value of a failure counter for a failed node is unbounded in another live node. The failure counter for a failed node is increasing whenever a message is sent to that node. Since s_j has failed, there is a time t' after which no node receives any messages from s_j. Those live nodes may be still sending messages or probe packets to s_j. Since live nodes are not receiving any acknowledgements or messages, corresponding failure counters for s_j in all live nodes are increasing. When the failure counter reaches the threshold c_{max}, a node, say s_i, sends a "node suspect" message to other gateway nodes to initiate the consensus procedure. Gateways that receive the message verify the suspected node either by checking its failure counter or by probing, and eventually identify the node as unreachable. Finally, s_i announces the failure by broadcasting the failure confirmation message, and all other live neighbours update their neighbour table accordingly. This implies that there is a finite time after which every live neighbour detects s_j as failed.

5.5.2 Achieving Accuracy

Accuracy is ensured, if there is a time after which no live node suspects another live node s_j. That is, there is a time after which no node will mark s_j as failed when s_j is alive. To show the accuracy of AFSD, we have to show following two things.

1. A sensor node that is alive cannot take any decision alone, instead it can only suspect a node as failed.

2. A decision is made after consensus.

Lemma 5.5.2 *A live sensor node only suspects another sensor node as failed.*

Proof Let s_j be any node. We have to show that if no node suspects s_j as failed before time t, no node can declare node s_j as failed before time t.

According to the properties of AFSD describes in Section 5.4.1, if s_j is a live node, the value of corresponding failure counters at neighbouring nodes is between 0 and c_{max} as shown in Equation 5.5. If the transmission is obstructed, some of the neighbours can fail to receive acknowledgements or messages from s_j. After a certain time t, the increasing failure counters for node s_j may cross the threshold c_{max}. According to AFSD, a live node only suspects a node, if the corresponding failure counter reaches c_{max}. The node that first identifies the failure counter for s_j reaches c_{max}, sends a suspect message to other cluster heads within that region to initiate the consensus procedure. This implies that no node declares a node as suspected before time t, and no node can declare node s_j as failed before that time.

Lemma 5.5.3 *Every node must agree before a suspected node is marked as failed.*

Proof To reach consensus, each node s_i begins from the undecided state, and it progresses to a common decision value for example, the *state* of a suspected node where $Node_{State} = \{Alive, Failed\}$. The node s_i communicates with other cluster heads and exchanges its *state* decision on a suspected node. Based on gathered information, node s_i decides the final *state* value of that suspected node.

Coulouris et al. [2005] define the requirements of a consensus algorithm, which are given below:

- *Termination :* Eventually each live gateway sets its state decision value for a suspected node.

- *Agreement :* The decision value of all live gateway nodes is the same.

- *Integrity:* If all live gateways propose the same value, any live node that has already chosen a decision value, has chosen that value.

In the proposed consensus procedure described in Section 5.4.3, there are three explicit phases. In the first phase, a gateway node checks its failure counter vector for the suspected node. If the failure counter reaches the threshold c_{max}, it sends a node suspect message to its live gateway neighbours and waits for a predefined time to get replies from gateway neighbours. During the waiting period, if the node receives any reply, this implies that the suspected node may not have failed yet, so it refrains from deleting the node from its live neighbour list. If the node does not receive such messages within the waiting time, the suspected node is deleted from the neighbour list, and a failure confirmation message is sent to all neighbours. Eventually the live node sets its decision value for the suspected node either way which satisfies the *termination* condition.

In the second phase, a gateway checks its own failure counter when it receives a node suspect message. If the counter value is already greater than or equals to c_{max}, it does not send any reply to the node suspect message which is supporting the value that it receives. Otherwise, it probes s_j and waits for the reply. If the suspected node replies within the expected time, the gateway sends a disagreeing reply to the node suspect message. To reach the decision, the logical *AND* is performed. In this method, if any one disagrees, everyone will refrain from suspecting. This implies that the decision at all live nodes is the same which satisfies the *agreement* condition.

In the third phase, after receiving a failure confirmation message and only then will the gateway delete the suspected node from its live neighbour node list. This implies that the decision is taken based on the final message from the consensus originating node, and *integrity* is ensured.

Theorem 5.5.4 *AFSD Method satisfies the Accuracy.*

Proof Lemma 5.5.2 and lemma 5.5.3 prove that the proposed failure detection method satisfies the accuracy.

5.6 Performance Modelling

Simple analytical models are developed to quantitatively compare the performance of failure detection methods. Since Keep-alive algorithms can be applied to any distributed networks, Keep Alive Sharing Negative (KASN) [Zhuang et al., 2005] method is considered for comparison. The Cluster method [Ranganathan et al., 2001] and Cluster with Backpointers (CB) [Tai et al., 2004] are two other prominent failure detection methods for asynchronous systems which are also considered and analysed together with Asynchronous Failed Sensor node Detection (AFSD) method. All these methods are analysed and a comparative study is performed. Symbols used for the performance model computation are given in Table 5.1.

Table 5.1: Symbol Table for Analysing Failure Detection Methods

Symbol	Denoting
n	Number of average neighbours
Δ	Probing rate
SN	Failed information sharing packets
τ	Average node failing time
g	Number of gateways in a cluster
U	Detection time of a failed node
k	Number of nodes sending probe packets after a node fails
δ	Time to generate a packet
c_{max}	Failure counter threshold
w_p	Waiting time for consensus

AFSD uses an existing message passing system to detect failed nodes, where sent and received messages are compared. In KASN, nodes periodically send keep-alive messages to their neighbours and update the neighbour table by receiving acknowledgements. If a failed node is found, the method shares the information with other neighbours [Zhuang et al., 2005]. By contrast, in a cluster based failure detection method only cluster heads send keep-alive messages to their neighbours and check node availability [Ranganathan et al., 2001]. To minimise the control overhead more, cluster heads can propagate failure information to other interested nodes. In CB [Tai et al., 2004], cluster heads use the keep-alive messages to identify failed nodes, and failure information is shared with other interested cluster heads. The computational complexity of each of the failure detection methods in terms of network traffic and required time are analysed in the following.

5.6.1 Calculating Control Overhead

The control overhead is important for any sensor network protocol because it affects energy efficiency. Overheads are computed for various failure detection methods with some assumptions, and the results are summarised in Table 5.2 for comparison.

Let us assume that packet sizes are the same for data, probe, acknowledgement, and

Table 5.2: *Analytical Results of Failure Detection Methods - Control Overhead*

Methods	Control Overhead
AFSD	$g(n + c_{max})$
Cluster method	$2g(\frac{\tau}{\Delta}n + 1)$
CB	$g(\frac{\tau}{\Delta}2n + 3)$
KASN	$n(\frac{\tau}{\Delta}2n + 1)$

information sharing. It is also assume that a node fails at every τ time. Since clusters are overlapped (Chapter 3), a cluster may contain multiple cluster heads or gateways. The worst case scenario is considered that there are an average g number of gateways within a cluster, and each gateway has n number of neighbours or cluster members.

Asynchronous Failed Sensor node Detection (AFSD)

AFSD starts failure detection when a gateway node suspects a cluster member. To suspect a node, a gateway needs a constant number ($c_{max} + 1$) of sent messages. If all the gateways within the cluster are communicating with the failed node, the number of messages required to suspect a node is $g(c_{max} + 1)$. The suspecting node initiates the consensus procedure with other $(g - 1)$ gateways by sending $(g - 1)$ node suspect messages. The consensus procedure can consist at most $3(g-1)$ packets because gateways can probe the suspected node and send a dispute to the consensus initiator should they receive any reply from the suspected node. If the node is found failed, the consensus originator should not receive any reply from those gateways, so the control overhead for a failed node to reach a consensus becomes $2(g - 1)$. The consensus originator then shares the negative information with its n neighbours. Each gateway also shares the information with its n neighbours. Then the maximum control overhead to detect a failed node is $g(c_{max} + 1) + 2(g - 1) + gn$. This can be approximated as $g(n + c_{max})$ where c_{max} is a constant.

The Cluster Method

In the Cluster method, cluster heads or gateways probe their neighbours and receive acknowledgements from cluster members [Ranganathan et al., 2001]. If the probing rate is Δ, g gateways will send and receive $2gn$ messages during that time. A node is failing in

133

every τ times, so the average control overhead for a failed node is $\frac{\tau}{\Delta}2gn$. Since the cluster-based failure detection method is asynchronous, a failure validation mechanism is needed. For the Cluster method, the same consensus mechanism that is proposed in this chapter is considered. The consensus method takes another $2(g-1)$ messages to confirm a failure, and the control overhead increases to $\frac{\tau}{\Delta}2gn + 2(g-1)$. The control overhead for the clustering method can be approximated as $2g(\frac{\tau}{\Delta}n + 1)$.

Cluster with Backpointers (CB)

In the CB [Tai et al., 2004] method, in addition to detect a failed node, gateway nodes also share negative information with other gateways within the cluster. If SN is the overhead for sharing the negative information, the control overhead for CB becomes $2g(\frac{\tau}{\Delta}n + 1) + SN$. For simplicity, let us assume that the method shares the negative information with only gateways within the cluster, that is, $SN = g$. Finally, the average control overhead to detect a failed node becomes $g(\frac{\tau}{\Delta}2n + 3)$.

Keep-Alive Sharing Negative (KASN)

In Keep-Alive algorithms [Zhuang et al., 2005], the control overhead consists of probes, acknowledgements and sharing failed information with neighbours. A node probes its neighbours every Δ times. During that time, the average number of keep-alive messages sent and received by each node with n neighbours is $2n$. Since there are n nodes probing each other, the control overhead for a cluster of n nodes during Δ times is $2n^2$. If τ is the average time to occur a failure, the control overhead for a failed node is $\frac{\tau}{\Delta}\left(2n^2\right)$. If a node is encountered as failed, the information is also shared with other live neighbours. The information sharing requires SN packets. For computational simplicity, let us assume that the information is shared with all cluster members, that is, $SN = n$. Then the control overhead to detect a failed node becomes $n(\frac{\tau}{\Delta}2n + 1)$.

Table 5.2 summarises the required control overheads for all methods. AFSD, like two other clustering methods, has linear control overhead in the order of number of gateways and cluster members. KASN requires control overhead in the order of the square of the number of cluster members. On the other hand, control overheads for all three existing methods depend on the probing rate. AFSD is free of such dependency because it keeps track of messages sent and received to identify a failed node.

Table 5.3: *Analytical Results of Failure Detection Methods - Detection Time*

Methods	Detection Time
AFSD	$\delta(c_{max} + 1) + w_p$
Cluster method	$\frac{\Delta}{2} + w_p$
CB	$k\frac{\Delta}{g} + w_p$
KASN	$\frac{k\Delta}{n}$

5.6.2 Calculating Detection Time

In the following, failed node detection times for various failure detection methods are analytically computed. A method should detect a failed node as soon as it fails, to minimise the effect of failed nodes such as futile communications with a failed neighbour. The analytically computed detection times are summarised in Table 5.3 for comparison.

Asynchronous Failed Sensor node Detection (AFSD)

In AFSD, nodes modify failure counters based on data packets sent and received, and a failed node is only suspected when the failure counter reaches the threshold c_{max}. How fast a failure counter reaches the threshold depends on the packet generation rate at each node. That means that the failed node detection time for AFSD depends on the packet generation rate. If the time to generate a packet at each node is δ, approximated failure detection time is the time to generate $(c_{max} + 1)$ packets and the time to reach a consensus. A gateway that suspected a node informs the other gateways and waits for a predefined time w_p. The average failed node detection time for AFSD method then becomes $\delta(c_{max} + 1) + w_p$.

The Cluster Method

In the Cluster method, cluster heads periodically probe their neighbours to monitor failed nodes. Let us assume that the probe interval is Δ. If a node fails at time t_1, and a cluster head is scheduled to probe at time t_2, the detection time U has a uniform distribution on $[0, \Delta]$. The expected value of U is $\frac{\Delta}{2}$. To reach a consensus, it takes w_p time as noted above, so that the failure detection time of the Cluster method is given as $\frac{\Delta}{2} + w_p$.

135

Cluster with Backpointers (CB)

In CB, cluster heads share information of overlapped neighbours with other cluster heads. Using order statistics, Zhuang et al. [2005] showed that if the probe interval is Δ and there are g number of gateways within a cluster, it will take on average $k\frac{\Delta}{g}$ time for the first k out of g gateways to send a probe to a failed node after it fails. This is also the time to suspect a node as failed. To reach consensus, another w_p time is required. With that, the average time to detect a failed node is approximated as $k\frac{\Delta}{g} + w_p$.

Keep-Alive Sharing Negative (KASN)

In KASN, if a node fails at t_1 time, and t_2 is the time when a neighbour detects it, the detection time U will be $t_2 - t_1$. If Δ is the probe interval, the detection time has a uniform distribution on $[0, \Delta]$ with an expected value of $\Delta/2$. Since the information is shared, the expected value of U is $k\Delta/n$ for the first k neighbours to send a probe to the failed node which is also the failure detection time of KASN [Zhuang et al., 2005].

Table 5.3 summarises the detection times for all the failure detection methods. While the detection time for AFSD depends on the packet generation rate, for the other methods it depends on the probing rate. For CB and KASN it also depends on the backpointer list, where the failure information is propagated.

5.7 Experimental Analysis

In this section, simulation and experimental results are presented evaluating the benefits and cost of the proposed AFSD method for sensor networks. Existing methods to detect failed nodes such as Keep-Alive Sharing Negative (KASN) [Zhuang et al., 2005], the Cluster method [Ranganathan et al., 2001] and Cluster with Backpointers (CB) [Tai et al., 2004] were also implemented to compare against AFSD.

5.7.1 Simulation Environment

For implementing failure detection methods, a simulation testbed is created where a base station was considered at a corner of the testbed collecting data. The base station was a node with unlimited resources. The network was formed with 500 sensor nodes randomly distributed. Nodes within the transmission range are considered neighbours of each other and the transmission range was set to 4 units. Nodes were organised using the Energy Balanced

Clustering (EBC) mechanism described in Chapter 3 where they were broadly classified as gateways and non-gateways. Clusters were formed around gateway nodes and neighbours of such a node were cluster members (gateways and non-gateways). To maintain network connectivity, each cluster contained at least two but no more than three gateways.

Different failure detection protocols were implemented on different nodes (for example, gateway and non-gateway nodes). AFSD has different detection protocols for gateway and non-gateway nodes so that the failure detection module activated appropriate protocols according to the node state. The Cluster method and CB were only implemented on gateway nodes as gateway nodes were regarded as cluster heads. Since KASN nodes detect failures by probing each other, KASN was implemented on every deployed node.

The simulation was performed with some fixed parameters such as the node failure rate τ was set to 100 simulation times (simtimes). Existing methods depend on probing rate Δ to detect a failed node. Δ was set to 50 simtimes to maintain the failure to probing rate ratio of two as mentioned in [Zhuang et al., 2005]. An AFSD node only needs to probe a neighbour after not receiving any message from that neighbour for a period t_{max}. The value of t_{max} was set 50 simtimes similar to node probing rate Δ times. An AFSD node becomes suspected when its failure counter reaches the threshold c_{max} at another live node. c_{max} was set to 5 considering network congestions.

5.7.2 Simulation Methodology

Three different cases with various network conditions were considered. To vary the network condition, three parameters were varied:

- Number of neighbours per node.

- Number of failed nodes.

- Data packet generation rate.

The number of neighbours per node has an effect on control overhead because most of the existing methods are based on periodic probing of neighbours. For a dense network, the control overhead for existing schemes should be higher than for a sparse network because of the higher number of neighbours. A dense network, in contrast, can identify failed nodes earlier than a sparse network because the number of interacting neighbours of a failed node is higher. The overhead for all methods should be decreasing with the increasing number of

137

failed nodes as failed nodes decrease the number of active neighbours. Since AFSD detects a failed node by comparing the sent and received messages, the data packet generation rate effects the detection time.

For each experiment, three performance metrics are considered - average *control overhead*, *energy overhead* and *detection time* per failed node. Results were observed when 70% of deployed nodes have failed similar to some of the existing work (such as [Zhuang et al., 2005; Parikh et al., 2006]). The network was assumed effective up to this point. Experimental conditions for observing those performance metrics are described below.

- In the first experiment, the data packet generation rate was set to 1 packet/simtime, and the size of the neighbour set was varied by varying the area of the sensor field from 100×100 to 50×50 square units. Performances of various methods were observed for 2 to 10 neighbours per node when 70% of deployed nodes became failed.

- In the second experiment, the average number of neighbours per node was set to five, and performance metrics were observed for 10% to 70% of deployed nodes as failed.

- In the last experiment, the network state was fixed, similar to the second experiment, and only the packet generation rate was varied. Results were observed for packet generation rates from 1 packet/simtime to 10 packets/simtime when 70% of deployed nodes have failed.

Case 1: Effects of Node Density

The node density or the average number of neighbours per node has an effect on failed node detection performance. Sensor nodes communicate with each other, so a relatively dense sensor network should able to identify a failed node faster than a sparse network. However, the control or energy overhead for a dense network will be higher as the number of monitored nodes per detector is higher. Various failure detection schemes were implemented to observe performance, and the number of neighbours per node was varied from 2 to 10. Results are described in the following.

Figure 5.2 shows the control overhead per detected failed node within a cluster. The figure shows that AFSD only needs around 10 control packets to detect a failed node at low node density. When a non-gateway node fails, gateway nodes keep communicating with that node until the failure counter reaches C_{max}. At low node density, the number of gateway nodes within a cluster is small, so the control overhead is also less. The overhead increases

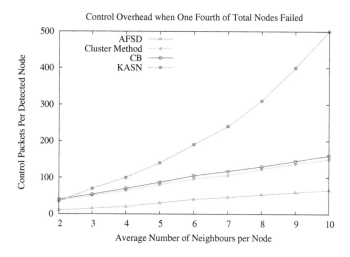

Figure 5.2: Control Overhead to Detect a Failed Node when the Number of Neighbours Varied.

to 60 control packets at high node density because more gateway nodes are communicating with the failed node (while also incrementing their failure counters). AFSD only counts messages up to c_{max} which keeps the change in overhead linear. Control overheads for the Cluster method and CB are also linear, however they need three times more control packets than AFSD to detect a failed node. The periodical probing mechanism also increases their overhead more than AFSD. The figure also shows that the control overhead is polynomial for KASN, because each node probes all others within the cluster. KASN requires about 20 control packets when the number of neighbours per node is 1, and it increases to 500 control packets when the number of neighbours per node increases to 10. This is about three times greater than the Cluster and CB need.

The energy overhead shown in Figure 5.3 shows a similar trend to that in Figure 5.2. The energy overhead is the energy consumption incurred by control packets that detect failed nodes. It is directly proportional to the control packet overhead. The figure clearly shows that for all network densities, AFSD outperforms both clustering methods by consuming only about $\frac{1}{3}$ of the energy those methods consume. This is a direct consequence of using fewer control packets to detect a failed node. In Cluster and CB methods, cluster heads

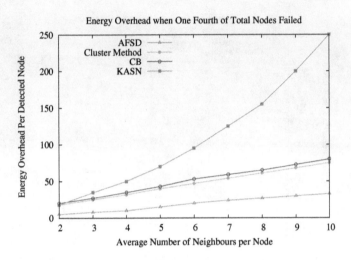

Figure 5.3: Energy Overhead to Detect a Failed Node when the Number of Neighbours Varied.

periodically broadcast probe messages to their neighbours thus consuming more energy than AFSD. KASN performs badly here by consuming on average ten times more energy than AFSD. KASN's energy inefficiency due to its periodical probing mechanism.

The detection time of AFSD depends on the packet generation rate, and in this experiment, the rate is only 1 packet/simtime. This can be considered the worst case scenario for AFSD. Figure 5.4 shows that the required time to detect a failed node for AFSD is about three times more than the time required for the Cluster method. A cluster head in a cluster method periodically probes its neighbours. If a failure is detected, a consensus procedure is initiated to confirm the failure. This implies that detection time for the Cluster method is constant. The figure also shows that the failed node detection time for the Cluster method is fairly stable from low to high node densities at about 20 simtimes. KASN closely follows the Cluster method and requires on average 2% more simtimes to detect a failed node than the Cluster method does. CB takes 5% more simtimes than the Cluster method because a CB node, like a KASN node, has to propagate the failure information to other interested nodes.

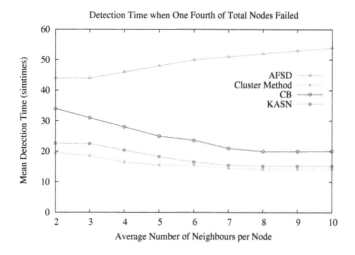

Figure 5.4: *Average Detection Time of a Failed Node when the Number of Neighbours Varied.*

Case 2: Effects of Percentage of Failed Nodes

In this case, the performance metrics for various failure detection methods are observed when 10% to 70% of deployed nodes are failed. The network was fixed with each node having on average five neighbours.

Figure 5.5 shows the effect of percentage of failed nodes on control overheads for various methods. As nodes are failing, the number of neighbours per node is also decreasing. In the previous case, it was noticed that the control overhead is low for all methods when the network is sparse. Something similar can also be observed in Figure 5.5, the increasing number of failed nodes reduces the control overhead for all methods. AFSD takes about 30 control packets to identify a failed node until about 10% of deployed nodes fail, and it gradually reduces to 15 control packets when the number of failed nodes reaches 70%. For the same percentage of failed nodes, the control overhead for both of the clustering methods is decreased from about 80 packets to 40 packets. CB performs about 5% better than the Cluster method because it shares the failure information with other cluster heads. KASN is more sensitive to the percentage of failed nodes than other methods. It relies on periodical broadcasting, so reducing the number of neighbours also reduces broadcast traffic. It takes

141

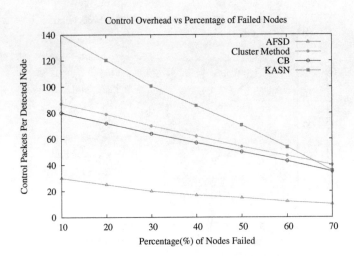

Figure 5.5: Control Overhead to Detect a Failed Node for Various Percentage of Failed Nodes.

140 control packets to detect a failed node when 10% of deployed nodes fail, and takes 60 packets when the number of failed nodes reaches 70%.

When energy efficiency was considered, Figure 5.6 shows that AFSD outperforms others by consuming the least energy to detect a failed node. It takes 18 energy units when 10% of deployed nodes fail, and the energy requirement reduces to 10 units when 70% of deployed nodes fail. Both of the clustering methods vary from 40 energy units to 20 units for the same percentage of failed nodes range. Because of the individual node probing, KASN proves the most energy inefficient method by consuming 70 energy units when 10% of deployed nodes failed. However, the energy consumption reduces to 20 energy units when 70% of deployed nodes failed.

Figure 5.7 shows the required time to detect a failed node after the failure occurred. The figure demonstrates that the Cluster method is the most time efficient. It requires about 5 simtimes to detect a failed node when the number of failed nodes is small, and the detection time gradually increases to about 25 simtimes as the number of failed nodes increases from 10% to 70% of deployed nodes. In the Cluster method, only cluster heads are periodically monitoring their members and, unlike other methods, a failure detector does not share the

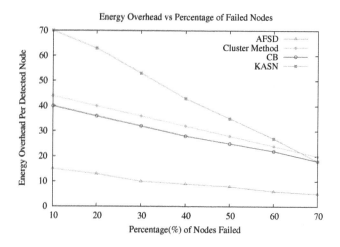

Figure 5.6: Energy Overhead to Detect a Failed Node for Various Percentages of Failed Nodes.

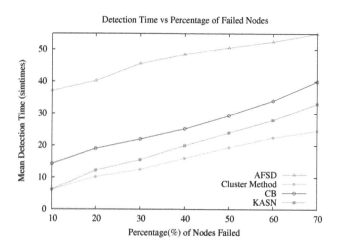

Figure 5.7: Average Detection Time for a Failed Node for Various Percentages of Failed Nodes.

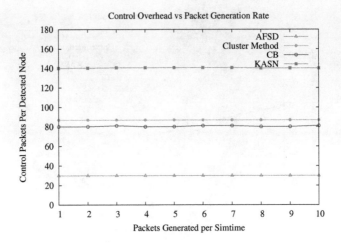

Figure 5.8: Control Overhead to Detect a Failed Node when the Packet Generation Rate Varied.

failure information with other nodes. KASN takes about 15 simtimes more than the Cluster method when 70% of deployed nodes failed. KASN shares the failure information with other live nodes, so it takes more time than the Cluster method. CB requires 35 simtimes to detect a failed node when 70% of deployed nodes become failed, which is more than KASN due to the propagation time to create backpointers and inform those nodes. AFSD does not perform well in this respect when compared to existing methods, the figure shows that the detection time varies from 38 to 65 simtimes. AFSD depends on the packet sent and received between nodes so packet loss increases with increasing number of failed nodes.

Case 3: Effects of Packet Generation Rate

To examine the effect of packet generation rate all parameters, except the packet generation rate, were fixed (as described in case 2). The packet generation rate was varied from 1 packet/simtime to 10 packets/simtime.

Figure 5.8 shows that the control overheads for all methods are constant and do not depend on the packet generation rate. Methods either probe or count messages to detect a failed node. Results show that AFSD takes only 18 control packets to identify a failed node

144

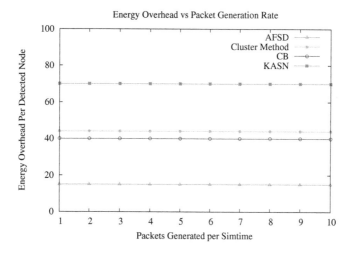

Figure 5.9: Energy Overhead to Detect a Failed Node when the Packet Generation Rate Varied.

and outperforms other methods. The Cluster method and CB take almost double amount of control packets than AFSD to detect a failed node, and KASN takes almost five times more than AFSD. Because of their periodic probing, those methods take more control packets than AFSD.

The energy overheads for various failed node detection methods shown in Figure 5.9, are also constant and follow the same trend as control packet overheads shown in Figure 5.8. AFSD is the most energy efficient solution for all data packet rates. The method outperforms clustering methods by 10% and the KASN approach by about 40%.

Figure 5.10 shows the failed node detection time when the packet generation rate is varied. In the figure, AFSD shows strong sensitivity to the failure detection time with the varied data generation rates. It takes 50 simtimes to detect a failed node when the data packet generation rate is 1 packet/simtime. This is also the worst case scenario for AFSD, and it is the longest detection time among the compared failure detection methods. For AFSD, a gradual decrease in detection time is noticed when packet generation rate is increased. The detection time decreases about 70% and eventually reaches a minimum time of 18 simtimes. On the other

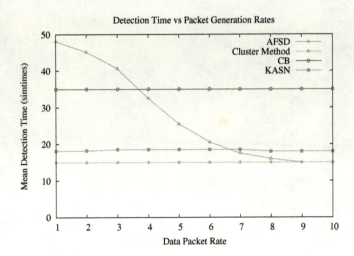

Figure 5.10: Average Failure Detection Time when the Packet Generation Rate Varied.

hand, existing failure detection methods are insensitive to data packet generation rate. The figure also shows that the failure detection time for methods other than AFSD is constant. The Cluster method takes the shortest time to detect a failed node, followed by KASN. CB takes almost twice longer to detect a failed node than the Cluster method which is caused by creating backpointers and propagating failure information to those backpointers. Interestingly, the minimum detection time of AFSD converges with the Cluster method for this simulation testbed.

5.8   Discussion

The focus in this chapter, is the detection of failed sensor nodes that should be replaced in order to maintain network effectiveness. The difficulty here is attributed to limited node resources, especially energy constraints. Furthermore, lack of a global clocking mechanism makes it hard to synchronise failure detectors. Energy-aware, asynchronous failure detection techniques can overcome these difficulties. Through the design of the proposed AFSD scheme, it has been demonstrated that the overhead of monitoring sensor nodes can be reduced by utilising the data packets exchanged between nodes. A consensus mechanism is used to synchronise failure detectors, instead of energy intensive distributed clocking. Another advantage of the method is that failure detection time is minimum when data packet generation rate is sufficiently high. A theoretical study proved that AFSD is *complete* by detecting all the failed nodes, and *accurate* by avoiding any false positives.

It was found from the analytical study that for existing Keep-Alive algorithm based methods, the control packet overhead for detecting a failed node is heavily dependent on the node probing rate Δ. It is proportional to $\frac{\tau}{\Delta}$, where τ is the node failure rate. To reduce this overhead, Δ can be increased, but this will increase failure detection time. Zhuang et al. [2005] show that the probing rate should be related to the node failure rate. For example, they find their best results when the ratio of those two rates was two. One possible solution to avoid such dependency is relying on data packets exchanged between nodes, instead of periodic probing. In AFSD, a failure detector only suspects a node when the detector fails to receive a certain number of data packets from that node.

The analytically determined detection time of a failed node showed that it depends on the node probing rate Δ for existing methods. The smaller the probing rate, the sooner these methods can detect a failed node. Small probing rate, however, will increase the control and energy overheads. In contrast, when data packets are used as in AFSD, the detection time depends on the packet generation rate and the required time to detect a failed node is inversely proportional to the data packet generation rate.

Simulation has shown that for AFSD and other existing failure detection schemes, except KASN, the control and energy overheads are linearly proportional to the number of nodes that a failure detector is monitoring. KASN showed a quadratic increase because each node was probing each other node in this technique. The simulation has also revealed that the failure detection times for existing approaches mostly depend on the probing rate. On the other hand, AFSD was sensitive to the node packet generation rate.

Simulation results were consistent with the analytical studies, and it showed that the performance of existing techniques depended on node density while it has little effect on AFSD. Energy efficiency for existing techniques was significantly affected by the number of neighbours per node but AFSD showed minimum change in energy overhead when node density was varied. The results have also shown that with high packet generation rate AFSD can detect failed nodes very fast, but with lower packet generation rates it is slower than other methods. Although packet generation rate may not be very high in sensor networks, arguably energy saving is more important for sensor networks than failure detection time.

147

5.9 Conclusion

In this chapter, a failure detection method is described, called Asynchronous Failed Sensor node Detection (AFSD) for sensor networks. Unlike existing methods, where periodical probing is used, AFSD utilises exchanged data packets between nodes to monitor neighbours. Each AFSD node maintains integer counters, called failure counters, to monitor every sent and received message between neighbours. The protocol proposed is different for gateway and for non-gateway nodes. In AFSD nodes maintain counters in such a way that, for a live neighbour, the counter value is between zero and a predefined threshold value while for a failed neighbour, it is unbounded. When a failure counter at a gateway reaches a predefined threshold for a node that node is suspected to have failed. After suspecting a node, a gateway initiates a consensus procedure between gateway nodes to validate the suspicion.

Analysis demonstrated that AFSD can accurately identify all the failed nodes with low control and energy overhead and within a reasonable time. A theoretical proof demonstrated its completeness and accuracy and the analytical study showed that control overhead, energy consumption and detection time for AFSD are linearly proportional to the average number of nodes and gateways within a cluster. An extensive simulation was also performed and AFSD was consistent with the analytical result. Simulation results were consistent with the analytical ones and demonstrated that AFSD is at least three times more energy efficient than other examined methods, such as Keep-Alive Sharing Negative (KASN) [Zhuang et al., 2005], Cluster [Ranganathan et al., 2001] and Cluster with Backpointers (CB) [Tai et al., 2004]. Interestingly, AFSD detected failed nodes as quickly as other methods do when the packet generation rate was high.

In this chapter, the focus was on identifying failed nodes energy efficiently. The next chapter will present policies for replacing failed nodes with redundant ones to extend the network lifetime.

Chapter 6

Failed Node Replacement Policies

6.1 Introduction

Due to limited energy capacity and hostile deployment environments, a sensor node can often fail. As a result, the network may become ineffective because of the coverage and connectivity holes created by failed nodes. Even though nodes are unattended in the field, applications for sensor networks require an extended network lifetime. For example, a wild-life monitoring network should be operationally effective in a hostile forest for a relatively longer period of time [Mainwaring et al., 2002]. To maintain the network effectiveness, this chapter proposes policies to replace failed nodes by utilising redundant node deployments for self-configuring sensor networks.

In a sensor network, a subset of nodes that can provide complete network coverage and connectivity is kept active to optimise the deployed node set. In such a network, a failed node may create coverage and connectivity holes also called holes or network holes. The replacement of a failed node can extend network operational lifetime by repairing network holes. Zhang et al. [2006] show that complete coverage can ensure complete connectivity under some constraints. Therefore, a coverage hole includes both coverage and possible connectivity holes. This simplifies the failed node replacement problem as identifying and repairing coverage holes.

In order to replace a failed node, the coverage holes created by that failed node should be identified. Existing work on coverage hole detection relies on the coverage degree of sensing points inside a node's sensing region [Huang and Tseng, 2005]. In a different approach, each node's sensing region is represented as a Voronoi polygon. The distance between a point and a sensor node in a Voronoi polygon is used to identify a hole boundary node [Wang et al., 2006]. Any of these techniques can be used to assist failed node replacement policies to identify holes created by a failed node.

In this research, repairing coverage holes created by failed nodes is considered as failed node replacements. Repairing holes is a relatively new area of research in sensor networks. Most existing hole repairing techniques either use mobile sensors [Wang et al., 2006] or node redeployment [Howard et al., 2002; Bulusu et al., 2004]. However, sensors are usually distributed in a hostile environment where using mobile robots or additional node deployment may not be feasible.

In contrast, to replace a failed node, redundant node deployment of a sensor network is exploited. To meet coverage and connectivity requirements, redundant deployment of nodes is common where nodes are randomly distributed. Redundant nodes are identified and deactivated from the network to minimise the energy wastage (see Chapter 4). This chapter gives policies to use such inactive nodes as replacements for failed nodes.

Three failed node replacement policies are proposed, these are - Directed Furthest Node First (DFNF), Weighted Directed Furthest Node First (WDFNF) and Best Fit Node (BFN) policies. The aim of these policies is to repair a hole created by a failed node using redundant but deactivated nodes. To identify the proper replacement location, existing perimeter based hole checking techniques such as [Huang and Tseng, 2005; Zhang and Hou, 2005] are extended. Using a perimeter based hole checking method, holes are bounded, in other words, hole regions with boundary nodes and their boundary edges are identified. Once a hole is bounded, the policies select redundant nodes to cover that hole. Under the DFNF policy, a live node that has detected a failed node replaces it by activating its furthest inactive neighbours. Since a hole is created outside a live node's coverage region, an inactive neighbour with the longest distance from the live node's centre to the hole direction has the higher probability of covering the hole. WDFNF is an extension of DFNF where the replacement of a failed node is selected by considering both distance and direction of a redundant neighbour. Each of the inactive neighbours is given a weight value with respect to a hole direction and distance. Based on the weight values, an inactive neighbour is reactivated to cover the hole. In BFN policy, all hole boundary nodes are involved in the replacement decision process. Hole boundary nodes send their boundary edge information to the node that has first detected the failed node. Boundary edges are used to create a polygon approximating the coverage hole. The "minimum covering circle" of that polygon is the smallest circle that can entirely cover the hole. BFN activates a previously deactivated node that is close to the centre of the minimum covering circle to replace a failed node.

Analytically calculated energy and time overheads for each policy demonstrate that for the best case scenario, the energy overheads of DFNF and WDFNF are $O(N)$ where N is the number of active neighbours per node. This is because only a live node that has detected the failed node first involves in the replacement procedure. Since all the hole boundary nodes participate in the replacement process, BFN has an overhead of $O(N^2)$. For the worst case, the energy overhead for DFNF and WDFNF are $O(N^2)$ because all the live boundary nodes are trying to replace the hole. For BFN, the energy overhead is in the cubic order of the number of active neighbours per node due to the fact that all the live boundary nodes communicate with each other to replace a hole. Since a hole boundary node performs a fixed set of instructions to replace a failed node, the time complexity for DFNF and WDFNF are constant for the best case. For BFN, time complexity is linear in the order of the number of active neighbours per node. For the worst case, the time complexity for all policies are the same - in the order of the number of active neighbours per node.

An extensive simulation was performed to compare performances of various failed node replacement policies. The simulation result shows that when the performances were measured using network lifetime, Quality of Coverage (QoC) and redundant node usage, BFN outperformed DFNF and WDFNF at low network density. BFN activated redundant nodes that were close to the centre of the minimum covering circles of coverage holes, so the probability of completely repairing the hole was higher than other policies. WDFNF had longer network lifetime and better redundant node usage than DFNF. This is because, to replace a failed node, WDFNF considered distance and direction of a deactivated node while DFNF considered only distances of a deactivated node in a particular direction. WDFNF required more time per failed node replacement than DFNF due to additional weight computations. Interestingly, when the network was sufficiently dense, DFNF and WDFNF maintained the same network lifetime as BFN with less energy and time overhead, because the higher number of inactive neighbours per live node helped to identify the best replacement node efficiently.

The rest of this chapter is organised as follows. Existing coverage identification and their recovery schemes are described in section 6.2. Section 6.3 introduces the preliminaries of the proposed policies. The failed node replacement policies are described in Section 6.4. A detailed analytical comparison of those policies is also presented in section 6.4.4. This is followed by the simulation results and performance evaluation in section 6.5. Finally, comparative results are discussed and conclusion is drawn in Sections 6.6 and 6.7, respectively.

6.2 Background and Related Work

This section discusses important research solutions for coverage and connectivity hole discovery and their recovery techniques. Since a failed node affects the network by creating a hole, the failed node replacement is considered as repairing the hole. Nodes are usually randomly distributed in a sensor network, so nodes may not cover the entire sensor field. Holes due to random node deployment can be avoided by redeployment of sensors however, in this research, node redeployment is not considered. It is assumed that nodes are deployed all at one time, and only holes created due to arbitrary node failures are addressed. In the following, various existing hole detection mechanisms are discussed, and then their recovery techniques are analysed.

6.2.1 Hole Detection

Whenever a node fails there is a possibility of having a coverage and/or connectivity hole. A network hole should be detected to repair. Since the coverage range of a sensor is assumed half of the transmission range coverage hole also includes possible connectivity holes [Zhang et al., 2006]. For this reason, only coverage holes are used to represent the effect of a failed node. In the literature, two different approaches to identifying coverage holes from sensor networks are found. One is the perimeter checking approach, and another is the computational geometric approach. Both of the approaches are discussed below.

Perimeter Checking Approach

In a perimeter checking coverage hole detection approach, all live sensors monitor their sensing regions to predict any possible coverage holes. The localised boundary node detection algorithm [Huang and Tseng, 2003; 2005] is a well known technique for such approaches. This technique collects node local information to detect a coverage hole. It determines a hole boundary node s_i, if there exists a point v inside the sensing region of s_i which is not covered by a predefined number of neighbours of s_i. To identify a hole boundary node, the method uses only the neighbour information so this method is distributed and scalable. Huang and Tseng [2005] identifies that the complexity of the algorithm as $O(N \log N)$ where N is the number of neighbours.

For a k-covered sensor network, where each of the sensing points is covered by at least k sensors, a subset of sensing points on a node perimeter is used for checking the hole boundary node. This reduces the computational overhead of the localised boundary node detection algorithms [Huang and Tseng, 2003]. An example of such techniques is Optimal Geographical Density Control (OGDC) [Zhang and Hou, 2004; 2005] where a subset of sensing points is selected from the intersection of two nodes' sensing regions. OGDC identifies hole boundary nodes by checking only those sensing points. In this method, a node s_i is adjudged as a boundary node if, and only if, at least one sensing point v belongs to the sensing region of s_i and s_j is not covered by k-1 neighbours of s_i. Like the localised boundary node detection algorithm [Huang and Tseng, 2003], the complexity of OGDC is also in the order of N, the number of active neighbours per node.

Computational Geometric Approach

Computational geometry is another approach to find the coverage holes. In this approach, based on closeness of neighbouring sensors, the sensor field is divided into polygons such as Voronoi diagram [Wang et al., 2004] and Delaunay triangulation [Fang et al., 2006]. Some of the well known computational geometric approaches to identify coverage holes are discussed below.

To identify coverage holes, Carbunar et al. [2006] divides the sensor field into polygons, called Voronoi polygons (VPs), based on deployed node set V. VPs are denoted by $Vor(s_i)$ for $s_i \in V$, such that all the points in $Vor(s_i)$ are closer to s_i than any other node in V. This method identifies coverage holes based on the closeness property of Voronoi polygons. According to that property, if some area of a VP is not covered by the node inside the VP, that area is not covered by any other nodes. This implies that there is a coverage hole. This technique is not entirely distributed because Voronoi polygons of nodes reside at the boundary of a sensor field may not be created locally [Zhang et al., 2006].

In a different approach, Zhang et al. [2006] propose a Localised Voronoi Polygon (LVP) method where each node keeps track of its neighbours by storing direction and distance information. LVP divides each Voronoi polygon into four quadrants, and points inside each of those quadrants are compared to neighbours in that direction. The distance between each point and each neighbours are used to find a coverage hole. Although LVP uses neighbour local information, LVP has higher complexity than the typical localised perimeter checking approaches due to complex geometrical computations.

Delaunay triangulation is another geometric computational approach where a Delaunay triangulation is obtained from Voronoi diagrams [Preparata and Shamos., 1985]. Delaunay triangulations are called dual graph of Voronoi diagrams because they are created by connecting nodes whose corresponding Voronoi polygons are adjacent. Edges of the triangulation are the distances between two vertices or sensor nodes. Fang et al. [2006] show that if any of these edges are greater than the coverage range that corresponding node is a weakly stuck node, and all the weakly stuck nodes are hole boundary nodes. The technique is based on distances between nodes which is similar to perimeter checking approaches, however creating Voronoi diagram and Delaunay triangulation increases the computational complexity of such approaches - their complexity is higher than perimeter checking based approaches.

6.2.2   Repairing Holes

To ensure the required QoS, a hole must be recovered from a network. In literature, two types of hole repairing techniques are found - repairing with mobile sensors and repairing with static sensors. Although mobile sensors are not considered in this research, repairing a hole using mobile sensors are discussed for the sake of completeness.

In a mobile sensor hole repairing technique, sensor robots are used which are continuously monitoring the sensor field for any possible coverage holes. Once a hole is detected, mobile robots move to that place to repair the hole. Movement-Assisted Node Deployment (MAND) [Wang et al., 2004; 2006] is an example of such a technique. Three different protocols are given to calculate the target position where the mobile sensors should move to repair holes. VEC (VECtor based algorithm) is motivated by the electro-magnetic particles where mobile nodes move away from a dense area if coverage hole exists in their Voronoi polygon. VOR (VORonoi based algorithm) pulls mobile nodes to their local maximum coverage holes. Similar to VOR, Minimax fixes holes by moving mobile sensors closer to the farthest Voronoi vertex, but it does not move as far as VOR to avoid the situation that the vertex which was originally close becomes a new farthest vertex. The simulation result shows that those techniques can maintain a predefined amount of coverage percentage for a certain period of time, however even a mobile node in a sensor network is vulnerable and can be exhausted. In this research, to replace failed nodes redundant deployment of sensors is used instead of special sensors such as mobile robots.

In a different approach, Howard et al. [2002] assume that GPS or other localised information for a sensor node may not be available, so they propose to deploy each node one by one. A new node is deployed within the line of sight of another node, and each time a node is deployed it sends back deployment information to the base stations. Based on that, the position of the next deployment node is predicted. Even if there is any coverage or connectivity hole, the base station recovers that while deploying nodes. This is a centralised approach where the base station is continuously monitoring node deployment to avoid and repair network holes. In practice, nodes are assumed to be randomly deployed, and they self-organise themselves to form the network in a distributed manner.

The radio beacon based adaptive node deployment is another well known approach to repair holes. For example, in Self-Configuring Localisation Systems (SCLS) [Bulusu et al., 2004], the radio beacon density is used as a parameter to re-enforce sensor nodes. This method automates the additional node deployment system with the radio beacon density. New beacons are placed at low density regions to balance the number of beacons all over the sensor field. This centralised node deployment technique gradually deploys nodes whereas this research assumes that all the sensor nodes are deployed at one time.

6.2.3 Summary

In summary, by using node local information, perimeter checking based coverage hole detection techniques can identify a network hole with a linear computational complexity. Geometric computational approaches are also found to identify a coverage hole where the computational complexity is higher compared to perimeter checking approaches. Most of the existing hole repairing techniques are based on either mobile robots [Mei et al., 2006; Le et al., 2006] or node redeployments [Wu and Yang, 2005]. Mobile robot based approaches need a special type of node in the network with mobility, and node redeployment techniques need a centralised approach to determine the appropriate location of node replacements.

6.3 Effects of a Failed Node

In this section, coverage and connectivity holes are determined and a hole bounding technique is identified for the understanding of the suitable replacement position of a failed node. A coverage measuring formula is given to calculate the network effectiveness in terms of network coverage measuring the effect of failed nodes (see Section 6.5). To assist failed node replacement policies, the hole boundary nodes and edges are identified.

6.3.1 Coverage and Connectivity Holes

Coverage and connectivity holes are defined because failure of an active node creates network coverage and/or connectivity holes. Sensor networks dynamically re-configure their topology by keeping a minimum number of node set active at a time providing complete network

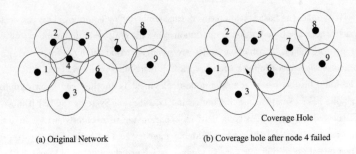

(a) Original Network   (b) Coverage hole after node 4 failed

Figure 6.1: Coverage Hole.

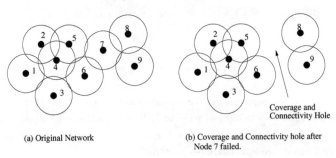

(a) Original Network

(b) Coverage and Connectivity hole after Node 7 failed.

Figure 6.2: Coverage and Connectivity Hole.

coverage and connectivity. In such a network, a failed node can leave some of the area uncovered and, as a result, coverage and connectivity holes may be created.

Coverage is the ability to sense a region, and complete coverage is the ability to sense throughout the sensor field. Huang and Tseng [2003] defines the coverage hole as an area in the sensor field that cannot be sensed. Coverage holes are often related to the degree of coverage as well. Let us assume that k is the required coverage degree. For a set of sensors and a sensor field, there is a coverage hole if an area is not covered by at least k sensors [Huang and Tseng, 2003]. The definition of coverage hole is application dependent because different applications may have different coverage degree requirements. In this chapter, for simplicity, the coverage degree requirement is assumed to be one. Figure 6.1 shows that a coverage hole is created when node 4 fails.

The network connectivity is another important requirement for a sensor network which is the ability to forward the sensed data to base stations. Like redundant coverage requirement, many applications may also need redundant connectivity to prevent accidental network partitioning. Connectivity or routing hole is defined as a region where nodes cannot participate in the routing due to failure of nodes. Figure 6.2 shows that the failure of node 7 disconnects node 8 and 9 from others so a coverage and connectivity hole is created.

6.3.2 Determining the Hole Area in a Sensor Network

In this section, the effect of a failed node is measured as network coverage. The effectiveness of a sensor network depends on the area of a sensor field that the network can cover. When a node fails, it may or may not create a partition in the network. In the following, both cases are addressed by identifying two equations measuring the failed node effect.

If the failure of node i does not partition the network (Figure 6.1), the area of the coverage hole is found by deducting intersecting regions between the failed node and other live node's sensing regions. Let the sensing coverage of a sensor node be uniform in all directions and is circular [Cardei and Wu, 2006]. Let us also assume that there are n nodes in the sensor field and the sensing region of node i is A_i. If CH is the coverage hole, the equation calculating the hole area created by a failed node i is given below:

$$CH \quad = \quad A_i - (A_i \cap A_0 + A_i \cap A_1 + ... + A_i \cap A_n) \qquad (6.1)$$

$$= \quad A_i - \sum_{j=0}^{n} A_i \cap A_j \qquad (6.2)$$

CH cannot be measured using equation 6.2 when there is a network partition. If a failed node creates network partitions (Figure 6.2), it disconnects a subset of live nodes. Although those nodes are alive, they are considered failed because of their inability to forward sensed data. Parikh et al. [2006] present a generalised method for calculating the area of a coverage hole created by a failed node when there is a partition. The method treats all disconnected nodes as failed, hence the created hole is measured by deducting the intersection regions created by live nodes and failed nodes from the sum of all the failed node sensing regions. If failure of node i causes k nodes (A_{fk}) to disconnect from the network, equation 6.2 becomes as follows.

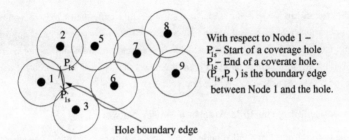

With respect to Node 1 –
P_{1s}– Start of a coverage hole
P_{1e}– End of a coverate hole.
(P_{1s},P_{1e}) is the boundary edge
between Node 1 and the hole.

Hole boundary edge

Figure 6.3: Bounding a Hole.

$$
\begin{aligned}
CH &= A_i - (A_i \cap A_0 + A_i \cap A_1 + ... + A_i \cap A_n) + \\
&\quad \sum_{l=1}^{k} A_{fl} - (A_{fl} \cap A_0 + A_{fl} \cap A_1 + ... + A_{fl} \cap A_n) \qquad (6.3) \\
&= A_i + \sum_{l=1}^{k} A_{fl} - \sum_{j=0}^{n} A_i \cap A_j - \sum_{l=1}^{k}\sum_{j=0}^{n} A_{fk} \cap A_j \qquad (6.4)
\end{aligned}
$$

6.3.3 Bounding a Hole

In this section, hole boundary nodes are identified to determine the dispersion and direction of the hole. Identifying hole boundary and direction are important because, by using that information replacement nodes can be selected to repair the hole. In this research, one of the existing perimeter based hole checking approaches is used to identify hole boundary nodes and edges because of their less computational complexity. The technique is given below.

A node is defined as a boundary node if its coverage region has a boundary with the hole region. If a node s_i is a boundary node of a coverage hole, s_i will have two intersecting points, called bounding points, with the hole. Such points are indicating the start and the end of a hole boundary with respect to a live node. Figure 6.3 shows that node 1, encountering a hole due to failure of node 4, has two bounding points P_{1s} and P_{1e}. In a special case, the start and end point can be the same where the coverage region of a live node has only one intersecting point with the coverage region of a failed node. These points are important, indicating in which direction the hole has been created with respect to a live node s_i.

The existing localised boundary node detection algorithm [Huang and Tseng, 2005] is modified to identify boundary points of a coverage hole with respect to a live node. It is assumed the sensor field is a sensing grid, and each sensor covers a subset of grid points called sensing points. Coverage degree requirement is set to the minimum so, instead of entire sensing perimeter, sensing points on the circumference of a sensing region are checked to identify hole boundary points. When a node fails, neighbours of that node check the distances of other live neighbours from their circumference points. If the minimum distance between a circumference point and all of its neighbours is greater than the sensing range, that point is in the hole boundary. The start and end of such points are stored as boundary points. For a coverage hole, there will be at most two such points for each hole boundary node.

The boundary points of each boundary node are used to approximate the hole as a polygon where the line connecting these two points, called the boundary edge, is one of the edges of that polygon. This edge is also the approximating boundary between the coverage hole and a live node. Figure 6.3 shows the boundary edge between node 1 and the hole. Once the boundary edges are identified, the polygon that approximating the hole can also be determined.

6.4 Proposed Policies to Replace a Failed Node

In this section, different failed node replacement policies for sensor networks are proposed by using redundant deployed nodes. This will help to extend network lifetime. Each node maintains neighbour tables consisting of neighbour coordinate and current neighbour state information such as active or inactive. Using that information, a node can identify the hole boundary should a coverage hole be created by a failed node (Subsection 6.3.3). The failed node replacement policies use hole boundary information to identify the replacement of a failed node. Those policies are -

- Directed Furthest (inactive) Node First (DFNF)

- Weighted Directed Furthest (inactive) Node First (WDFNF)

- Best Fit (inactive) Node (BFN)

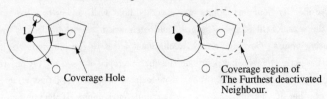

○ – Deactivated Neighbours of Node 1

Coverage Hole

Coverage region of
The Furthest deactivated
Neighbour.

Figure 6.4: Directed Furthest Node First (DFNF) Policy.

6.4.1 Directed Furthest Node First (DFNF) Policy

DFNF is the simplest policy to replace a failed node. A live hole boundary node re-activates one of its inactive neighbours based on the (deactivated) neighbour distance and the direction of a hole created by a failed node. A coverage hole always occurs outside the sensing range of a live node, so that an inactive neighbour in the same hole direction and situated outside the sensing range has a higher probability to cover the hole. A DFNF live node finds such a neighbour to replace a failed neighbour.

In DFNF policy, the node to first identify a coverage hole selects an inactive node from its neighbour list to cover the hole. It chooses the neighbour that has the longest distance from its centre but in the same direction to the coverage hole. The presence of an inactive neighbour in the same direction may not be always found. If a replacement node partially covers the hole, other neighbours will still experience holes outside their coverage range. Nodes anticipating coverage holes reactivate their redundant neighbours using the same DFNF policy until the hole disappears. Figure 6.4 shows that node 1 is a hole boundary node, and it has three inactive neighbours. In the second figure (in Figure 6.4), it is noticed that if the furthest inactive neighbour in the same hole direction is reactivated, it can cover the hole. DFNF implementation procedure is given below.

A node that first detects a failed node is called the initiator node. An initiator node follows the following steps.

- Using the boundary node detection technique (see Subsection 6.3.3), the initiator checks its circumference points for a possible coverage hole.

- If there is a coverage hole, the initiator detects the bounding edge with the coverage

160

hole by identifying bounding points as shown in Figure 6.3.

- The initiator determines the direction of the coverage hole using the hole boundary information. The sensing region of a node is circular, and the direction of a coverage hole is the centre angle created by the cord connecting the start and end points (bounding points) of that coverage hole. If the sensing range of a node is t_s, and the distance between the centre and the midpoint of a cord is d, the centre angle α is identified using the following equation:

$$\alpha = 2 \arccos\left(\frac{d}{r}\right) \tag{6.5}$$

- The direction and distance information for all the inactive neighbours are compared.

  - For simplicity, it is sufficient to find the direction of an inactive neighbour (with respect to a hole) from the mid-point of the boundary edge. If the coordinate of an inactive neighbour and the boundary edge mid-point are (x_i, y_i) and (mx, my) respectively, the direction angle β is computed using the following equation.

$$\beta = \arctan\left(\frac{x_i - mx}{y_i - my}\right) \tag{6.6}$$

- Direction angle to the hole controls the number of inactive neighbours to be considered to repair the hole. Any inactive node within a specified direction to the hole and furthest from the node centre is the replacement node (see Figure 6.4), and a reactivation signal is sent to that node.

- The reactivated node sends a neighbour announcement message to nodes within its communication range. Nodes that receive the message, update their neighbour table accordingly.

- If there is still a coverage hole, other hole boundary nodes run the entire procedure as if there is another failed node.

6.4.2 Weighted Directed Furthest Node First (WDFNF) Policy

Weighted DFNF (WDFNF) is a variant of DFNF, where the direction and distance to the hole of an inactive neighbour with respect to a live node are combined to select a failed node replacement. An inactive neighbour with longer distance from a boundary node and lesser deviated angle from the hole direction is considered the pseudo ideal replacement for a failed node.

In WDFNF, a weight is assigned to the distance and direction between a node and the inactive neighbour. The weight is assigned in such a way that an inactive node with the same direction to the hole has the highest weight value, and a node with the opposite direction has the lowest weight in a weight scale. For example, a node with the same direction to the hole has the weight value one in the zero to one scale. Similarly, an inactive node with a distance of the communication range (that is, the maximum possible distance) has the highest weight value. On the other hand, if the distance is zero, the weight is also zero in the zero to one scale. The product of these two weights indicates how close the inactive node is to cover the hole.

The implementation for WDFNF is the same as DFNF except for the best replacement node finding step. In this policy, all inactive nodes are assigned a weight value based on their distance and direction to a coverage hole. The highest weighted inactive node is the replacement for a particular failed node. The procedure is given below.

A node that has encountered a failed node (and a coverage hole) is called the WDFNF initiator. An initiator node follows the following steps.

- The initiator node calculates the direction to a coverage hole from its centre as mentioned in Subsection 6.4.1.

- It also identifies the direction of all of its inactive neighbours and compares against the direction to the coverage hole to assign a weight value (for example, between zero and one). An inactive neighbour with the same direction as the hole has the highest weight value, and if it is in the opposite direction to the hole, its weight value is the least.

- The distances of initiator and inactive neighbours are calculated and compared to the communication range to assign another weight value. The inactive node that has the longest distance has the highest weight value. If an inactive node has the zero distance, its weight value is zero in the zero to one scale.

- The product of these two weights is calculated, and the inactive neighbour that has the highest value is the replacement node.

- The initiator node sends a reactivation signal to that highest weight value node.

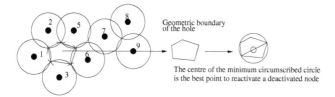

Figure 6.5: Best Fit Node (BFN) Policy.

- After reactivation, the node sends a neighbour announcement message to nodes within its communication range. Nodes that receive the message update their neighbour table accordingly.

- If there is still a coverage hole, other hole boundary nodes run the whole procedure as if there is another failed node.

6.4.3 Best Fit Node (BFN) Policy

In the Best Fit Node (BFN) policy, all the hole boundary nodes participate in the failed node replacement procedure to identify an appropriate replacement. A node may not have an inactive neighbour at an ideal place to cover the hole whereas another live nodes may have. BFN identifies the replacement node by collecting inactive neighbour information from all the boundary nodes of a hole.

In this policy, as soon as a live node identifies a hole, that node initiates a procedure to find the ideal replacement position inside the hole such that if a node is placed at that point, the hole will be covered as much as possible. The procedure has two steps - building a polygon that approximates the hole, and calculating the appropriate replacement position. To approximate the hole, a node collects the boundary edges from hole boundary nodes. These are the edges of a polygon approximating the hole. Once the geometric shape of a hole is found, the minimum bounding circle of that hole is identified. The centre of that circumscribed circle is the ideal point to reactivate a node covering the hole. This is also described in Figure 6.5.

Each boundary node has a boundary edge with a coverage hole and the node that has detected the failed node first, called initiator node, collects those edge information. To collect the boundary edge information, an initiator node broadcasts a message seeking boundary information to its neighbours. Neighbours having a boundary with the coverage hole further broadcast the message to their neighbours and so on. To optimise the broadcast overhead, it is a directed broadcast toward the coverage hole, and if a node already has broadcast a message, it does not broadcast again. All the boundary nodes reply the message with their boundary points, start and end points of the boundary edge. When all the edge information is received, the initiator node constructs the polygon. The node also calculates the minimum circumscribed circle and its centre. The ideal position to replace the failed node is the centre of the minimum circumscribed circle of that polygon.

Figure 6.5 illustrates BFN where node 1, 2, 5, 6 and 3 are the boundary nodes of a hole created due to failure of node 4. Let us assume that node 1 is the initiator node that first identified the hole. Node 1 collects all the boundary edge information and draws the polygon approximating the hole as shown in Figure 6.5. The minimum circumscribed circle is drawn for that polygon and the centre of that circle is sent to hole boundary nodes to find the inactive neighbour closest to the centre.

The BFN implementation detail is given below.

- There is an initiator node that identifies the coverage hole first.

- The initiator node broadcasts a message seeking hole boundary information to its neighbours, and a hole boundary neighbour broadcasts to its neighbours, and so on.

- Nodes, having the hole boundary, forward their boundary points to the initiator node. Considering the hole as a polygon, the line connecting those two points is an edge of that polygon.

- The initiator node draws the minimum circumscribed circle of that polygon and identifies the centre of that circle.

- The initiator node forwards another message informing the best fit point (the centre coordinate of the circumscribed circle) to the nodes having a boundary with the hole.

- Hole boundary nodes identify and forward their inactive neighbour information located close to the best fit point.

- The initiator node chooses the inactive node closest to the best fit point.

164

- The best fit node is reactivated and, after reactivation, the node sends an announcement message to nodes within its communication range. Nodes that receive the message update their neighbour table accordingly.

- If there is still a coverage hole, other boundary nodes run the whole procedure as if there is another failed node.

Special Cases for BFN

Although BFN identifies a suitable failed node replacement that can repair the hole most, it does not work for two network conditions - when the sensor field is infinite and when a network partition occurred in an infinite sensor field.

- *Sensor field boundary*: BFN does not work for an infinite sensor field because nodes at the field boundary may not determine their hole boundary edges. In this research, the sensor field is assumed to be a finite plane (a X×Y rectangle), so the field has a fixed boundary as shown in Figure 2.5, Chapter 2. Nodes at the sensor field boundary consider the intersection points between their sensing regions and field boundary edge as hole bounding points.

- *Network partition*: BFN does not work when there is a network partition because a network partition creates an infinite hole region. However, if the sensor field is finite, the hole region is also finite and bounded, and BFN works.

6.4.4 Overhead Analysis

In this section, the required energy and time to replace a failed node of above mentioned policies are identified. Protocols designed for sensor networks need to be efficient in terms of energy and time because sensor nodes are resource limited. Three different policies - Directed Furthest Node First (DFNF), Weighted Directed Furthest Node First (WDFNF) and Best Fit Node (BFN) are given for replacing failed nodes using redundant but inactive nodes. The energy and time overhead for those policies are analysed and compared.

Let us assume that the energy requirement for internal calculation of a replacement procedure is 1 unit. It is also assumed that if there are N active neighbours per node, a broadcast process requires N units of energy [Zou and Chakrabarty, 2005]. The execution time of a single instruction including broadcast is fixed, say T time units.

Directed Furthest Node First (DFNF)

In DFNF, if a node n_i identifies a failed node, it tries to replace that with its inactive neighbours. To minimise the overhead, n_i does not interact with other active neighbours when finding the replacement. Instead, n_i calculates the direction of the coverage hole created due to the failed neighbour, and computes distances between n_i and its inactive neighbours. Directions between n_i and those inactive nodes are also calculated using the available node information. If multiple inactive nodes are found within a specified direction angle to the coverage hole, the inactive node n_j having the maximum distance is reactivated as a replacement of the failed node. If there is no inactive neighbour within the specified angle, n_i refrains from replacing the failed node, assuming that another hole boundary node will replace it. When n_j is reactivated, it sends a broadcast message to its neighbours, and they update their neighbour tables accordingly.

In the best case scenario, the first node that has detected a failed node is able to replace that failed node. In this case, the energy overhead of DFNF is linear - in the order of N. Because it requires internal distance and direction computation to select a replacement node, and the replacement node broadcasts the reactivation information to its N neighbours. On the other hand, when no proper replacement is found by any of the N boundary nodes, this is the worst case scenario. The energy complexity increases to $O(N^2)$ in this case, because each of the boundary nodes activates one of their inactive neighbours to cover the hole.

For the best case scenario, if a live node executes η such instructions to replace a failed node, the time requirement is constant which is ηT. For the worst case, each of the N neighbours tries to repair the hole one by one and executes the same set of instructions, so the time requirement is ηNT which is in the order of N, that is $O(N)$.

Weighted Directed Furthest Node First (WDFNF)

WDFNF is an extension of DFNF where the direction and distance of inactive neighbours are used to replace a failed node. Each inactive neighbour is quantified by a weight value based on the distance and direction with respect to a coverage hole and an active node. The inactive node having the highest weight value replaces the failed node. The technique is similar to DFNF, so the energy requirement for WDFNF is the same as DFNF. For the best case, the energy requirement is in the order of average number of active neighbours N, that is $O(N)$. For the worst case, it is in the order of square of N, that is $O(N^2)$ where all the hole boundary nodes perform WDFNF.

Table 6.1: *Analytical Results of Failed Node Replacement Policies - The Best Case*

N is the average number of neighbours per node		
T is the time to do a unit task		
η and η' are integer constants		
	Energy Overhead	**Time Overhead**
DFNF	$O(N)$	ηT
WDFNF	$O(N)$	$\eta' T$
BFN	$O(N^2)$	$O(N)$

Although WDFNF takes more time than DFNF for additional weight calculations, the time requirement of WDFNF is still in the same order of DFNF. If the number of instructions required to replace a failed node is η', the time requirement is $\eta' T$ for the best case. In the worst case, the time requirement increases to the order of average number of active neighbours, that is $\eta' N T$ or $O(N)$.

Best Fit Node (BFN)

In contrast to DFNF or WDFNF, all hole boundary nodes are involved in the failed node replacement process in BFN. When a node n_i identifies a failed node, it asks its neighbours having a boundary with the hole to send the boundary information. A hole boundary node relays that message to their respective neighbours and so on. In response, active boundary nodes forward their boundary information to the replacement initiator n_i. The initiator node calculates the centre of the minimum circumscribed circle of the hole and notifies others. Nodes identify their respective inactive neighbour closest to that centre and forward that information to n_i again. Finally, n_i chooses the best fit node among them and forwards the information to reactivate that.

In BFN, nodes participating in the node replacement procedure require at most three directed broadcasts - for identifying boundary nodes, collecting boundary information and informing the appropriate replacement node position. If N is the average number of active neighbours per node, the maximum number of boundary nodes for a coverage hole created by a failed node is also N. The best case of BFN is when the first replacement node can cover the entire hole. Since each of those N nodes needs to broadcast a message finding

167

N is the average number of neighbours per node		
	Energy Overhead	**Time Overhead**
DFNF	$O(N^2)$	$O(N)$
WDFNF	$O(N^2)$	$O(N)$
BFN	$O(N^3)$	$O(N^2)$

other boundary nodes, the energy requirement for BFN is in the order of square of number of neighbours, that is $O(N^2)$. If all the boundary nodes need to run the procedure to cover the hole, it is the worst case. Since there are N boundary nodes trying to repair the hole one by one, the energy complexity becomes $O(N^3)$ for the worst case.

The time requirement also depends on the number of neighbours, hence it is in the order of N or $O(N)$ for the best case. In the worst case, with each of the N nodes running the same procedure, the complexity increases to $O(N^2)$.

The comparative overhead analysis for three different failed node replacement policies is given in tables 6.1 and 6.2.

6.5 Experimental Performance Analysis

An extensive simulation study has been performed evaluating the performances of the proposed failed node replacement policies which are Directed Furthest Node First (DFNF), Weighted Directed Furthest Node First (WDFNF) and Best Fit Node (BFN). The No Replacement policy has also been implemented where failed nodes are not replaced. The No Replacement policy is considered the base case for performance comparisons. For different failed node replacement policies network lifetime redundant node usage, time complexity and energy efficiency are compared.

Network lifetime is defined as the time up to which a network is operationally effective. The effectiveness of a network is redefined based on Quality of Coverage (QoC) that it can provide [Parikh et al., 2006]. QoC is measured as the percentage of sensor field covered by a network. In the experiment, each time a failed node was replaced by different policies,

QoC was computed using equations 6.2 and 6.4. Redundant node deployment is exploited for replacing failed nodes. How efficiently redundant nodes are reused by different failed node replacement policies is also shown. An important issue for protocols devised for sensor networks is time and energy efficiency. These metrics are measured by implementing failed node replacement policies in the simulation testbed.

6.5.1 Simulation Model

The simulation testbed used for experiments had following parameters to vary the network conditions. A sensor field (Q) of 50×50 square units was considered where sensor nodes were randomly deployed. S is the set of sensor nodes deployed where all the sensor nodes were homogeneous, however they had unique IDs. The number of deployed nodes $|S|$ was varied from 100 to 1000 to vary the node density. The network was considered "sparse" when $|S| = 100$, "dense" when $|S| = 500$ and "extremely dense" when $|S| = 1000$.

It was assumed that nodes were identical having the same energy, memory and processing powers. The initial node energy (E) was set to 30K energy unit. The energy requirement for internal computations to find a replacement node was 1 energy unit. For transmitting (E_{tx}) a single data packet, the energy consumption was set to 1 energy unit and for receiving (E_{tr}) the value was set to 0.5.

Zhang and Hou [2005] showed that complete coverage ensures complete connectivity when the transmission range of a sensor node is at least twice of its sensing range. For this reason, the transmission range (t_r) and the sensing range (t_s) of a sensor node were set to 8 and 4 units respectively.

The network was formed from a base station - a node with limitless resources. After deploying nodes, redundant nodes whose sensing area was already covered by their neighbours are identified. Redundant nodes were identified and deactivated to reuse them as replacements for failed nodes. Active nodes continuously sensed the sensor field and forwarded the sensed data to the base stations using the shortest path routing algorithm.

The network performed sensing and data communication until it became ineffective. The network effectiveness was measured by QoC where a minimum coverage threshold C_{th} was set. The value of C_{th} was 70% coverage. (The value of C_{th} was taken from [Parikh et al., 2006].) The simulation program was stopped when the coverage reduced below C_{th}.

In every simulation seconds (simtimes), an active node was randomly selected from the network and made it failed. Failed node replacement policies replaced that node using redundant but inactive nodes.

Node replacement policies do not need any implementation parameters, except DFNF. Nodes using DFNF find replacement nodes in the hole direction. Any inactive node within a specified angle and furthest from the node centre is the replacement node. In this simulation, a DFNF node considered inactive neighbours that were within 45° to the hole direction, assuming that on average a hole boundary edge creates central angle equivalent to 45°. BFN and WDFNF are based on neighbour distance and/or direction information between nodes so, nodes using those policies, do not need any such implementation parameters. Followings are the important parameters of our simulation model.

- Sensor field (Q) = 50 × 50 square grid.

- Sensing range of a sensor node (t_s) = 4 units.

- Transmission range of a sensor node (t_r) = 8 units.

- Initial node energy (E) = 30 K energy unit.

- Transmission cost of a single packet (E_{tx}) = 1 energy unit.

- Receiving cost of a single packet (E_{tr}) = 0.5 energy unit.

- Coverage threshold (C_{th}) : 70% of Q [Parikh et al., 2006].

- Deployed node set (S) : |S| Nodes are randomly deployed in the sensor field. |S| ranges from 100 to 1000 nodes.

- Inactive nodes per transmission range (I) : I is the average number of redundant neighbours per node. I ranges from 1 to 20.

- Active nodes per transmission range (N) : N is the average number of active neighbours per node. At $N = 5$, the sensor field is found fully covered by the active node set, so in this simulation average value of N is 5.

6.5.2 Network Lifetime

Now the effect of inactive nodes on network lifetime for various node replacement policies is shown. Network lifetime is defined as the time up to which the network can cover at least

170

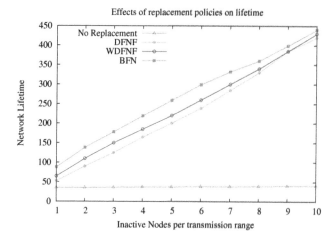

Figure 6.6: Network Lifetime for Various Node Replacement Policies when Inactive Nodes per Transmission Range Varied from 1 to 10.

70% of the sensor field. Failed nodes are replaced using redundant (and previously deactivated) nodes to extend network operational lifetime. As nodes are immovable and randomly deployed, the perfect replacement may not be found. If there is more than one redundant node to replace a failed node, it helps find a better replacement. For this reason, although the average number of active nodes per transmission range was fixed at 5, experiments were performed for various inactive node densities.

Figure 6.6 and 6.7 shows the effects of replacement policies on lifetime when the number of inactive nodes per transmission range is varied. For the No Replacement policy lifetime does not depend on the density of the network and the policy is considered the base case for comparison. In the figures, the base case lifetime is found constant at 38 time units. For BFN, network lifetime is about three times of the base case at the lowest node density. BFN shows an increase in the lifetime with the increase of inactive nodes per transmission range. Because increase of the number of inactive neighbours, increases the probability of having more appropriate replacement nodes. When the number of inactive nodes increases to 10 per transmission range, BFN improves the lifetime 12 times than the base case. When the network is extremely dense, BFN extends the lifetime about 20 times more than the

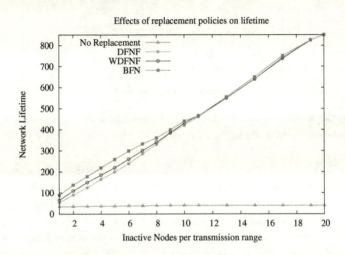

Figure 6.7: Network Lifetime for Various Node Replacement Policies when Inactive Nodes per Transmission Range Varied from 1 to 20.

base case as shown in Figure 6.7. WDFNF extends the lifetime twice the base case at low node density, and it also shows a gradual increase with the increase of inactive nodes per transmission range. When the number of inactive neighbours per node is 10, network lifetime for WDFNF is about 50 time units less than the network lifetime of BFN. When the inactive node density increases extremely (Figure 6.7), WDFNF matches with BFN. DFNF has network lifetime at least 10 time units less than WDFNF and about 60 time units less than BFN at low network density. Interestingly, when the density of inactive nodes increased, DFNF reduces the lifetime differences and is able to extend the lifetime similar to WDFNF. When the number of inactive nodes is increased, all the policies find appropriate replacement nodes using their respective node replacement policies.

6.5.3   Redundant Node Usage

Usage of redundant nodes is important to extend network lifetime because those nodes can replace failed nodes. Failed node replacement policies given in this chapter are using redundant nodes to repair network holes. To measure the redundant node usage, the percentage of redundant nodes that has been reactivated was considered. For various failed node replacement policies, the redundant node utilisation results are given below.

Figure 6.8 shows the redundant node usage graph in percentage for various node replacement policies. Understandably, the No Replacement policy has zero usage of redundant nodes. The result shows that BFN uses 100% of redundant nodes when the number of inactive nodes is low. With the increase of inactive nodes per transmission range, the usage gradually decreases to about 80%. This is because redundant nodes are static and randomly distributed in the network, therefore redundant nodes in one place cannot repair coverage holes created in other places. WDFNF and DFNF show an opposite tendency to BFN because they may not always find appropriate replacement nodes at low node density. With the increase of the number of redundant nodes, they increase the redundant node usage. For example, the redundant node usage percentage for WDFNF is about 55% when the number of inactive nodes per transmission range is only 1. When the number of inactive nodes is 10 per transmission range, the redundant node usage is about 75% for WDFNF. After that, the usage matches with BFN. The result also shows that DFNF uses only 30% of redundant nodes when the inactive node density is the minimum, that is 1 inactive node per transmission range. DFNF reactivates a redundant node if it is within the $45°$ to the hole

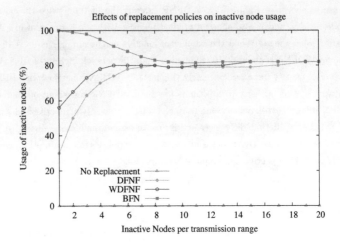

Figure 6.8: Usage of Redundant Nodes when Coverage reduces to Less than 70% of Entire Sensor Field.

direction. When the number of inactive neighbours per node is only one, DFNF may not be able to replace the coverage hole. For this reason, the coverage drops below the threshold C_{th} while still 75% of redundant nodes are unused. Interestingly, DFNF gradually improves the redundant node usage with the increase of inactive nodes and matches with WDFNF at high node density.

6.5.4 Energy/Time Overhead

Average energy and time required to replace a failed node for various replacement policies are measured. In Subsection 6.4.4, the best case and the worst case scenarios to replace a failed node are analysed. The analytical expectations are validated using simulation results.

Figure 6.9 shows the average energy consumption to replace a failed node by different replacement policies. In this simulation, the number of active nodes per transmission range was fixed at 5 so the average energy requirements to replace a failed node for BFN were steady at 21 energy units. This is because all the active boundary BFN nodes participated in the hole repairing procedure. In WDFNF and DFNF, the node that has detected the failed node tries to replace it with one of its inactive neighbour. The figure shows that compared to a

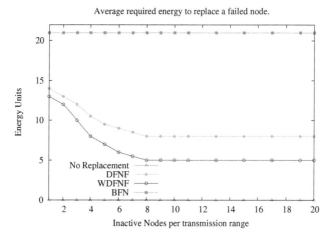

Average required energy to replace a failed node.

Figure 6.9: Required Energy to Replace a Failed Node while the Number of Inactive Nodes per Transmission Range is varied.

dense network, WDFNF and DFNF both take more energy to replace a failed node when the number of inactive nodes per transmission range is low. For WDFNF, required energy per failed node replacement is about 13 energy units at low node density, and the average energy requirements reduces and stabilises at about 5 energy units with the increase of node density. When the number of inactive neighbours increases, the probability of getting a replacement node at the first replacement initiator node also increases (the best case). DFNF shows a similar tendency as WDFNF, however it takes at least 3 energy units more than WDFNF. DFNF only relies on distances of inactive nodes which do not guarantee full coverage of a hole. For this reason, some other boundary nodes may have to reactivate their neighbours to repair the rest.

Figure 6.10 shows the time requirements to replace a failed node during the simulation. A BFN node needs to communicate with other live boundary nodes, hence it takes more time than other policies. BFN is almost constant at 16 time units because of the fixed number of active nodes per transmission range. DFNF and WDFNF show sensitivity to the increasing inactive neighbours. Initially both policies take about 12 and 15 time units respectively to replace a failed node. When the number of inactive nodes per transmission range reaches

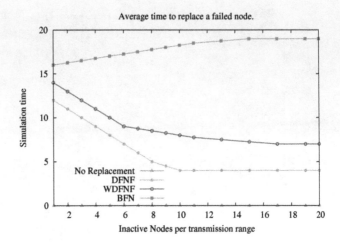

Figure 6.10: Required Time to Replace a Failed Node while the Number of Inactive Nodes per Transmission Range is varied.

5, DFNF stabilises at 5 time units and WDFNF stabilises at 8 time units which are almost $\frac{1}{3}$ and $\frac{1}{2}$ of BFN time requirements respectively. DFNF takes the least time because of its simpler computation technique than other policies.

6.5.5 Quality of Coverage (QoC)

Quality of Coverage (QoC) of a sensor network shows the effectiveness of a network [Parikh et al., 2006]. Sensors are deployed to sense the sensor field, so providing the complete coverage is extremely important. Since sensors are stochastically distributed, 100% coverage of a sensor field may not be possible. In addition, nodes may become exhausted anytime for various reasons, which can also reduce the coverage percentage of the sensor field. A coverage threshold is set to define the effectiveness of a sensor network. The threshold is set at 70% coverage of the sensor field. The network remains effective when the network coverage is $\geq 70\%$, otherwise ineffective. For various network conditions namely, sparse, medium dense, dense and extremely dense network, lifetime was measured as the time when coverage became $< 70\%$ of the sensor field. Above mentioned node replacement policies used redundant nodes to keep the network effective. The results of QoC for those failed node replacement policies

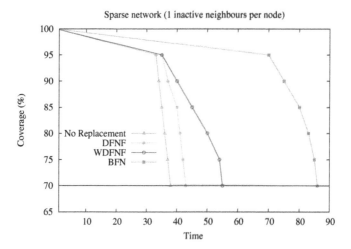

Figure 6.11: Quality of Coverage with Time when the Network is Sparse.

are given below.

Figure 6.11 shows QoC achieved by different failed node replacement policies. The results were obtained when the network was sparse that is, each active node on average had only one inactive neighbour. In this experiment, a randomly selected active node was intentionally made exhausted in every time unit. Failed node replacement policies recovered the hole due to that failed node. QoC of the No Replacement policy is calculated as the base case for others. The No Replacement policy shows that it starts with 100% coverage and when nodes start failing, the network effectiveness degrades sharply. The network using the No Replacement policy becomes ineffective at about 38 time units. DFNF can maintain the required coverage up to 43 time units. It tries to replace the failed node with inactive neighbours, however it may not always find the appropriate replacement because of the low network density and that has an effect on QoC. Although WDFNF uses a better failed node policy than DFNF, it cannot improve the lifetime significantly because of the very few inactive neighbours to replace. The result shows that WDFNF only maintains QoC 12 time units more than DFNF. BFN chooses the inactive node that has the higher probability to cover the hole most. The effect also reflects in the result where it shows that BFN can maintain QoC for the longest

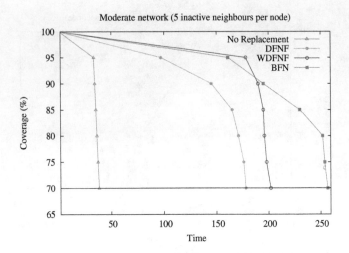

Figure 6.12: Quality of Coverage with Time when the Network is Moderately Dense.

period of time, which is about two times more than the base case and DFNF and about 30 simtimes more than WDFNF.

Figure 6.12 shows QoC of various node replacement policies at medium network density. The average number of inactive neighbours was set to 5 in this experiment. The No Replacement policy understandably had the same lifetime as it showed in Figure 6.11. DFNF and WDFNF extend network lifetime by maintaining the coverage threshold up to 180 and 200 time units respectively. With the increase of inactive neighbours, the probability of finding better replacement nodes is also increased. BFN, due to its superior replacement policy, still outperforms others and has a lifetime of about 250 time units. This is about 25% more than WDFNF and about 40% more than DFNF.

Figure 6.13 shows QoC of replacement policies when the average number of redundant neighbours for each active node is 10. Since the number of inactive nodes increases, DFNF and WDFNF have more inactive neighbours to select a failure replacement node. Both policies narrowed the lifetime gaps with BFN from sparse and medium dense network conditions. In this case, DFNF differs by 20% from BFN and by 5% from WDFNF which maintains QoC up to about 350 time units but still about 15% less than BFN.

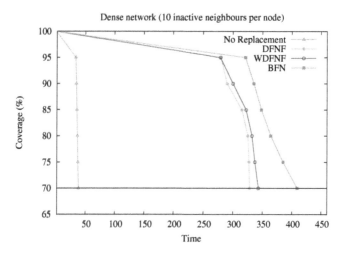

Figure 6.13: *Quality of Coverage with Time when the Network is Dense.*

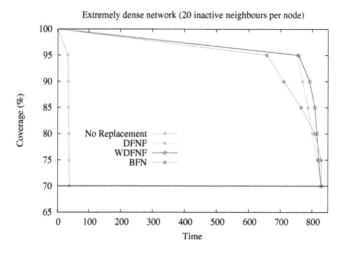

Figure 6.14: *Quality of Coverage with Time when the Network is Extremely Dense.*

When the number of inactive nodes per transmission range was set to 20 per transmission range, the quality of coverage provided by each failed node replacement policies is shown in Figure 6.14. The average number of inactive nodes per transmission range is also the average number of inactive neighbours per node. Each node has sufficient number of inactive neighbours to properly repair coverage holes created at its neighbouring region. The effect is also visible in the figure for DFNF and WDFNF. Both techniques can maintain QoC as long as BFN. The result shows that, except for the No Replacement policy, lifetimes of all policies almost converge at 830 simtimes. Nodes were static and were failing at a regular interval. Although replacement policies tried to replace failed nodes, result shows that the maximum lifetime of the simulated network was about 830 simtimes.

6.6 Discussion of the Result

In this chapter, three failed node replacement policies are given to repair holes using redundant but deactivated nodes. The aim of those policies is to extend network lifetime by maximum utilisation of limited resources including redundant node deployment. In the first policy, called Directed Furthest Node First (DFNF), distances of inactive neighbours to the hole direction is used to replace a failed node. However, this policy may not find the most appropriate replacement node, especially at low network density. In Weighted Directed Furthest Node First (WDFNF), a method using distance and direction of inactive nodes is given to find better failed node replacements where complexity is higher compared to DFNF. Finally, a policy, called Best Fit Node (BFN), is proposed where all the inactive neighbours of a failed node are considered to find the appropriate replacement with a higher energy and time overhead. Extensive simulation was performed to assess their performances using network lifetime, redundant node usage and computational overhead. The results are summarised in Tables 6.3, 6.4, 6.5 and 6.6.

Network lifetime was redefined according to the effectiveness of the network. It was assumed that a network is effective up to the time when it is still able to cover at least 70% of the sensor field [Parikh et al., 2006]. Summary Tables 6.3, 6.4, 6.5 and 6.6 show that BFN maintains the coverage threshold longer than any other techniques in all network conditions due to a more accurate failed node replacement technique than others. When all the neighbours of a failed node participate in the replacement process, appropriate replacements among the potential inactive nodes are found. In DFNF and WDFNF, the node to first identify a failed node replaces the failed node using its inactive neighbours. The node may

Table 6.3: Comparison of Failed Node Replacement Policies - When the Network is Sparse

Policies	Lifetime	Redundant Node Usage	Energy Overhead	Time Overhead
No Replacement	34	0%	NA	NA
DFNF	51	30%	14	12
WDFNF	55	55%	13	14
BFN	87	100%	21	16

Table 6.4: Comparison of Failed Node Replacement Policies - When the Network is Medium Dense

Policies	Lifetime	Redundant Node Usage	Energy Overhead	Time Overhead
No Replacement	34	0%	NA	NA
DFNF	172	70%	10	6
WDFNF	205	75%	7	11
BFN	265	90%	21	17

Table 6.5: Comparison of Failed Node Replacement Policies - When the Network is Dense

Policies	Lifetime	Redundant Node Usage	Energy Overhead	Time Overhead
No Replacement	34	0%	NA	NA
DFNF	355	75%	8	5
WDFNF	365	75%	5	9
BFN	405	80%	21	18

Table 6.6: Comparison of Failed Node Replacement Policies - When the Network is Extremely Dense

Policies	Lifetime	Redundant Node Usage	Energy Overhead	Time Overhead
No Replacement	34	0%	NA	NA
DFNF	830	82%	8	4
WDFNF	829	82%	5	7
BFN	831	82%	21	18

not find the appropriate replacement because only one hole boundary node involves in the replacement process. There is a possibility that the replacement node may be able to partially cover the hole. In this scenario, other hole boundary nodes that are still experiencing a hole, try to repair it with their inactive neighbour set. The experiment showed that, when there was sufficient number of inactive neighbours per active node, both techniques significantly improved their network lifetimes. For example, Table 6.6 shows that the network lifetimes of DFNF and WDFNF are similar to that of a BFN network when the network was extremely dense.

Failed node replacement policies reused redundant deployed nodes to replace a failed node. The simulation results showed that better utilisation of the redundant nodes resulted in a better network lifetime for BFN compared to other policies. When each of the live nodes had sufficient number of inactive neighbours, WDFNF and DFNF were able to find appropriate replacements, and that increased the redundant node usage (Tables 6.6).

Any network protocols designed for sensor networks should be energy and time efficient. The analytical study showed that, in the best case, the energy overhead for DFNF and WDFNF is linearly proportional to the average number of active neighbours per node. Both the policies perform fixed instructions to replace a failed node so the time overhead is constant in this case. In contrast, BFN tries to find a replacement node by collecting information from all the active hole boundary nodes. In the best case, appropriate replacement node is found with the energy overhead in the quadratic order of the number of active neighbours. The time complexity for BFN is linearly proportionate to the number of active neighbours. In the worst case, the energy and time overheads for BFN increases in the cubic and in the quadratic order of the number of active neighbours respectively. In this case, energy overhead for WDFNF and DFNF is proportional to the square of the number of active neighbours per node. The time complexity for those policies is linearly proportional to the number of active neighbours per node.

The simulation results conform to the analytical outcomes. Table 6.3 shows that the time and energy overhead for all three cases are close to each other when the network was sparse. At low inactive node density, DFNF and WDFNF could not find a proper replacement at the first try, so multiple hole boundary nodes reactivated their inactive neighbours to cover the same hole. This increases the time and energy overhead. The result shows that with the increase of the number of inactive neighbours, the relative time and energy overheads for those techniques decreased and stabilised at a minimum value. The differences of time and energy overheads between BFN and other two techniques were noticeable at high inactive node density.

6.7   Conclusion

This chapter addresses the problem of failed node replacement to maximise network operational lifetime. The replacement process is considered as repairing the coverage hole created by a failed node. Whenever a hole is created, hole boundary nodes and edges are identified. Using that information, the hole is repaired by reinstating already deployed but redundant nodes. Three failed node replacement policies have been proposed. Directed Furthest Node First (DFNF) is the simplest policy, as the failed node identifier replaces that by its inactive neighbours based on distances toward the hole direction. Weighted Directed Furthest Node First (WDFNF) is an extension of DFNF where the direction and distance both are used to

183

select a replacement node. In the Best Fit Node (BFN) policy, all the active neighbours of a failed node participate in the decision process to identify the appropriate replacement node.

Analytical and simulation studies showed that there is a trade-off between energy efficiency and finding the appropriate replacement node. Analytical results showed that DFNF and WDFNF have energy overhead linearly proportionate to the number of active neighbours while BFN has energy overhead in the cubic order of the number of active neighbours in the worst case. The simulation of those policies showed that BFN maintained the network quality of coverage for a longer period of time than other policies when the network was sparse. DFNF performed badly among the three policies at low inactive node density but was able to match with others when the network was extremely dense. WDFNF perhaps is the best policy to replace failed nodes in sensor networks because it had energy and time overhead close to DFNF and network lifetime same as BFN when the network was dense or extremely dense.

This research only considers sensors which are static however, sensors with mobility may also be available in near future. Policies to replace failed nodes using mobile sensors can be investigated further.

Chapter 7

Conclusion

7.1 Research Aim and Achievements

This research has investigated sensor node organisation techniques for maximising the lifetime of sensor networks. The issues related to network formation, such as energy balancing, redundant nodes, node failure and failed node replacement have been addressed. Some of these issues have been studied in the context of node energy efficiency, however a sensor network needs to consider more than the energy consumption of individual nodes in order to remain effective for a longer period of time. This is because any energy remaining in a live node after the network has failed is wasted energy. The research goal was set to form a network where limited resources, including energy, are considered when organising sensor nodes. The best utilisation of resources resulted in maximised network lifetime.

In particular, this book demonstrated the sensor networking issues and challenges in Chapter 1 and Chapter 2 and then addressed those by balancing energy while organising nodes (Chapter 3). Chapter 4 provided a method to identify redundant nodes and Chapter 5 identified failing nodes in an energy efficient manner. Finally, Chapter 6 gave policies to replace failed nodes by redundant nodes.

Research achievements that help to extend sensor network operational lifetime are summarised below.

Energy Balanced Clustering (EBC)

A node self-organisation method, called Energy Balanced Clustering (EBC), was proposed to demonstrate that a balanced network can maximise network lifetime. In EBC, tasks are redistributed among high energy nodes to relieve low energy nodes. EBC classifies nodes based on an energy level threshold - a node having energy reserves above the threshold is called an Excess Energy Node (EEN), otherwise it is a Necessary Energy Node (NEN). EBC forms connected clusters of small groups of nodes by selecting cluster heads from EENs. Neighbours attached to those EENs become cluster members. An EEN leaves the cluster head task when it becomes a NEN, and thus extends network lifetime by avoiding early exhaustion.

Network lifetime analytical models developed for various node organisation techniques demonstrated that the lower bound of an EBC node lifetime is at least 15% higher than that of existing techniques such as All-Active [Cerpa and Estrin, 2004], LEACH [Heinzelman et al., 2002] and ASCENT [Cerpa and Estrin, 2002]. Extensive simulation has also been performed and results showed that network lifetime has a strong relationship with energy balancing. Compared to existing techniques, EBC extends network lifetime by at least 10%, while EBC's standard deviation of residual energy levels is at least 20% lower for various lifetime definitions.

Self Calculated Redundancy Check (SCRC)

Redundant node deployment has an impact on network lifetime because redundant nodes consume excess energy by performing unnecessary repetitious tasks. A distributed node redundancy identification method, called Self-Calculated Redundancy Check (SCRC), was proposed to eliminate redundant tasks. A grid is laid over the field to help each node to calculate its own redundancy measure by checking the coverage degree of its sensing region. Before deactivating a potentially redundant node, a coverage and connectivity check is performed to avoid network holes. This optimises the active node set and minimises network energy consumption while providing complete network coverage and connectivity.

Analysis showed that the time, message and space complexity of SCRC is linearly proportional to the number of neighbours of a node. An extensive simulation study demonstrated that, compared to existing redundant node identification techniques, SCRC can identify 5 to 10% more redundant nodes for different node distribution schemes, namely uniformly random and Poisson distributions.

Asynchronous Failed Sensor node Detection (AFSD)

In order to maintain network effectiveness, failed sensor nodes should be detected and replaced. A failure detection method, called Asynchronous Failed Sensor node Detection (AFSD), was proposed to support sensor nodes monitoring neighbours. To lower energy overhead, AFSD does not perform periodic probing, but nodes compare the numbers of messages sent to and received from other nodes, and in case of discrepancy node failure is predicted. The prediction is verified using a consensus mechanism among detectors.

A theoretical study proved that AFSD is complete by detecting all the failed nodes and is accurate by avoiding false positives. The complexity analysis showed that the control, energy, and time overhead of AFSD are linearly proportional to the number of neighbours and gateways within a cluster. An extensive simulation showed that AFSD's performance is consistent with the analytical result, and that it is at least three times more energy efficient than compared methods. It also demonstrated that with high packet generation rate AFSD can detect failed nodes very fast.

Policies for Replacing Failed Nodes

A new concept, called policy for failed node replacement, was given and three failed node replacement policies were proposed to improve network operational lifetime by repairing network holes created by failed nodes. In the Directed Furthest Node First (DFNF) policy, an active node repairs the hole using one of its deactivated neighbours which is selected based on neighbour and hole location. Compared to DFNF, Weighted Directed Furthest Node First (WDFNF) selects better replacements by considering both the distance and direction of an inactive neighbour. Finally, Best Fit Node (BFN) policy was proposed where all the active nodes adjacent to the coverage hole participate in the replacement procedure. BFN identifies the best replacement node in terms of covering the longest part of the hole.

Analytical study of failed node replacement policies showed that the energy and control overhead of DFNF and WDFNF are constant, while it is in the quadratic order of node density for BFN in the best case. In the worst case, the overhead increases linearly in the order of node density for DFNF and WDFNF, while it increases in the cubic order for BFN. The simulation result showed that DFNF and WDFNF can maintain the same network lifetime as BFN when network condition was extremely dense.

7.2 Future Work

In this section, the future research directions in sensor networks are described. Future work that is specific to the techniques proposed in this book is also discussed.

7.2.1 Research Directions in Sensor Networks

With the emergence of Micro Electro Mechanical Systems (MEMS) technology, the number of applications available on sensor networks will continue to grow [Akyildiz et al., 2002]. However, cost constraints and the need for ubiquitous deployments results in small sized resource-constrained, especially energy limited, sensor nodes. Since these low end nodes are unattended in the sensor field, their energy reserves are generally irreplaceable. For this reason, nodes can affect network operational lifetime due to finishing their limited energy reserves. To prolong the network operational lifetime, energy efficiency must be considered in almost every aspect of network designing. Energy efficiency is needed not only at the physical layer (such as low power transceiver, sensing and processing units) and the link layer (for instance, energy efficient medium access control), but also at the network layer (for example, energy efficient routing) and higher layers (such as query optimisation). In this research, issues of node organisation have been addressed to form a lifetime maximising network but other research areas are still open to address. In terms of research directions, the following areas will require extensive research efforts in the future:

Network Protocol Stack

Unlike the Internet where TCP/IP is the standard transport protocol upon which all the Internet applications are built, a common protocol stack is yet to be defined for sensor networks on which most applications can be implemented. Although currently IEEE 802.11 is used, a new protocol architecture is needed to combine energy awareness and promote cooperative efforts of sensor nodes. It is also likely that not every application will need the entire protocol stack, hence cross-layer optimisation may be required [Marron et al., 2004; Sichitiu, 2004].

In the literature, some research efforts can be noticed on these very issues such as time shared modem architecture [Chien et al., 2001] at physical layer, S-MAC (Sensor Medium Access Control) [Ye et al., 2002] at data link layer and power aware routing [Singh et al., 1998; Chang and Tassiulas, 2004] at network layer. Still a combined effort is needed to realise a complete protocol stack for sensor networks. In summary, some of the future protocols for sensor networks can be listed as follows.

- *Physical layer*: Low power signal modulation schemes for sensor networks.

- *Data link layer*: Reliable and energy-aware medium access control and error control techniques for sensor networks.

- *Network layer*: Energy-efficient and network lifetime maximising routing protocols for sensor networks.

- *Transport layer*: Efficient transport protocols such as energy efficient broadcasting for a resource limited sensor network.

Query and Data Aggregation

Sensors are deployed for the purpose of monitoring and collecting sensory data based on specific queries. This has been put forward as an essential paradigm for query and data forwarding in sensor networks [Intanagonwiwat et al., 2000; Krishnamachari et al., 2002]. To minimise the energy consumption, the idea is to combine the data coming from different sources enroute, eliminating redundancy and minimising the number of transmissions. This paradigm shifts the focus from the traditional address-centric routing approaches such as finding shortest paths between pairs of addressable end-nodes to a more data-centric approach, for example, finding routes from multiple sources to a single destination that allows internal mechanism of eliminating redundant data. This leads to more specific research challenges of query and data optimisation to extend network lifetime.

7.2.2 Future Work Specific to this Research

This section describes future work specific to the implementation and performance analysis of the techniques proposed in this book. Due to time and length constraints, it was not possible to explore these directions in this book. Instead, they are described briefly below.

In this research, the performance analyses of all the proposed techniques are based on static sensors. On the other hand, if node mobility is allowed, network re-organisation will actually lead to higher overheads compared to the All-Active method. To deal with the mobile sensors, a movement restricted clustering method can be used where cluster heads are not allowed to move. Another issue to be addressed in future work is the heterogeneity of sensor nodes. The scenarios studied in this research assumed that all the nodes are identical from the node architectural point of view. While this assumption is true for many applications, it does not hold in environments where different sensors are used for sensing different objects. For example, a weather sensor network sensing moisture and temperature has two types of nodes with different sensing ranges.

The proposed self-configuring node organisation mechanism extends the node and network lifetime by balancing energy consumption over the network. In the implementation, it is assumed that each sensor is randomly sensing and generating data however, to conserve the node energy, a sensor may be activated only when a particular sensing phenomenon occurred. For example, when an intruder enters into a restricted area, only a subset of deployed sensors should sense and forward data. For future work, the effect of target location dependent node organisation needs to be investigated.

The models developed in this work assume that a network is effective if it can provide complete coverage and connectivity. The required degree of coverage and connectivity was set to the minimum for the sake of simplicity. A fault-tolerant and reliable service may need higher degree of redundancy. Creating a fault-tolerant and reliable node organisation technique is also our future aim.

Lastly, very little empirical data is currently available for large scale sensor networks. In fact, very few sensor network applications are implemented so far in real life, and many potential applications are yet to come. So, in order to perform realistic analysis, sensing query patterns were modelled using either the Poisson or Uniformly random distributions obtained from past research. However, as the number of sensor networks is increasing, real traces of sensing query patterns will be available. In future work, real work traces will be used for the simulations to obtain more realistic and accuracy results. Depending on resource availability, prototypes of the techniques proposed may also be developed to obtain deeper understanding of their strengths and weaknesses.

7.3 Final Remarks

This research has demonstrated that sensor node organisation can maximise the lifetime of a sensor network. It has been found that by taking into account limited resources, particularly energy, a sensor network can survive a longer period of time. Technological advancements can contribute significantly to the improvement of network lifetime, however, these advances are being made slowly. The increasing requirements of long serving networks will always place a heavy demand on energy-aware sensor networks. The node organisation techniques proposed are significant because they address the network lifetime maximisation problem, and they create a network upon which other issues such as query and data aggregation and network protocol stacks, can be addressed.

Bibliography

O. B. Akan and I. F. Akyildiz. Event-to-sink reliable transport in wireless sensor networks. *IEEE/ACM Transactions on Networking*, 13(5):1003–1016, Oct. 2005.

I. F. Akyildiz, W. Su, Y. Sankarasubramaniam, and E. Cayirci. A survey on sensor networks. In *IEEE Communications Magazine*, pages 102–114, Aug. 2002.

ALERT. Automated local evaluation in real-time (ALERT), 2007. URL http://www. alertsystems.org/.

K. Alzoubi, P. Wan, and O. Frieder. Distributed heuristics for connected dominating sets in wireless ad hoc networks. *Journal of Communications and Networks*, 4(1):1–8, 2002.

E. Arjomandi, M. Fischer, and N. Lynch. Efficiency of synchronous versus asynchronous distributed systems. *Journal of the ACM (JACM)*, 30(3):449–456, 1983.

S. J. Baek, G. D. Veciana, and X. Su. Minimizing energy consumption in large-scale sensor networks through distributed data compression and hierarchical aggregation. *IEEE Journal on Selected Areas in Communication*, 22(6):1130–1140, Aug. 2004.

S. Bandyopadhyay and E. J. Coyle. An energy efficient hierarchical clustering algorithm for wireless sensor networks. In *The 22nd International Annual Joint Conference of the IEEE Computer and Communications Societies (INFOCOM'03)*, pages 1713–1723, San Francisco, CA, USA, 2003.

E. Biagioni and K. Bridges. The application of remote sensor technology to assist the recovery of rare and endangered species. *International Journal of High Performance Computing Applications*, 16(3):112–121, 2002.

N. Bulusu, J. Heidemann, D. Estrin, and T. Tran. Self-configuring localization systems:

Design and experimental evaluation. *ACM Transactions on Embedded Computing Systems*, 3(1):24–60, Feb. 2004.

M. Burns, A. D. George, and B. A. Wallace. Simulative performance analysis of gossip failure detection for scalable distributed systems. *Journal of Cluster Computing, Springer Netherlands*, 2(3):207–217, July 1999.

Z. Butler, P. Corke, R. Peterson, and D. Rus. Virtual fences for controlling cows. In *IEEE International Conference on Robotics and Automation*, pages 4429–4436, New Orleans, USA, Apr. 2004.

Z. Butler, P. Corke, R. Peterson, and D. Rus. From robots to animals: Virtual fences for controlling cattle. *International Journal on Robotics Research*, 25(5-6):485–508, May 2006.

B. Carbunar, A. Grama, and J. Vitek. Distributed and dynamic voronoi overlay maintenance for coverage detection and distributed hash tables in ad hoc networks. In *The 10th IEEE International Conference on Parallel and Distributed Systems (ICPADS'04)*, pages 1–8, Newport Beach, USA, July 2004.

B. Carbunar, A. Grama, J. Vitek, and O. Carbunar. Redundancy and coverage detection in sensor networks. *ACM Transactions on Sensor Networks*, 2(1):94–128, Feb. 2006.

M. Cardei and J. Wu. Energy efficient coverage problems in wireless ad-hoc sensor networks. *Journal of Computer Communications, Elsevier*, 29:413–420, 2006.

A. Cerpa and D. Estrin. ASCENT: Adaptive Self-Configuring sEnsor Networks Topologies. In *The 21st International Annual Joint Conference of the IEEE Computer and Communications Societies (INFOCOM'02)*, pages 1278–1287, New York, NY, USA, June 2002.

A. Cerpa and D. Estrin. ASCENT: Adaptive Self-Configuring sEnsor Networks Topologies. *IEEE Transactions on Mobile Computing*, 3(3):272–285, July 2004.

A. Cerpa, J. Elson, D. Estrin, L. Girod, M. Hamilton, and J. Zhao. Habitat monitoring: application driver for wireless communications technology. In *ACM SIGCOMM Computer Communication Review*, pages 20–41, San Jose, Costa Rica., Apr. 2001.

K. Chakrabarty, S. Iyengar, H. Qi, and E. Cho. Grid coverage for surveillance and target location in distributed sensor networks. *IEEE Transactions on Computers*, 51(12):1448–1453, Dec. 2002.

T. Chandra and S. Toueg. Unreliable failure detectors for asynchronous systems. In *The 10th annual ACM symposium on Principles of distributed computing (PODC'91)*, pages 325–340, Montreal, Quebec, Canada, Aug. 1991.

T. Chandra and S. Toueg. Unreliable failure detectors for reliable distributed systems. *Journal of the ACM*, 43(2):225–267, Mar. 1996.

T. Chandra, V. Hadzilacos, and S. Toueg. The weakest failure detectors for solving consensus. In *The 11th annual ACM symposium on Principles of distributed computing (PODC'92)*, pages 147–158, Vancouver, British Columbia, Canada, Aug. 1992.

J. Chang and L. Tassiulas. Maximum lifetime routing in wireless sensor networks. *IEEE/ACM Transactions on Networking*, 12(4):609–619, Aug. 2004.

B. Chen, K. Jamieson, H. Balakrishnan, and R. Morris. SPAN: An energy-efficient coordination algorithm for topology maintenance in ad-hoc wireless networks. *ACM Journal of Wireless Networks*, 8(5):481–494, 2002.

H. Chen, B. Cheng, C. Cheng, and L. Tsai. Smart home sensor networks pose goal-driven solutions to wireless vacuum systems. In *International Conference on Hybrid Information Technology (ICHIT'06)*, pages 364–373, Cheju Island, Korea, Nov. 2006.

X. Cheng, B. Narahari, R. Simha, M. Cheng, and D. Liu. Strong minimum energy topology in wireless sensor networks: NP-completeness and heuristics. *IEEE Transactions on Mobile Computing*, 2(3):248–256, July 2003.

C. Chien, 1. Elgorriaga, and C. McConaghy. Low-power direct-sequence spread-spectrum modem architecture for distributed wireless sensor networks. In *International Symposium on Low Power Electronics and Design (ISLPD'01)*, pages 251–254, Huntington Beach, California, USA., Aug. 2001.

C. Chong and P. Kumar. Sensor networks: Evolution, opportunities, and challenges. *Proceedings of the IEEE*, 91(8):1247–1257, Aug. 2003.

T. Collier and C. Taylor. Self-organization in sensor networks. *Journal of Parallel and Distributed Computing (JPDC)*, 64(7):866–873, July 2004.

C. Cordeiro and D. Agrawal. *Ad Hoc & Sensor Networks - Theory and Applications*. World Scientific Publishing Co. Pte. Ltd, 2006.

P. Corke, P. Sikka, P. Valencia, C. Crossman, G. Bishop-Hurley, and D. Swain. Wireless adhoc sensor and actuator networks on the farm. In *The 5th international ACM symposium on Information processing in sensor networks (IPSN'06)*, pages 492–499, Nashville, Tennessee, USA, Apr. 2006.

G. Coulouris, J. Dollimore, and T. Kindberg. *Distributed Systems, Concepts and Design*. Addison-Wesley, fourth edition, 2005.

Crossbow. IMOTE2 data sheet, 2007a. URL http://www.xbow.com/Products/Product_pdf_files/Wireless_pdf/Imote2_Datasheet.pdf.

Crossbow. MICA2 data sheet, 2007b. URL http://www.xbow.com/Products/Product_pdf_files/Wireless_pdf/MICA2_Datasheet.pdf.

CSIRO. Sensor solution for environmental monitoring, 2007. URL http://www.csiro.au/solutions/pps7f.html.

D. Culler, D. Estrin, and M. Srivastava. Overview of sensor networks. *IEEE Computers*, 37(8):41–49, Aug. 2004.

Q. Dai and J. Wu. Computation of minimal uniform transmission range in ad hoc wireless networks. *Journal of Cluster Computing, Springer*, 8(2–3):127–133, 2005.

B. Das and V. Bharghavan. Routing in ad hoc networks using minimum connected dominating sets. In *IEEE International Conference on Communications (ICC'97)*, pages 376–380, Montreal, Qukbec, Canada, June 1997.

J. Deng, Y. S. Han, W. B. Heinzelman, and P. K. Varshney. Scheduling sleeping nodes in high density cluster-based sensor networks. *ACM/Kluwer MONET: Special Issue on Energy Constraints and Lifetime Performance in Wireless Sensor Networks*, 10(6):813–823, Apr. 2005. URL http://web.ntpu.edu.tw/~yshan/monet04.pdf.

S. Dhillon and K. Chakrabarty. Sensor placement for effective coverage and surveillance in distributed sensor networks. In *IEEE Wireless Communications and Networking Conference (WCNC'03)*, pages 1609–1614, New Orleans, Louisiana, USA, 2003.

D. Dolev, C. Dwork, and L. Stockmeyer. On the minimal synchronization needed for distributed consensus. *Journal of the ACM (JACM)*, 34(1):77–97, 1987.

195

Q. Dong. Maximizing system lifetime in wireless sensor networks. In *The 4th international ACM symposium on Information processing in sensor networks (IPSN'05)*, number Article-3, Los Angeles, California, USA, Apr. 2005.

X. Du and F. Lin. Efficient energy management protocol for target tracking sensor networks. In *The 9th IFIP/IEEE International Symposium on Integrated Network Management*, pages 45–58, Nice, France, May 2005.

E. Duarte-Melo and L. Mingyan. Analysis of energy consumption and lifetime of heterogeneous wireless sensor networks. In *IEEE Global Communications Conference (GLOBECOM'02)*, pages 21–25, Tai Pei, Taiwan, Nov. 2002.

A. Dunkels, B. Gronvall, and T. Voigt. Contiki - a lightweight and flexible operating system for tiny networked sensors. In *The 29th Annual IEEE International Conference on Local Computer Networks (LCN'04)*, pages 455–462, Tampa, Florida, USA, Nov. 2004.

T. ElBatt. On the scalability of hierarchical cooperation for dense sensor networks. In *The 3rd international ACM symposium on Information processing in sensor networks (IPSN'04)*, pages 287–293, Berkeley, California, USA, Apr. 2004.

D. Estrin, R. Govindan, J. Heidemann, and S. Kumar. Next century challenges: Scalable coordination in sensor networks. In *The 5th ACM/IEEE Mobicom Conference (MobiCom'99)*, pages 263–270, Seattle, WA, USA, Aug. 1999.

Q. Fang, J. Gao, and L. Guibas. Locating and bypassing holes in sensor networks. *Journal of Mobile Networks and Applications (MONET)*, 11(2):187–200, Apr. 2006.

C. Fetzer. Enforcing perfect failure detection. In *IEEE 21st International Conference on Distributed Computing Systems (ICDC'01)*, pages 350–357, Phoenix (Mesa), Arizona, USA, Apr. 2001.

C. Fetzer. Perfect failure detection in timed asynchronous systems. *IEEE Transactions on Computers*, 52(2):99–112, Feb. 2003.

M. J. Fischer. The consensus problem in unreliable distributed systems (a brief survey). In M. Karpinsky, editor, *Foundations of Computation Theory, Spring-Verlag*, volume 158, pages 127–140, 1983.

A. Fox, S. D. Gribble, Y. Chawathe, E. A. Brewer, and P. Gauthier. Cluster-based scalable network services. *The 16th ACM symposium on Operating systems principles SOSP '97*, 31(5):78–91, Oct. 1997.

D. Ganesan, A. Cerpa, W. Ye, Y. Yu, J. Zhao, and D. Estrin. Networking issues in wireless sensor networks. *Journal of Parallel and Distributed Computing (JPDC), Special issue on Frontiers in Distributed Sensor Networks*, 64(7):799–814, July 2004.

A. Ghosh and S. Das. *Mobile, Wireless and Sensor Networks: Technology, Applications and Future Directions.* John Wiley & Sons, 2006. Chapter 9: Coverage and Connectivity Issues in Wireless Sensor Networks.

R. Guerraoui, M. Larrea, and A. Schiper. Non blocking atomic commitment with an unreliable failure detector. In *IEEE 14th Symposium on Reliable Distributed Systems*, pages 41–50, Bad Neuenahr, Germany, Sept. 1995.

S. Guha. Approximation algorithms for connected dominating sets. *Algorithmica.*, 20(4): 374–387, Apr. 1998.

I. Gupta, T. Chandra, and G. Goldszmidt. On scalable and efficient distributed failure detectors. In *The 20th annual ACM symposium on Principles of distributed computing (PODC'01)*, pages 170–179, Newport, Rhodes Island, USA, 2001.

P. Gupta and P. Kumar. The capacity of wireless networks. *IEEE Transactions on Information Theory*, 46(2):388–404, Mar. 2000.

S. N. Haaser. *Real Analysis.* Courier Dover Publications., jan 1991.

P. Hall. *Introduction to the Theory of Coverage Process.* John Wiley and Sons Publications., 1988.

S. Han and K. G. Shin. Fast restoration of real-time communication service from component failures in multi-hop networks. In *ACM Conference on Applications, technologies, architectures, and protocols for computer communications (SIGCOMM'97)*, pages 77–88, Cannes, French Riviera, France, Sept. 1997.

N. Hayashibara, A. Cherif, and T. Katayama. Failure detectors for large-scale distributed systems. In *The 21st IEEE Symposium on Reliable Distributed Systems (SRDS'02)*, pages 404–409, Osaka, Japan, Oct. 2002.

W. Heinzelman, J. Kulik, and H. Balakrishnan. Adaptive protocols for information dissemination in wireless sensor networks. In *The 5th ACM/IEEE Mobicom Conference (MobiCom'99)*, pages 174–185, Seattle, WA, USA, Aug. 1999.

W. Heinzelman, A. P. Chandrakasan, and H. Balakrishnan. An application specific protocol architecture for wireless micro-sensor networks. *IEEE Transactions on Wireless Communications*, 1(10):660–670, Oct. 2002.

J. Hellerstein, W. Hong, and S. Madden. The sensor spectrum: technology, trends, and requirements. *ACM SIGMOD Record*, 32(4):22–27, Dec. 2003.

J. Hill, R. Szewczyk, A. Woo, S. Hollar, D. E. Culler, and K. S. J. Pister. System architecture directions for networked sensors. In *ACM Architectural Support for Programming Languages and Operating Systems (ASPLOS-IX)*, pages 93–104, Cambridge, MA, USA, 2000.

X. Hong, M. Gerla, R. Bagrodia, T. Kwon, P. Estabrook, and G. Pei. The mars sensor network: efficient, energy aware communications. In *IEEE Military Communications Conference (MilCom'01)*, pages 418–422, McLean,Virginia USA, Oct. 2001.

X. Hong, M. Gerla, and H. Wang. Load-balanced, energy-aware communications for mars sensor-networks. In *IEEE Aerospace Conference*, pages 3–1109–3–1115, Bigsky, MI, USA, Mar. 2002.

A. Howard, M. J. Matari, and G. S. Sukhatme. An incremental self-deployment algorithm for mobile sensor networks. *Autonomous Robots Special Issue on Intelligent Embedded Systems (Kluwer)*, 13(2):113–126, 2002.

L. Hu and D. Evans. Localization for mobile sensor network. In *The 10th annual international conference on Mobile computing and networking (MobiCom'04)*, pages 45–57, Philadelphia, PA, USA, Sept. 2004.

C. Huang and Y. Tseng. The coverage problem in a wireless sensor network. In *ACM International Workshop on Wireless Sensor Networks and Applications (WSNA'03)*, pages 115–121, San Diego, California, USA, Sept. 2003.

C. Huang and Y. Tseng. The coverage problem in a wireless sensor network. *Journal of Mobile Networks and Applications (MONET), Springer*, 10(4):519–528, 2005.

C. Huang, L. Lo, Y. Tseng, and W. Chen. Decentralized energy-conserving and coverage-preserving protocols for wireless sensor networks. *ACM Transactions on Sensor Networks*, 2(2):182–187, May 2006.

L. Huyse. Solving problems of optimization under uncertainty as statistical decision problems. In *The 42nd AIAA Structures, Structural Dynamics and Materials Conference*, number AIAA-2001-1519, Seattle, WA, USA, Apr. 2001.

C. Intanagonwiwat, R. Govindan, and D. Estrin. Directed Diffusion: A scalable and robust communication paradigm for sensor networks. In *The 6th ACM/IEEE annual international conference on Mobile computing and networking (MobiCom'00)*, pages 56–67, Boston, MA, USA, Aug. 2000.

Intel Corporation. Intel Mote: Sensor Nets/RFID, 2007. URL http://www.intel.com/research/exploratory/motes.htm.

J. Jiang and W. Dou. A coverage-preserving density control algorithm for wireless sensor networks. In *The 3rd International Conference on AD-HOC Networks & Wireless (ADHOC-NOW'04)*, pages 42–55, Vancouver, Canada, July 2004.

D. Johnson. *Optimization Theory*. Connexions, July 2003. URL http://cnx.rice.edu/content/m11240/1.2/.

B. Krishnamachari and S. Iyengar. Distributed bayesian algorithms for fault-tolerant event region detection in wireless sensor networks. *IEEE Transactions on Computers*, 53(3): 241–250, Mar. 2004.

B. Krishnamachari, D. Estrin, and S. Wicker. The impact of data aggregation in wireless sensor networks. In *IEEE International Workshop on Distributed Event-Based Systems (DEBS'02)*, pages 575–578, Vienna, Austria, July 2002.

L. Krishnamurthy, R. Adler, P. Buonadonna, J. Chhabra, M. Flanigan, N. Kushalnagar, L. Nachman, and M. Yarvis. Design and deployment of industrial sensor networks: Experiences from the north sea and a semiconductor plant. In *The 3rd ACM Conference on Embedded Networked Sensor Systems (SenSys'05)*, pages 64–75, San Diego, California, USA, Dec. 2005.

S. Kumar, T. H. Lai, and J. Balogh. On k-coverage in a mostly sleeping sensor network. In *The 10th annual international conference on Mobile computing and networking (MobiCom'04)*, pages 144–158, Philadelphia, PA, USA, Sept. 2004.

M. Larrea, A. Fernndez, and S. Arvalo. On the implementation of unreliable failure detectors in partially synchronous systems. *IEEE Transactions on Computers*, 53(7):815–828, July 2004.

L. Lazos and R. Poovendran. Stochastic coverage in heterogeneous sensor networks. *ACM Transactions on Sensor Networks*, 2(3):325–358, Aug. 2006.

T. Le, N. Ahmeed, and S. Jha. Location-free fault repair in hybrid sensor networks. In *The 1st International Conference on Integrated Internet Ad hoc and Sensor Networks, (InterScience'06)*, number Article-23, Nice, France, May 2006.

P. Levis, S. Madden, J. Polastre, R. Szewczyk, K. Whitehouse, A. Woo, D. Gay, J. Hill, M. Welsh, E. Brewer, and D. Culler. *Ambient Intelligence*. Springer-Verlag, Berlin, Heidelberg, Germany, 2005. Chapter: TinyOS - An Operating System for Sensor Networks (Pages 115–148).

Q. Li and D. Rus. Global clock synchronization in sensor networks. In *The 23rd International Annual Joint Conference of the IEEE Computer and Communications Society (INFOCOM'04)*, pages 574–584, Hong Kong, China, Mar. 2004.

K. Lorincz, B. Kuris, S. Ayer, S. Patel, P. Bonato, and M. Welsh. Wearable wireless sensor network to assess clinical status in patients with neurological disorders. In *The 6th international conference on Information processing in sensor networks (IPSN'07)*, pages 563–564, Cambridge, Massachusetts, USA, Apr. 2007.

C. Lynch and F. OReilly. Processor choice for wireless sensor networks. In *Workshop on Real-World Wireless Sensor Networks (REALWSN05)*, Stockholm, Sweden, June 2005.

Y. Ma and J. H. Aylor. System lifetime optimization for heterogeneous sensor networks with a hub-spoke topology. *IEEE Transactions on Mobile Computing*, 3(3):286–294, July 2004.

A. Mainwaring, D. Culler, J. Polastre, R. Szewczyk, and J. Anderson. Wireless sensor networks for habitat monitoring. In *The 1st ACM Workshop on Wireless Sensor Networks and Applications (WSNA'02)*, pages 88–97, Atlanta, Georgia, USA, Sept. 2002.

P. Marron, A. Lachenmann, D. Minder, J. Hahner, K. Rothermel, and C. Becher. Adaptation and cross-layer issues in sensor networks. In *International Conference on Intelligent Sensors, Sensor Networks and Information Processing (ISSNIP'04)*, pages 623–628, Melbourne, Australia, Dec. 2004.

S. Megerian and M. Potkonjak. *Wireless Sensor Networks*. Wiley Encyclopaedia of Telecommunications, Editor: John G. Proakis, Dec. 2002.

S. Megerian, F. Koushanfar, M. Potkonjak, and M. B. Srivastava. Worst and best-case coverage in sensor networks. *IEEE Transactions on Mobile Computing*, 4(1):84–92, Jan. 2005.

S. Meguerdichian, F. Koushanfar, M. Potkonjak, and M. Srivastava. Coverage problems in wireless ad-hoc sensor networks. In *The 20th International Annual Joint Conference of the IEEE Computer and Communications Societies (INFOCOM'01)*, pages 1380–1387, Anchorage, Alaska, USA, June 2001.

Y. Mei, C. Xian, S. Das, Y. Hu, and Y. Lu. Replacing failed sensor nodes by mobile robots. In *The 26th IEEE International Conference on Distributed Computing Systems Workshops (ICDCSW'06)*, number 87, Lisboa, Portugal, July 2006.

C. Mendis, S. Guru, S. Halgamuge, and S. Fernando. Optimized sink node path using particle swarm optimization. In *The 20th International Conference on Advanced Information Networking and Applications (AINA'06)*, pages 388–394, Vienna, Austria, Apr. 2006.

E. Miluzzo, N. D. Lane, and A. T. Campbell. Virtual sensing range. In *The 4th ACM Conference on Embedded Networked Sensor Systems (SenSys'06)*, pages 397–398, Boulder, Colorado, USA, Dec. 2006.

R. Min, M. Bhardwaj, N. Ickes, A. Wang, and A. Chandrakasan. The hardware and the network: Total-system strategies for power aware wireless microsensors. In *IEEE CAS Workshop on Wireless Communications and Networking Power Efficient Wireless Ad Hoc Networks*, Pasadena, California, USA, Sept. 2002.

E. C. Nishimura and M. Dennis. IUSS Dual Use: Monitoring whales and earthquakes using SOSUS. *Journal of Marine Technology Society*, 27(4):13–21, 1994.

H. Oh, H. Bahn, and K. Chae. An energy-efficient sensor routing scheme for home automation networks. *IEEE Transactions on Consumer Electronics*, 51(3):836–839, Aug. 2005.

S. Parikh, V. Vokkarane, L. Xing, and D. Kasilingam. Node-replacement policies to maintain threshold-coverage in wireless sensor networks. Technical Report UMASSD-CIS-TR-2006009, University of Massachusetts, Dartmouth, 2006.

D. A. Patterson and J. L. Hennessy. *Computer Organization and Design: The Hardware/Software Interface 2nd Edition.* Morgan Kaufmann Publishers, Inc., 1998.

J. Polastre, R. Szewczyk, and D. Culler. Telos: Enabling ultra-low power wireless research. In *The 4th international ACM symposium on Information processing in sensor networks (IPSN'05)*, pages 364–369, Los Angeles, California, USA, Apr. 2005.

F. P. Preparata and M. I. Shamos. *Computational Geometry: An Introduction.* Springer-Verlag, New York, 1985.

S. Ranganathan, A. D. George, R. W. Todd, and M. C. Chidester. Gossip-style failure detection and distributed consensus for scalable heterogeneous clusters. *Journal of Cluster Computing, Springer Netherlands*, 4(3):197–209, July 2001.

R. V. Renesse, Y. Minsky, and M. Hayden. A gossip-based failure detection service. In *International Conference on Distributed Systems Platforms and Open Distributed Processing, (Middleware'98)*, pages 55–70, England, 1998.

K. Romer and F. Mattern. The design space of wireless sensor networks. *IEEE Transactions on Wireless Communications*, 11(6):54–61, Dec. 2004.

K. Sakib, Z. Tari, and I. Khalil. Energy balancing in the self-configuring sensor networks. In *The 2nd International Conference on Intelligent Sensors, Sensor Networks and Information Processing (ISSNIP'05)*, pages 39–44, Melbourne, Australia, Dec. 2005.

P. Santana, J. Barata, H. Cruz, A. Mestre, J. Lisboa, and L. Flores. A multi-robot system for landmine detection. In *The 10th IEEE International Conference on Emerging Technologies and Factory Automation (ETFA'05)*, page 8 pp, Facolta' di Ingegneria, Catania, Italy, Sept. 2005.

P. Santi. Topology control in wireless ad hoc and sensor networks. *ACM Computing Surveys*, 37:164–194, June 2005.

C. Schurgers, V. Tsiatsis, S. Ganeriwal, and M. Srivastava. Optimizing sensor networks in the energy-latency-density design space. *IEEE Transactions on Mobile Computing*, 1(1): 70–80, Jan. 2002.

L. Schwiebert, S. Gupta, and J. Weinmann. Research challenges in wireless networks of biomedical sensors. In *The 7th ACM/IEEE annual international conference on Mobile computing and networking (MobiCom'01)*, pages 151–165, Rome, Italy, July 2001.

N. Shrivastava, S. Suri, and C. D. Toth. Detecting cuts in sensor networks. In *The 4th international ACM symposium on Information processing in sensor networks (IPSN'05)*, number Article-28, Los Angeles, California, USA, Apr. 2005.

M. L. Sichitiu. Cross-layer scheduling for power efficiency in wireless sensor networks. In *The 23rd International Annual Joint Conference of the IEEE Computer and Communications Society (INFOCOM'04)*, pages 1740–1750, Hong Kong, China, Mar. 2004.

S. Singh, M. Woo, and C. S. Raghabendra. Power-aware routing in mobile ad hoc networks. In *ACM/IEEE Mobicom Conference (MobiCom'98)*, pages 181–190, Dallas, Texas, USA, 1998.

P. K. Sinha. *Distributed Operating Systems, Concepts and Design.* IEEE Press, 1997.

B. Sinopoli, C. Sharp, L. Schenato, S. Schaffert, and S. Sastry. Distributed control applications within sensor networks. *Proceedings of the IEEE*, 91(8):1235–1246, Aug. 2003.

R. Sivakumar, B. Das, and V. Bharghavan. Spine-based routing in ad hoc networks. *Journal of ACM/Baltzer Cluster Computing*, 1:237–248, 1998.

K. Sohrabi, W. Merrill, J. Elson, L. Girod, F. Newberg, and W. Kaiser. Methods for scalable self-assembly of ad hoc wireless sensor networks. *IEEE Transactions on Mobile Computing*, 3(4):317–331, Oct. 2004.

M. Srivastava, R. Muntz, and M. Potkonjak. Smart kindergarten: sensor-based wireless networks for smart developmental problem-solving enviroments. In *The 7th ACM/IEEE annual international conference on Mobile computing and networking (MobiCom'01)*, pages 132–138, Rome, Italy, Aug. 2001.

W. Stallings. *Data and Computer Communications, 8/E.* Prentice Hall., 2007.

T. Starner. Powerful change part 1: Batteries and possible alternatives for the mobile market. In *IEEE pervasive computing*, pages 86–88, Oct. 2003.

D. Steere, A. Baptista, D. McNamee, C. Pu, and J. Walpole. Research challenges in environmental observation and forecasting systems. In *The 6th ACM/IEEE annual international conference on Mobile computing and networking (MobiCom'00)*, pages 292–299, Boston, MA, USA, Aug. 2000.

I. Stoica, R. Morris, D. Karger, M. Kaashoek, and H. Balakrishnan. Chord: A scalable peer-to-peer lookup service for internet applications. In *ACM Conference on Applications, technologies, architectures, and protocols for computer communications (SIGCOMM'01)*, pages 149–160, San Diego, California, USA, Aug. 2001.

L. Subramanian and R. H. Katz. An architecture for building self-configurable systems. In *IEEE/ACM symposium on Mobile and Ad hoc networkig and computing*, pages 63–73, Boston, MA, USA, Aug. 2000.

K. J. Taek, M. Gerla, V. Varma, M. Barton, and T. Hsing. Efficient flooding with passive clustering an overhead-free selective forward mechanism for ad hoc/sensor networks. *Proceedings of the IEEE*, 91(8):1210–1220, Aug. 2003.

A. Tai, K. Tso, and W. H. Sanders. Cluster-based failure detection service for large-scale ad hoc wireless network applications. In *IEEE International conference on Dependable Systems and Networks (DSN'04)*, pages 805–814, Los Angeles, CA, USA, June 2004.

D. Tian and N. D. Georganas. A coverage-preserving node scheduling scheme for large wireless sensor networks. In *The 1st ACM Workshop on Wireless Sensor Networks and Applications (WSNA'02)*, pages 32–41, Atlanta, Georgia, USA, Sept. 2002.

D. Tian and N. D. Georganas. Energy efficient routing with guaranteed delivery in wireless sensor networks. In *IEEE Wireless Communications and Networking Conference (WCNC'03)*, pages 1923–1929, New Orleans, USA, 2003.

D. Tian and N. D. Georganas. Connectivity maintenance and coverage preservation in wireless sensor networks. *ACM Transactions on Adhoc Networks, Elsevier Science*, 3:744–761, 2005.

M. Tubaishat and M. Madria. Sensor networks: an overview. *IEEE Potentials*, 22(2):20–23, Apr. 2003.

University of California, Berkeley. TinyOS, 2007. URL http://www.tinyos.net/.

University of California, Los Angeles. SOS: Embedded operating systems, 2007. URL https://projects.nesl.ucla.edu/public/sos-2x/doc/.

G. Wang, G. Cao, and T. Porta. Movement-assisted sensor deployment. In *The 23rd International Annual Joint Conference of the IEEE Computer and Communications Society (INFOCOM'04)*, pages 2469–2479, Hong Kong, China, Mar. 2004.

G. Wang, G. Cao, and T. Porta. Movement-assisted sensor deployment. *IEEE Transactions on Mobile Computing*, 5(6):640–652, June 2006.

X. Wang, G. Xing, Y. Zhang, C. Lu, R. Pless, and C. Gill. Integrated coverage and connectivity configuration in wireless sensor networks. In *The 1st ACM Conference on Embedded Networked Sensor Systems (SenSys'03)*, pages 28–39, Los Angeles, California, USA, Nov. 2003.

J. Wu. Extended dominating-set-based routing in ad hoc wireless networks with unidirectional links. *IEEE Transactions on Parallel and Distributed Systems*, 13(9):866–881, Sept. 2002.

J. Wu and S. Yang. SMART: A scan-based movement-assisted sensor deployment method in wireless sensor networks. In *The 24th International Annual Joint Conference of the IEEE Computer and Communications Societies (INFOCOM'05)*, pages 2313–2324, Miami, FL, USA, Mar. 2005.

G. Xing, X. Wang, Y. Zhang, C. Lu, R. Pless, and C. Gill. Integrated coverage and connectivity configuration for energy conservation in sensor networks. *ACM Transactions on Sensor Networks*, 1(1):36–72, Aug. 2005.

W. Ye, J. Heidemann, and D. Estrin. An energy-efficient MAC protocol for wireless sensor networks. In *The 21st International Annual Joint Conference of the IEEE Computer and Communications Societies (INFOCOM'02)*, pages 1567–1576, New York, NY, USA, June 2002.

O. Younis and S. Fahmy. HEED: a hybrid, energy-efficient, distributed clustering approach for ad hoc sensor networks. *IEEE Transactions on Mobile Computing*, 3(4):366–379, Oct. 2004.

C. Zhang, Y. Zhang, and Y. Fang. Localized coverage boundary detection for wireless sensor networks. In *The 3rd international conference on Quality of Service in Heterogeneous Wired/Wireless Networks (QShine'06)*, number Article-12, Waterloo, On, Canada, Aug. 2006.

H. Zhang and J. Hou. On deriving the upper bound of α-lifetime for large sensor networks. In *The 5th ACM International Symposium on Mobile Adhoc Networking and Computing (MobiHoc'04)*, pages 121–132, Roppongi, Japan, May 2004.

H. Zhang and J. Hou. Maintaining sensing coverage and connectivity in large sensor networks. *Journal of Ad-hoc and Wireless Sensor Networks, OCP Science*, 1:89–124, Mar. 2005.

Z. Zhou, S. Das, and H. Gupta. Connected k-coverage problem in sensor networks. In *IEEE International Conference on Computer Communications and Networks (ICCCN'04)*, pages 373–378, Chicago, IL, USA, Oct. 2004.

S. Zhuang, D. Geels, I. Stoica, and R. Katz. Exploring tradeoffs in failure detection in routing overlays. Technical Report UCB/CSD-3-1285, University of California, Berkeley, 2003.

S. Zhuang, D. Geels, I. Stoica, and R. Katz. On failure detection algorithms in overlay networks. In *The 24th International Annual Joint Conference of the IEEE Computer and Communications Societies (INFOCOM'05)*, pages 2112–2123, Miami, FL, USA, Mar. 2005.

Y. Zou and K. Chakrabarty. Sensor deployment and target localization in distributed sensor networks. *ACM Transactions on Embedded Computing Systems*, 3(1):61–91, Feb. 2004.

Y. Zou and K. Chakrabarty. A distributed coverage- and connectivity-centric technique for selecting active nodes in wireless sensor networks. *IEEE Transactions on Computers*, 54 (8):978–991, Aug. 2005.

VDM publishing house ltd.

Scientific Publishing House

offers

free of charge publication

of current academic research papers, Bachelor´s Theses, Master's Theses, Dissertations or Scientific Monographs

If you have written a thesis which satisfies high content as well as formal demands, and you are interested in a remunerated publication of your work, please send an e-mail with some initial information about yourself and your work to *info@vdm-publishing-house.com*.

Our editorial office will get in touch with you shortly.

VDM Publishing House Ltd.
Meldrum Court 17.
Beau Bassin
Mauritius
www.vdm-publishing-house.com

www.ingramcontent.com/pod-product-compliance
Lightning Source LLC
LaVergne TN
LVHW042333060326
832902LV00006B/145